BAND ON THE BUS

AROUND THE WORLD IN A DOUBLE-DECKER

RICHARD KING

The
History
Press

Front cover: Artwork by Adrian Teal.

Back cover: Author's collection.

First published 2017

The History Press
The Mill, Brimscombe Port
Stroud, Gloucestershire, GL5 2QG
www.thehistorypress.co.uk

British Library Cataloguing in Publication Data.
A catalogue record for this book is available from the British Library.

ISBN 978 0 7509 7020 4

Typesetting and origination by The History Press
Printed and bound in Malta by Melita Press

Contents

I Arrive in New York

The Vickers VC10 banked gently over the wintery salt marshes, lining up for its final approach to New York's JFK Airport. It had gradually been losing height on its journey south along the snowy New England coast. The long line of Manhattan skyscrapers that had been visible in the distance through the window sank behind the horizon, and we landed with a screech as the plane's tyres touched the tarmac. BOAC flight BA 501 from Heathrow had arrived in America.

I'd never visited the United States before, although I was sure that there would be a familiarity about it all from years of watching American TV programmes and Hollywood films. 'Business?' the immigration official asked as he glanced at the multiple entry business visa that had been stamped in my passport eighteen months before. 'Yes,' I replied. Then he looked at me. I was wearing my smart new business suit with matching tie and handkerchief and carrying my coat and hand baggage. 'How long will you be staying?' he asked. I wasn't sure, but my business shouldn't take more than a couple of weeks, I thought. The truth was that I had no idea. I was here until my money ran out. 'Welcome to America,' he said, swiftly stamping my passport. 'Enjoy your stay.'

I was in! I waited by the luggage carousel for my suitcases. There were two large ones, a smaller overnight case and some other bags. The bigger one I could hardly lift. It was so heavy I'd had to pay an excess baggage fee when I'd checked in. I put them on a trolley, wheeled them through customs and headed for the bus that would take me to the East Side Airlines Terminal. It was cold outside, with heaps of snow everywhere. Little flurries were picked up by the wind as my bags were loaded under the floor of the Carey airport bus. I bagged a window seat and we pulled away. The ride was soft and spongy as the bus swung into the stream of traffic heading away from the airport along the expressway. It was a dull, grey afternoon and the four-lane highway was full of traffic. We passed a large, colourless cemetery, the extravagant tombstones all shades of grey as if in a black-and-white movie. Then the skyscrapers I'd seen from the plane came into view. They made an impressive sight, their lights twinkling in the twilight.

We dived into the Midtown Tunnel and surfaced right next to the East Side Airlines Terminal building at 38th Street and 1st Avenue, inside which the airport bus abruptly ended its journey. I collected my bags and headed towards the exit. I checked the map I'd picked up when it suddenly struck me that I had a problem. I couldn't carry all my luggage in one go. It was fine with an airport trolley, but now I was on the street and had to cross 1st Avenue to a bus stop. I was so broke I couldn't afford a cab, so I heaved up the suitcases and other bags and with a great effort shuffled with them all across the road. I got to the bus stop and along came a bus. It took me a while to get the cases up the bus steps. I said to the driver that I wanted to get to East 64th Street. He told me to put 30 cents into the machine. I found the change I'd got at the airport and did what he said. The machine clicked and whirred, gobbling up my money. The door closed and the bus took off with the engine screaming as the automatic clutch slipped through the gears and we bounced along the potholed one-way avenue.

The bus stopped just down the road from East 64th Street. Once I'd struggled to offload the cases the bus pulled away, roaring off in a cloud of exhaust fumes into the gloom. I just couldn't manage all this luggage in one go, so I first carried the heaviest suitcase a few paces up the street, left it there, ran back to the remaining heap, lugged everything else past the first case, dumped them down a few yards further along the sidewalk, returned to move the first case again and continued like this until I reached the lights at the junction. I wasn't going to get very far like this. Fortunately, my destination, 340 E 64th Street, was on the corner of the street just across 1st Avenue.

340 E 64th Street turned out to be a modern thirty-four-storey condominium. Standing at the glass doors, a few steps down from the pavement, was a handsome young black man in a full-length bottle green coat with bright buttons and wearing gloves and a top hat. 'I'm visiting Mr Smith,' I said. 'Suite 17 S.' 'Mr Smith is out at the moment, sir,' he replied, 'but he is expected back within the hour. Do you have an appointment?' 'I've just arrived from London, but I'm sure he's expecting me,' I lied. I'd no idea if Joe Smith was expecting me or not. 'Can I leave these bags here?' 'Sure,' he said, and he helped me move them off the pavement into a storage room off the broad, stylish lobby. 'My name is Richard King,' I told him. 'I'll come back in half an hour.'

I stepped into the street and walked round the block. It was an upmarket, attractive neighbourhood, but it was cold, with the sky dark and overcast. My clothes were no match for the biting wind and I soon returned to the warmth of the lobby. 'Mr Smith has returned, sir,' I was told. 'He asked if you would go up.'

The lift took me to the 17th floor, and I walked along the deep pile carpet of the broad corridor to Suite 17 S and rang the bell. The door opened and there was Joe Smith, not as tall as I'd imagined, wearing smartly pressed slacks, a blazer and tie with a silk handkerchief prominent in the breast pocket. 'Mr Smith?' I said, 'I'm Richard King, a friend of the Houghs in England. I believe they've written to you about me.' With a warmth towards me that I didn't deserve, the impeccably mannered Joe Smith replied, 'Well come IN. Let me take your coat.' He led me through a wide hallway and into a very large L-shaped room, beautifully furnished with highly polished antiques. The view through the plate glass windows lining the side of the room was breathtaking. There in front of me was the whole of mid-town Manhattan, the skyscrapers alive with lights. 'This is Marie Bernolfo,' he said, introducing me to a tall, elegant woman in her mid-40s who stood up and shook my hand. 'We've just been to Bloomingdale's,' Joe said. 'Can I offer you a kir?' I'd no idea what a kir was. I was about to find out. 'Thank you,' I replied.

He disappeared into a well-equipped galley kitchen and returned with a large and expensive thin-stemmed wine glass filled with chilled, pink-tinged, white wine. 'How long have you been in New York?' they asked as we sat down on the broad, white sofas. I sank deep into the cushions. I explained that I'd just arrived that afternoon from London and that I was a friend of the Houghs' son, Tony. He and I with some other friends were travelling the world and I had come to New York to find sponsorship for our trip across America. They asked where I was staying. I said I didn't know, I had hoped that someone would put me up for a few days until I found my feet, as I hadn't much money. My bags were downstairs in the lobby. I was sure that Tony's mother would have put this in her letter. 'Well, Richard, I've not heard from Val since her Christmas card. But I do know about your travels with Tony.' My heart sank. What was coming next? 'WELL ...' he said, 'I guess you'd better stay here the night.'

Inwardly I heaved a massive sigh of relief. I was exhausted and very nervous about what lay ahead of me. I thanked him very much indeed. At least I now had a bed for the night. 'We'll get your luggage brought up from the lobby,' he said. Marie had a dinner engagement, said goodbye, and hoped we would meet again. Joe escorted her to the door. Then he showed me into the television room. There was a large sofa, which converted into a good-sized double bed, above which was a large mid-Victorian oil painting which took up most of the wall. It was a pastoral landscape showing a well-to-do American family – mother, father and several chubby little children with hoops and parasols with a colonial style house in the background. 'Relatives of yours?' I asked. 'I bought it in a sale. It fills the space on the wall quite nicely, doesn't it? This will be your room,' he said, as he unfolded and made up the bed.

He asked me if I would like a steak for supper and, in the meantime, how about another kir? We then sat down to eat. It was one of the best steaks I'd ever tasted, washed down with glasses of rich red wine. As we started eating, Joe said, 'Now you have to tell me EVERYTHING about your travels. I want to know ALL about it, right from the beginning,' and so I began telling Joe our story. It grew late and I was tired. Joe had his own bedroom with an antique four-poster bed and en-suite bathroom and dressing room, to which he retired. I climbed into bed. It was soft and comfortable. Outside it was snowing, but I was cozy and warm. Never in my wildest dreams could I have imagined my first night in New York would be like this, and I quickly fell asleep.

Over the next few days, I filled in the details of the story of our adventure, starting at the very beginning. What follows is what I told Joe, more or less, starting with how it all began.

How it all Started: An Aeroplane and 'Hairy Pillock'

The chances to meet girls in our village were rather limited. Mostly we met them on our way to and from school on the bus, but opportunities to socialise were few. In the 1950s, the Young Conservatives, known as YCs, had a reputation of being a marriage bureau and, although none of our gang in the Longmoor Road had any intention of getting married, the local YCs seemed as good a place to hang out as any. During the 1960s in Liphook, Hampshire, the place where I was born, the YCs was a highly successful youth organisation, run by its members. They met every Thursday evening in Liphook's Methodist Church Hall and each week we listened to talks, watched slides and films, held discussions and debates, took part in quizzes and mock trials or grappled awkwardly with ballroom dancing lessons, as well as putting on variety shows, organising donkey derbies, tennis competitions, dances and box cart races, making films and, very occasionally, getting involved in local politics. Oh, and we sometimes sang in pubs!

Our meetings ended with coffee, following which those who were lucky enough to own an old car or to borrow their father's, drove the rest of the gang to the pub. Originally this was The Plough at Redford, 5 miles over the border in Sussex, partly because the landlord, Wing Commander Jackson, had an attractive daughter, Natalie, who was a well-liked YC, but more probably because of the Sussex opening hours. Pubs in Hampshire closed at 10.30 p.m., while Sussex pubs stopped serving at 11 p.m. In 1963 Natalie married another YC, Brinsley Smith, and the gang transferred their allegiance to the Deers Hut, just outside Liphook down the Longmoor Road. The landlord, Bert Oram, took a paternal interest in our activities, and his wife Queenie soon thought of us as 'her boys'. Bert's opening hours were somewhat flexible, too!

The big social event of our year was the annual Liphook Carnival at the end of October. It involved the crowning of a Carnival Queen, a procession with dozens of floats entered by local clubs, pubs, businesses, families and friends, followed by a bonfire and firework display. Some of us had taken part since we were children, so it was only natural that each year the YCs entered a float. In 1967 we decided to do something really ambitious in an attempt to win the prize for the best float, and built an aeroplane. It was 20ft long, had a 15ft wingspan, a big twin-bladed propeller and a mock sixteen-cylinder radial engine. The frame, welded together from old gas piping, was covered with hardboard and sprayed silver. We called it the 'Discord'. Everyone dressed like aviators or first-class passengers. But our optimism was shattered when the League of Friends of King George's Hospital won the cup for the best float with 'St George and the Dragon'.

We were inconsolable. 'What are you going to do with your aeroplane now?' someone in the pub asked. 'You ought to enter it in a carnival somewhere else. There's one at Titchfield, a week on Monday. It's the biggest in the South of England. You might win a prize there.' We decided to take it to Titchfield. 'And how will you get it there?' said one of the pub's greatest cynics. We thought for a minute. 'We'll pull it there by hand and collect money for charity on the way!' At this point someone got out their wallet, took out a pound note and slapped it down on the counter. 'Here's a pound that says you can't pull your aeroplane to Titchfield in a day!' We took the bet. It was only then that we learned that Titchfield was 34 miles away!

To cut a long story short, we pulled the aeroplane to Titchfield in a day, won our bet, and also won the first prize. We brought it home a week later on the back of a lorry. Stopping at a pub for a bite to eat, we wondered what else we could do with our aeroplane. 'How about taking it on holiday? We could pull it round the lanes of Devon and raise money for charity?' someone suggested. 'You're mad,' was the response. 'We had enough problems pulling it to Titchfield.' 'All right, then,' said someone else, 'how about putting a real engine in it, strengthening the wings, taking it to Dover and flying the English Channel!' That didn't go down too well either. At this point I made a suggestion. 'Forget the aeroplane. Why don't we do what Cliff Richard did in that film and buy an old bus, kit it out with bunks, a cooker and kitchen sink and take it to Europe for a fortnight's holiday?' There was a stunned silence. Someone said: 'Why not?'

I'd always wanted to drive a double-decker bus. Here was a chance for me to drive a real bus, so I volunteered to find one. We bought a 20-year-old Leyland double-decker from Portsmouth Corporation. It cost us £70. My family's business, run by my uncle Arthur and my grandfather, was a haulage company, Three Counties Supplies and Transport Ltd, so one of the mechanics, Ernie Smithers, collected the bus and drove it back to Liphook, where we parked it on a hard-standing area we'd made for it on Andrew Luff's farm. Andrew was a YC and childhood friend. He and his mother ran a large market garden on the opposite side of the Longmoor Road to where we lived and where our family business was situated.

We converted the bus, with nine bunks and eight seats at the front upstairs, worktops, cupboards, a kitchen sink, gas cooker, and tables for twelve and sixteen seats downstairs. We even had a radio and record player. There were carpets on the floors, curtains at the windows and running water at the sink. The driver could talk to the navigator on the upper deck using an intercom. Our film group recorded all this activity, which took place every weekend and on several weekday evenings, and the whole team gradually bonded together. We christened the bus 'Hairy Pillock'. By mid-June it was ready and in July twelve of us took it to Spain for a two-week holiday.

With us went our musical instruments, and we enjoyed singing to the other holidaymakers at the campsite we'd found on Spain's Mediterranean coast. Peter Windibank, another childhood friend from the Longmoor Road, played guitar, as did Roland Hutchings, while Clive Hughes played guitar and banjo, and his brother Alan the accordion. Peter's friend from college, Wally Walsh, also played the accordion and guitar. I took my old double bass. Dick Hayes and John Wilson looked after the catering. John was the original 'Hairy Pillock', a nickname acquired when he was painting the 'Discord' and sprayed every car in the Deers Hut car park silver by mistake. Peter, Bob Hall and I shared the driving, and Adrian Bird, John Carver and Tim Palmer made up the rest of the crew. We felt that the world was our oyster, and returned home triumphant. And that, most of us thought, was that. But it wasn't.

3

What Happened Next: The Die is Cast

The autumn of 1968 was dreary, damp and miserable and our summer holiday in the bus seemed a distant memory. For the 1968 carnival we built a replica of a Roman stone-throwing machine, which we mistakenly called a 'ballista', which won the prize for the best float at both Liphook and Titchfield. The bus ventured out for the evening on most weekends, and when we were invited to play at nearby pubs, clubs and folk clubs, and we always took a busload of YCs with us. Some places gave us money for the charities we supported and, when we passed the hat round, it always came back full. We'd called ourselves 'The Procal Turdum', a name nicked from *Private Eye*.

While editing the film of our Spanish adventure, I daydreamed about taking our bus to other sunnier climes. Down at the pub, I sensed that many of the others felt the same. Most of us were fed up with our jobs and couldn't wait for work to end and to be in each other's company again. 'Next year we could drive the bus all over Europe' we said, thinking we should never have come back. Then, one dull winter's evening, we became even more expansive. 'We could even take it right around the world!' we thought. At this point

Bert Oram, our cheery but somewhat eccentric landlord, leant over the bar, wagged his finger at us and said, 'If you lot can drive a double-decker bus around the world, I'll give each of you a free pint of beer!' And that was really how it all started.

'Well, who would be up for it?' I asked. 'I'm willing to chuck everything up for a couple of years and go travelling if the rest of you are prepared to.' 'What have we got to lose? I'd do it,' someone said. 'You can count me out,' said someone else. 'A couple of weeks' holiday is fine, but I've got a good job and the thought of spending a year or two cooped up in an old bus with you lot isn't my idea of a good time.' 'Stuff the job,' said Tim, 'it would be the opportunity of a lifetime – how could you possibly pass it up?' Yet another said, 'I don't know. Do you really think we could do it?' 'Sure,' I replied with a new-found confidence, 'it's certainly worth giving it a go.' 'But how would we pay for it, then?' someone asked. Nobody spoke. We had another drink, then another, and by closing time the majority of us agreed that we should give it a try. 'Well, Bert, you've got a bet,' we said to him as we left, little knowing just what we had let ourselves in for. My mother was still up when I let myself in through our front door. 'Ma,' I said with a flourish, 'we're going to drive around the world in a double-decker bus!' 'Very nice, dear,' she replied, 'now go on upstairs and go to bed.'

In the weeks that followed, we spent our evenings discussing it. Of the twelve who went on the trip to Spain five were keen, four were not too sure and the remaining three not really interested. The first thing we had to address was how we would pay for it all. We might be able to sell advertising on the side of the bus and seek sponsorship. If we could afford to get to India and sail to Australia we could earn enough money there to pay for crossing the Pacific, driving from Panama to the USA, and back home to England.

We guessed it would take us around two years to complete the trip. The bus was owned by nine of us, but some of the owners were lukewarm. Besides, it was a Leyland PD1. The PD1 was built as a post-war stop-gap and was powered by the pre-war Leyland E181 7.4-litre diesel engine, for which spares would be hard to find. Also, the interior would have to be completely re-designed to include more storage space and better living accommodation for a lengthy overland journey. What we really needed was the Leyland PD2. This had the post-war 9.7-litre Leyland 600 engine, still in production in 1968 with spares available worldwide. Variants of PD2s and the 600 engine were used in many of the countries that we might visit.

Meanwhile, I'd finished the film, and we decided to hold a premiere. Parents and friends were invited to *Pillock Rides Out*, the story of our journey to Spain, in the old cinema in the upstairs room at the Railway Hotel. At the end of the evening I stood up, surrounded by the other boys, and announced that our next adventure would be to buy another double-decker bus and drive it around the world. This was reported in the local papers, but I don't think anyone really took us seriously.

The first thing to do was to find another bus. I got on the phone to Portsmouth Corporation, but they had none available. Ian Allen published a series of booklets entitled 'British Bus Fleets', costing 4s 6d each. Between them they listed the complete fleets of all the bus operators in the country. I started with No. 1, 'South Eastern', and worked my way northwards. In the space of eight weeks I must have contacted over a hundred bus companies, none of whom had any PD2s for disposal. I was at the end of Volume 6, 'Lancashire Municipal Operators', when I spoke to the general manager of Warrington Corporation's Passenger Transport Department, Fred Mantle. 'Well, yes,' he said, 'as a matter of fact we do have a Leyland PD2 we're thinking of getting rid of. It's 20 years old, it has over 700,000 miles on the clock, and it's on its third engine.' He wanted £100 for it.

I reported back to the group. We called ourselves 'The Hairy Pillock Organisation', and had been making money from bus trips around the South of England full of Liphook YCs. There was enough in the kitty to buy and start work on a new bus. Adrian, Andrew and I drove up to Warrington. FED 795, the bus for sale, was No. 10 in the Warrington fleet. We put it on their inspection pit. The running gear looked OK, so I gave Mr Mantle £100 in cash and he handed over the logbook. Using Three Counties' trade plates I drove it back to Liphook, where we parked it on Andrew's farm next to the Portsmouth bus and started work. We named it 'Hairy Pillock 2'.

We needed more funds, but most of us had very little money. We decided we should each put in the same amount, and that for the duration of the trip everything we earned would be paid into a central kitty, out of which all our costs and expenses would be taken. It was a system that was to work well for the entire trip. What we paid in initially would be determined by what the person with the least amount of money could afford. This was Clive Hughes, who had very little savings, but did have a Triumph Herald, which he eventually sold for £150, so each of us contributed £150, to be paid in instalments. As there were to be nine of us, this meant that our total resources would be £1,350.

The cynics and detractors began to have a field day. We were being foolish and unrealistic, they said. Why didn't we just accept our lot and settle down and get married? My uncle Arthur bet us a fiver that we would be back by Christmas. Others told us that nobody would back us and we couldn't afford to do it on our own. Anyway, the bus would surely break down as it was years old and worn out. One of my mother's cousins, a big wheel in the oil industry, told me that we would never be allowed into the US. 'You've no money and they'll never give you a visa,' he said. 'And have you any idea of the cost of shipping something as big as a bus across the Indian Ocean, the Pacific and the Atlantic? You'll never find the money to do it.'

Blissfully confident in our ability to overcome these problems, we set to and got on with converting the Warrington bus for our world trip. Upstairs there would be nine bunks arranged in tiers of three, with six on the nearside and three on the offside, each with its own light, individual lockers and shelves, and curtained off from the gangway. The gap between the top of the mattress and the bunk above was 18in. We only ever sat up in bed once! At the top of the stairs was a boxed-in 85-gallon water storage tank which fed the taps of the sink downstairs. It had a funnel through which water purification tablets could be added, and a gauge to indicate the water level. A tap allowed the tank to drain outside the bus and an attachment was devised to turn this into an external cold shower if we found it necessary. We never did. Above the tank there were lockers for nine. Towards the front on the left was a wardrobe, underneath which was a long storage cupboard. A curtain separated the sleeping quarters from the forward cabin, where there was a large cushioned seat on the left, with a desk opposite, the lid of which lifted to reveal a washbasin. There was also a filing drawer and a safe. The front seats, boxed in for additional storage, came from a scrapped coach. Above the front window was a bookshelf, and under it was the navigation table with a telephone handset connected to a telephonist's headset worn by the driver. Through this the navigator gave directions, and told the driver if the bus was likely to smash into the low bridge ahead. The emergency window at the back was altered so that when opened it formed a platform on which someone could kneel and look along the roof. A grab handle was added outside, and a jack socket connected another telephone handset to the driver and navigator.

The bus had an open platform, so Bob devised a sliding door using a roller shutter door from an old British Road Services delivery van from Three Counties' yard. It ran in channels in the platform floor and above the opening inside. Initially secured by a padlock, this was eventually replaced by a neater Yale lock. It was very efficient and didn't spoil the lines of the bus at all.

Downstairs were our living quarters. A Formica worktop on the nearside ran two-thirds of the length of the lower deck, with a large cupboard underneath and a hinged section which opened up to reveal a gas cooker with four burners, a grill and an oven. Next to the cooker was a gas-powered refrigerator. Above were cupboards with sliding doors and lights underneath. Opposite was a large floor-to-ceiling storage cupboard, next to which was an old double drainer aluminium sink unit. This had come from the bar at the Deers Hut, which Bert was refurbishing. It had hot and cold running water, the hot water being provided by a small gas heater. To the front, two seats faced the scrapped coach's five-seater back seat, and between them were two removable tables. The front seat was hinged so that the tables could be stowed behind it. Between the front seat and the bulkhead was another Formica top, this time with three hinged sections. The centre section lifted to reveal a record player and radio. To the right, behind a sliding window to the driver's cab, was space for our LP collection, whilst behind the window overlooking the bonnet was our cocktail cupboard. There were carpets on the floor, curtains at the windows, red lampshades with gold trim above the tables – and it was all rather reminiscent of a corner of the Deers Hut bar, so we felt very much at home. There was no toilet, as none of us felt up to the task of cleaning it!

Following some unfortunate incidents after eating out during our Spanish trip – which we sometimes referred to as 'le crapeau noir' – we decided it would be better, and cheaper, to take our own food with us, which we bought from the local cash and carry. Dick Hayes produced a lengthy shopping list of six months' supplies for nine. The main meals were dehydrated catering packs and came in five varieties: Farmhouse Stew, Bolognese Sauce, Savoury Mince and Beef and Chicken Curry. The packets, similar to a bag of flour, contained what looked like dried dog food, which you tipped into a large saucepan of boiling water, stirred well and simmered for forty minutes. This ended up looking like hot, wet dog food. After a few weeks it all began to taste the same. We tried mixing things with it, including some of the large quantities of catering-size packet soups we'd bought. When making soup the powder regularly congealed into lumps. As well as loads of dried foods we carried with us hundreds of tins, everything from vegetables, sausages, baked beans and kippers to fruit salad, prunes, peaches and pears – and inexplicably vast quantities of spam. Most of these had paper labels and we stowed them under the front seat downstairs, moving a few at a time to the larder cupboard as we needed them. The floor at the front of the bus wasn't watertight and after driving on wet roads and through puddles and fords, we found that water had soaked into the paper labels and turned them into a gooey mush. After it was wiped off there was nothing to show what the tins contained. The bus was eventually fully stocked with everything we would need for our six-month journey to India, from food to pan scourers, toothbrushes and toilet rolls. Provisioning cost over £250. We had everything now except money, and we were beginning to run out of cash!

4

The 'Round-The-World Bus Sell': How We All Become Directors

Eight of the twelve who had travelled to Spain in 1968 were committed to the world journey. We were a disparate bunch. The most enthusiastic of all were Alan Hughes and Tim Palmer. Alan, 23, was a technician at Pyestock, the government's National Gas Turbine Research Establishment near Farnborough, and had studied engineering. On the Spanish trip it became obvious that he wasn't the tidiest of people, and his rewiring of the Portsmouth bus left something to be desired. He certainly wasn't a committed Conservative, but was happy in the company he found in the YCs and enjoyed questioning everyone's political beliefs.

To Tim, 26, it was 'the opportunity of a lifetime'. He was an electronics engineer who would rather have been a writer and journalist. He was the Liphook YCs' scribe, writing the weekly scandal sheet and diary of events, his press releases being regularly published in the *Haslemere Herald*. His chronicle of our Spanish trip filled the paper for a couple of weeks the previous summer. He'd had a bad accident in the early 1960s when his moped was hit by a car at speed, following which he'd spent several weeks in hospital with broken arms and legs, which now had metal plates and pins in them, and we all made cracks about his 'bionic' legs. He displayed some strange eccentricities, but was bright, intelligent and always full of ideas. One evening at the pub a few months after leaving hospital, he hooked his wooden walking stick over the sprinkler pipe while using the gents' toilets and we all peed on it. He never used a stick again. His stick stayed hanging in the gents' for months.

I was the third enthusiast. I was also 26, and was becoming increasingly disillusioned working as an estate agent for Shaw & Byrne, an independent agency in Haslemere. I believed that I was good at my job, but Tony Byrne, the senior partner, and I didn't see eye to eye, and he was happy for me to submit my resignation. This enabled me to spend all my time sorting out the world trip, in between casual jobs including driving a lorry for my uncle, working for a local removal company, helping Andrew on his farm, and acting as a holiday relief manager for local estate agencies and Andrew's do-it-yourself shop. I'd studied business management and thought I knew a lot about it – I didn't – and was also a committed, though slightly disillusioned, Young Conservative who had been Branch and Constituency Chairman, Treasurer and Vice Chairman of the regional YCs and a member of the National Executive. Alan took every opportunity to challenge my political convictions and leadership skills.

Dick Hayes, 23, was also keen to be involved. He worked as a printer but had always wanted to run a pub and worked part-time behind the bar at The Duke of Cumberland, where we sang on winter Sunday evenings with a large and cheery singer called Cliff Giles. Living in Camelsdale in Sussex, just south of Haslemere, Dick was a peripheral member of the YC clan and had come on the scene more recently. With swarthy good looks, he was the only one of us who was regularly mistaken for a local in every country we visited.

John Wilson, 21, also wanted to go. Working in a builder's merchant's showroom in Guildford, he had recently been promoted to a heating and plumbing estimator. He was a skilled plumber and installed the bus water and gas systems. He was slight and wiry, the smallest of the group, and a good friend of Alan's younger brother Clive. We sometimes referred to him as 'Blidge' in recognition of John's habit of aggressively wagging his finger at people to reinforce his arguments.

The others were less sure. Adrian Bird, 23, was studying architecture at Cambridge and could only commit for a year, following which he would have to return for a post-graduate course. He was due to graduate in the summer, after which he could work full-time on getting the bus ready. His father worked in the City and they lived in Rectory Lane, Bramshott, traditionally the upmarket part of the parish. Adrian didn't find money as much of a problem as some, and was better educated and better connected than most of us. His easy-going personality concealed a stubborn streak, and he had a habit of doing his own thing in a laid-back sort of way, but he would prove to be a useful conciliator and creative member of the team.

Alan's brother Clive, 22, took some persuading. Grammar School educated, unlike his brother, Clive valued his job as an assistant engineer with the Farnborough Urban District Council, even if he didn't like it that much, and was sceptical about our likely success. He got on well with the girls and enjoyed driving around in his open Triumph Herald and playing his guitar. If we were going to sing songs, we needed Clive's guitar and banjo playing.

At 27, Bob Hall had been the oldest person on the Spanish holiday, and we badly wanted him on board. He was powerfully built, the strongest and most energetic, with the widest range of practical skills of all of us. Good-hearted, even-tempered, sometimes unpredictable, and with the ability to get on with most people, he preferred to avoid confrontation. He had been brought up with three brothers and a sister near Milland, in Sussex, and had worked in Durham for a family member in the mining business. There he'd married, and moved back south with his wife and children in the mid-1960s. To the rest of us it appeared that married life didn't seem to suit Bob at all. He played a leading part in the 'Discord' adventure and became one of the central figures around whom our group revolved. Should the bus break down, we felt sure that Bob would be able to fix it. We worked hard to persuade him to come and, in the end, he agreed, but we had to accept that he was unlikely to find all of the £150 the rest of us had already coughed up.

None of the others who went to Spain were interested. The leading guitar player of The Procal Turdum, Peter Windibank, wanted to marry his girlfriend, Alison. He enjoyed home comforts and couldn't understand why anybody would want to drive an old bus around the world. Easy-going John Carver, a talented professional carpenter, just couldn't be bothered – he liked his life at home too much. They were two old childhood friends whom I had known since they were in their prams. Wally Walsh and Roland Hutchings both had good career prospects which neither of them wanted to jeopardise. Then there was Andrew Luff, on whose land the buses lived. His farm work had prevented him from coming to Spain and he couldn't leave the farm he'd inherited. So that made eight so far. We still needed to fill the ninth bunk, if only to find another £150 towards our spiralling costs.

About this time a young man started knocking on my door. 'You must take me with you,' he pleaded, 'I'll do anything – please!' His name was Tony Hough. He came from Essex, and his family owned a local company, Temple Building Products Ltd. He'd recently arrived in Liphook to work at their factory in nearby Passfield. He lodged in the village and threw himself enthusiastically into our local YC life. John Wilson's father had worked for Tony's family setting up the factory and, until his death some years before, was general manager there. Tall, well-built with tousled hair and glasses, Tony had left school at 16 and joined the Royal Tank Regiment. His minor public school and army experience caused him to refer to himself as 'the incredibly tough Hough'. He wasn't, though – he was too good-natured – and army life didn't suit him, so he eventually joined the family firm as a management trainee. However, it seemed that Tony felt that working in Passfield was like being sent to Siberia. His great advantage, apart from being good company, was that his family were well off, his grandfather, Sir Patrick Hennessy, being Chairman of the British Ford Motor Company. Tony was 20, well-spoken and personable, had a somewhat aristocratic demeanour, mixed well, and was well connected. He seemed capable and reliable and we liked him, so we decided that, even though we didn't know him very well, if Tony could help us find some sponsorship and pay his £150 contribution, he should come with us.

We sat in the bar and mulled over how we could find some more money. 'You can't just write to ICI or BP and say, "My friends and I are going on a two-year holiday of a lifetime. We're going to enjoy ourselves, pull the birds and have a wonderful time, and we're writing to you to ask you to pay for it." We've got to think of something different, something unusual.' I'd come up with an idea. As bright young Englishmen, couldn't we become travelling salesmen and take samples of British-made products with us in our bus? We could meet importers in different countries, get orders for our products, sign them up as local agents and earn a commission on their sales, giving us an ongoing income to pay for the trip. Their retainers would pay for advertising on the side of the bus and help get the show on the road. As an overseas trade mission, British Embassies would assist us. We could wear pinstripe suits and bowler hats and carry briefcases and rolled umbrellas, which would also get us loads of publicity.

This got a mixed reception from the others. Tim thought it was brilliant, while Alan totally disagreed. 'I'm no salesman,' he grumbled, 'I'm a mechanic. You'd be taking money under false pretences. Just because you think you're good at selling things doesn't mean that the rest of us are. If we get short of money, then we should all go out to work. At least that's honest!' 'Hold on, maybe Richard's got something here,' said Bob. 'Even if it just got us some money for adverts it would help,' said someone else. Alan was adamant. 'It's just not honest,' he repeated. The debate went on for days but eventually the sceptics were worn down and we agreed to give it a go. All the major decisions we subsequently took were made in the same way, and when things didn't turn out quite as the enthusiasts had planned, the doubters took great delight in being able to say, 'I told you so!'

We became a limited company, with all nine of us as directors, each having an equal shareholding. Late one evening in the pub we decided on the company name. 'Pillock Limited' seemed rather appropriate.

Pillock Ltd wrote to over 700 manufacturers. Around 680 of them did not reply. But we signed contracts with ten of those that did, who paid us retainers and bought advertisements on the bus. Altogether, including the odd donation, this income amounted to just under £1,000. The products we represented were a bizarre collection of oscilloscope trolleys, sausage grilling machines, gramophone styli, stainless steel tableware, plastic 'pillow tanks', telephones and tartan-trousered teddy bears. We were also given razor blades and fire extinguishers, mountains of Tupperware and a collection of high-quality copper-bottomed cooking pans.

There were other advantages to having our own company. It limited our liability and gave us a corporate identity and a degree of respectability which was useful in opening doors which might otherwise remain closed. Our discussions with the Board of Trade ended with them actually recognising us as an 'overseas trade mission' and through them we were offered help by all the embassies and high commissions on our route. Because of this, the American Embassy, after a lengthy interview, gave all the directors of Pillock Ltd multiple entry business visas that were valid until September 1973, enabling us to visit the US whenever we liked. Adrian's father helpfully sorted out insurances and mail collection arrangements through his firm's overseas contacts. The national press began to take a serious interest. 'Hold tight, it's the round the world bus sell,' ran the headline in the *Daily Express*.

Nine sporting bachelors ... plan to back Britain with a two-year round-the-world 'Bus Sell' ... They gathered sales commissions and trade samples from several British firms and next month set out on the 50,000-mile trip. The Board of Trade has backed the venture and Government commercial counsellors abroad have been alerted to help the mission.

While I was organising all this, with help from Tony and Tim, the others were working away on the bus, but time was passing and we were still nowhere near ready. Two tall gas cylinders were installed under the stairs, and an additional 25-gallon fuel tank fitted underneath the bus, increasing its range to 500 miles. There were one or two setbacks, of course. When welding the brackets to hold the extra fuel tank, twenty years' worth of grime and grease under the bus caught alight and nearly brought the whole enterprise to an end. Before Bob could put it out, the fire had burned one of the body panels, which had to be repainted. Mr Mantle kindly sent us replacement Warrington Corporation crest transfers and lettering. We also had problems with the fuel pump, which we had rebuilt. Tony's grandfather arranged for the bus to be checked and overhauled at the AEC works at Southall, which was another expense.

Although plans for the start of our journey were firming up, people were beginning to wonder if we were ever going to leave. Originally we had intended to have another holiday in Spain, this time taking both buses. The Portsmouth bus would then return to England, while Pillock 2 would turn eastwards and continue on towards India. We planned to leave Liphook at the end of August, Andrew and our trusted friend David Fletcher driving Hairy Pillock 1, taking with them Uncle Arthur's sons, my young cousins Peter and Paul Johnson, along with Peter Harris, Rodick Mitchel – who'd answered an advert in the local paper – Trevor Meech and Wally Walsh – who had been on the first trip. In mid-August, hundreds of our friends turned up to a 'Mammoth Farewell Party' with a barbecue, jazz band and farewell performance by The Procal Turdum, in the paddock behind the Deers Hut. This proved somewhat premature.

As the end of August approached, it was obvious that we were not ready. We were still tying up loose ends with potential advertisers, waiting for visas and insurances, and various medical inoculations. Every day we were becoming increasingly frustrated as something else completely unexpected delayed us. Bob insisted that we take what was virtually a complete workshop, including oxyacetylene welding equipment, ropes, chains and winches, a generator, electric drills, a comprehensive tool kit, and a full set of spare parts, including four spare wheels, but we had nowhere left on board to put any of this. We also had all the sales samples, including two oscilloscope trolleys and some big display units. Bob's solution was to tow a trailer, but it would have to collapse and be stowed away when the bus was shipped to Australia. He and Alan set to work designing and building a magnificent trailer that was capable of doing all this and holding securely everything which we would be taking with us. The bus had to be fitted with a tow bar, causing even more delays. With 29 August, the day we were due to leave, looming we were forced to postpone our departure by a month. This meant losing our Spanish holiday with the others. There would be no sun, sea and sand for us, and so they set off without us, leaving behind nine frustrated young men who were beginning to wonder if those who had predicted that we would never leave England were going to be proved right after all.

5

We Set Off: Into the Unknown

After weeks of delay we finally re-booked the ferry for the morning of Wednesday 1 October, on the basis that if we didn't go then we never would.

We'd been working on the bus right up to the end and, in the last four weeks, time for everything had run out. It had taken two days to load everything on board. Upstairs we filled the lockers and wardrobe with our clothes and made up our beds. All the food, the melamine plates, bowls and cups we'd bought – more sensible than china as they wouldn't break – cutlery and kitchen utensils, favourite records, glasses (mostly pinched from the pub), washing powder, toothbrushes, tea towels, toilet rolls, medical supplies, musical instruments, Tim's typewriter, reams of paper, files, maps, permits, carnets and books were stowed in their allotted places. Our trailer groaned under the weight of all the tools, spares and samples we were taking with us.

On the evening of Tuesday 30 September the two buses were parked outside the Deers Hut and last drinks were taken in the pub. Hundreds of relatives, friends and well-wishers had come to see us off. Andrew Harvey, from BBC TV South, had interviewed us and filmed the bus leaving the

farm for the last time. Pictures were taken and stories written
by the press. Pillock 1 had limped home with a blown head
gasket following a successful trip to Spain and Andrew now
presented us with a visitors' book which everybody was
busy signing. The Petworth Silver Band played from the top
deck of the old Isle of Wight open-top bus that Adrian and
I had acquired with my Uncle Arthur and David Fletcher.
By 9.15 p.m. we had said our final farewells, with the cynics,
led by my Uncle Arthur, telling us we would be back before
Christmas, and pulled away down the crowded drive. As we
set out for Dover with Bob at the wheel, the milometer read
23,327. He and I shared the driving between us, being the
only ones over 25 – apart from Tim, who didn't drive – as
our insurance only covered drivers over 25. Suddenly, after
the melee at the pub, it was very quiet on board. Most of us
were taken up with our own private thoughts about leaving
home. With glass in hand, John announced to those who
were listening that he'd had the last shave he would take on
the trip.

At 2.30 a.m., we rolled to a halt on the seafront at Dover.
Unexpectedly, Esme Grimes and some other friends had
followed us, and sat up talking with us for most of the night.
Then it really was goodbye and, as we drove towards the
Eastern Docks, John took the very first shots for the film
we intended to make of our travels. Ten days before, Tony's
father had surprised us by loaning us a professional Bell &
Howell 16mm cine camera, and this was the first time we'd
used it. Delivered to us at the docks to avoid the purchase
tax were thirty spools of Kodachrome II film – all we could
afford – which we would use to make a record of our journey.
We boarded the 10.30 a.m. ferry. After months of planning
and getting the bus ready, we were at last on our way.
Although none of us were really aware of it yet, our differing
expectations about living together in a confined space and

how we should pay for what lay ahead of us would eventually be the cause of friction between some of us. If we were to keep the show on the road, it was something we would all ultimately have to confront and come to terms with.

Due to the height of the bus we were last on the ferry. I had to reverse the bus down the narrow loading ramp, the trailer having already been manhandled on board. Although we were first off at Calais, there was still a lengthy customs inspection before we were allowed into France. It was early afternoon when we headed up the coast towards Dunkirk, the destination blind, made for us by my sister Mary, boldly proclaiming 'Vienna', which we aimed to reach in mid-October for a British Week there. The sun shone as we crossed into Belgium, their customs officers failing to notice that the bus was 2ft 6in above the country's legal height limit. We stopped for the night at the gates of a campsite on the outskirts of Bruges.

The next afternoon found Bob driving the bus around the centre of Brussels looking for somewhere to park. We turned into Avenue de la Liberté and after a few yards drove onto the wide, sandy central reservation and stopped. It was an odd place for us to park but at the time it seemed the natural thing to do. Now was the time to start honing our skills as salesmen, and so Tim, Tony, Adrian and I changed into our suits, donned our bowler hats and set off on a tram clutching a tartan teddy bear and a bag containing a loud-speaking telephone, leaving Dick and Clive to find fresh provisions and Bob, Alan and John to sort out some minor problems with the bus. Tony and Tim took the telephone to the Belgian equivalent of the GPO, but arrived at their city centre headquarters at the end of the afternoon and were almost flattened as several hundred telephone engineers surged through the main doors on their way home. Speaking to a receptionist, they promised to return the next morning.

It was the rush hour and as Tim squeezed into a tram the door closed, leaving Tony on the pavement. Climbing onto the next tram, Tony found himself with no Belgian currency, offered the rather stern conductor a £10 note and was swiftly ordered off. Tony arrived back at the bus over an hour later, having walked the length of Boulevard Leopold feeling very conspicuous in his bowler hat. Meanwhile, Adrian and I were told at Bon Marché that our teddy bear was rather nice and, if the manufacturers would like to send them a sample next February, they would consider ordering some.

Back at the bus we found the others downing our whisky with an Englishman, Guy Hamilton, an employee of British Oxygen who lived across the street. Amazed to see a British double-decker bus parked outside his flat, he rashly offered us the use of his bathroom. Throughout the evening, while he and his wife entertained us, one by one we took advantage of his facilities.

Early the next afternoon, having seen nothing of Brussels and achieving little as export salesmen, we prepared to leave. At this point several problems surfaced. The sink drained out underneath the bus, and a great puddle had formed in the sandy soil, into which the back wheels had slowly sunk. We eventually overcame this by purchasing a flexible rubber pipe to carry the waste water further away, but that day it was a problem. We'd also flattened the batteries by using our internal lights the previous evening, and now there wasn't enough power to turn the starter motor. Everyone had to get round the back and, with a little effort – John having dug out the wheels first – we pushed the bus out of the mud we'd created and bump started it.

We followed the N3 through drab and dismal suburbs into Belgium's industrial heartland, past decaying steel plants and old factories. We drove along the cobbled streets of Liège, returning the cheery waves of a few people as we scraped under the local trolley bus wires, finally stopping for the night next to a derelict marshalling yard through a town called Hervé. Next morning we were driving in the countryside, with hedges, trees and open farmland, and by midday reached the border with Germany.

With Teutonic thoroughness, the German border officials insisted on seeing all our papers. We produced the 'Carnet de Passages en Douane', the 'Carnet de Declarations', the International Green Card, the Certificate of Motor Insurance, the Travel Insurance Certificate and various other official-looking documents, but they were not satisfied with anything we gave them and, as none of them spoke English and only Tim and Clive had a smattering of schoolboy German, it took some time to discover that they wanted to see an overheight vehicle permit from the West German Transport Ministry. Eventually a special 'Transit Document' was prepared which allowed us nine days to cross Germany and cost us 81 marks. An hour later we set off to spend the weekend in Cologne.

Two of us had family friends in Cologne, and visits to them had been arranged before we left. Our first stop was at the family home of Adrian's friend Liz Herweg. Liz had often stayed with the Birds in England, knew the Deers Hut, and was pleased to see us. After a drink, we drove to a pretty campsite on the banks of the Rhine, just outside the city. The Herwegs had invited us back for supper, but Tony's contact, Ernst Bismark, had invited him to dine with them. The rest of us enjoyed a wonderful supper at Liz's, washed down with liberal amounts of strong German beer, which fortified us sufficiently to get the musical instruments out for an impromptu concert in the Herwegs' drawing-room. We greatly appreciated their generous hospitality, and their enjoyment of our music. The following day the Von Bismark family entertained us, with drinks and a late lunch in their beautifully appointed home. The visitors' book was signed by everyone, after which we reluctantly set off along the autobahn towards Frankfurt. Discreet enquiries had been made with the police – they had been told that someone wanted to transport a boat down the autobahn – who advised that none of the bridges on the autobahn were lower than 4.3m, the height of the bus, so off we went. The sun shone, the new road was excellent and as evening fell we arrived at the campsite we'd selected just off the motorway – only to find it closed for the winter.

There was another campsite in nearby Koblenz, so we headed west towards the Rhine. A few hundred yards after crossing the river on a dual carriageway our way was blocked by a low railway bridge. We managed to reverse to an exit we'd just passed, went down it and plunged into the town's complicated road system. Without a street map we were totally lost, and a succession of roadworks, low bridges and a railway embankment blocked our way in one direction while the river and the elevated main road we'd just left closed off our options in the other. It got worse, as we had to drive down a one-way-street the wrong way, much to oncoming drivers' astonishment. At this point an English-speaking German couple, noticing our difficulty, offered to help. In front of us was a large arched girder bridge carrying the main road we'd left earlier and, if we could get under it, we could get back onto the eastbound carriageway and escape from the city. The sign said it was 4m high. We decided to attempt it. Dick looked along the roof from the upstairs emergency exit while Clive climbed the side girders of the bridge. With their guidance I slowly inched forward, missing the first three girders by less than an inch, but ground to a halt under the fourth with a loud crunch. We were stuck. With cars driving by on either side of us, Bob, Clive and our German friends let down the front tyres. It took fifteen minutes to let enough air out to free the bus, and the flat tyres made it impossible to steer. Fortunately there was a petrol station immediately in front of us, so I drove across the pavement and onto the forecourt within reach of their air line, and we reinflated the tyres. We decided to forget about finding a campsite. Our German friends led us across the Rhine, which glistened steely grey in the moonlight, and back to the autobahn, where we said goodbye. We pulled into the next lay-by and, with a great sigh of relief, quickly settled down for the night. The following day, we visited the German Automobile Association in Frankfurt and Adrian, our navigator, came away with a map and guidebook which gave the height of every low bridge in the country. Never again would we venture into a big city without getting a local street map.

We sped down the autobahn at 38mph – our top speed – on the smooth, recently resurfaced highway. John was taking a nap on his bunk when there was a loud bang and the bus shuddered. We'd hit a low bridge at speed, and John awoke with a start. The upright support for the wardrobe next to John's bunk had been forced through the roof, creating a hole about the size of a sardine tin just above his head. One of the ventilator covers had also been torn off. We pulled over, quickly patched up the hole, and thereafter became deeply mistrustful of any information we were given about bridge heights. By nightfall, after travelling 185 miles, we arrived at Munich's luxurious-looking campsite.

Our expectation that the annual beer festival would still be in full swing was dashed, as it had ended the week before. Our bridge height book said we should avoid the Munich–Salzburg autobahn as, being built in the 1930s, the bridges were too low for us. We showered and cleaned ourselves up before setting off the next day on a diversion that took us through some of the most beautiful scenery on our trip so far – the Bavarian Alps. The bus slowly climbed the steep alpine roads, taking them in its stride. Descending the pass towards

Salzburg, we stopped for the night in a coach park at Inzell and breakfasted the next morning in a fold of the Bavarian hills next to a bubbling mountain stream teeming with trout. We rejoined the autobahn just before the Austrian border. Four London Transport Routemasters had passed this way a few days before en-route to Vienna's British Week, so the Austrian authorities assumed we were to do with them and let us through without question. Another night in a lay-by and we were in Vienna, our log showing that in ten days we had travelled 1,135 miles. The first real test of our abilities as salesmen was about to begin.

6

Golden October: Austrian Days and Viennese Nights

'Welcome, welcome,' said Herr Lorenz in a thick German accent as he ushered us into his imposing high-ceilinged Viennese apartment, an impressive arcaded neo-renaissance building in Lichtenfelsgasse 5, next to the magnificent Rathaus, the city's richly decorated Victorian gothic town hall. Small, middle-aged, with steel-rimmed glasses and an old-world, formal manner, beneath which lay a kind-hearted and rather shy man, Herr Lorenz introduced us to his charming wife and offered us drinks. We'd arrived half an hour late, as we'd been told his address over the phone and turned up punctually at 6.30 p.m. at Liechtensteinstrasse 5, which was miles away! We were wearing our best suits and bowler hats for our first meeting with the agent for Hill, Thomson & Co., the distillers of Queen Anne Scotch Whisky, a product we advertised on the side of the bus. As well as being paid £200 for this, we were to receive a free American gallon bottle of Scotch wherever we came across one of their agents, who would also try to arrange promotional work for us, for which we would be paid. Queen Anne's Simon Reynolds, with whom we'd set up the deal in

London, had written to Herr Lorenz suggesting he might use us during the British Week. By the time we left Vienna, we had a lot to be grateful to Herr Lorenz for, and he was most helpful in getting us work there.

It soon became apparent that Herr Lorenz actually spoke very little English. Tim struggled manfully as our translator until Herr Lorenz's 26-year-old son Gunther, who spoke English perfectly, appeared, followed by his younger sister Sissy, an attractive, animated 22-year-old with long, dark hair, who also spoke English and immediately began to organise us. It was Friday night and, after the party had broken up and we had returned to the bus in the street outside to have our supper, Gunter and Sissy took us to a wine cellar where they entertained us for the rest of the evening. When strolling musicians came to our table – something we discovered was usual in this part of Europe – we sang a few songs with them rather loudly. By the time we'd said goodnight and driven to the campsite we'd found earlier in the day, all we were fit for was a good night's sleep.

It was the weekend and Gunther and Sissy, bringing along two Italian girls who were holidaying with them, had organised a day out for us. We headed for Klosterneuburg, a delightful town built on a hill overlooking the Danube just north of the city limits. It is best known for its impressive monastery, founded in 1114 and extensively remodelled in the eighteenth and nineteenth centuries, which dominated the town. We parked outside the monastery's ancient walls and, while some of us were inside viewing the magnificent building and its treasures, Sissy set about preparing a traditional Austrian meal for us. Displaying an uncharacteristic interest in cooking, Tony, Alan and Clive stayed behind to help her, but became distressed by the unfamiliar smell and enormous size of Sissy's mother's pale and unappetising-looking Wienerwurst sausages curled up and steaming in our saucepans. It took courage even to consider eating them, which eventually led to puns about them being the 'wurst' sausages we'd ever seen.

From the hill, we filmed the view over the Danube and the city below us in the hazy afternoon sunshine, and then readied ourselves for our first professional engagement promoting Scotch whisky. We were joined by Sissy and were dismayed to find that she had a boyfriend, Hubert, who was with her. We'd parked the bus outside Gerard's Bar in Kärntner Strasse, Vienna's Regent Street, which was decked out with hundreds of Union Jacks, limply hanging like washing high above the wide street. Passing trams carried the flags of Britain and Austria crossed above the front windows, and the occasional London Transport Routemaster sped past full of bemused Viennese being given a free ride and a souvenir ticket by their British conductor. Advertisements for the bar were placed on the front and rear of our bus, and white-shirted waiters offered small tots of Scotch to passers-by while we paraded in our pinstriped suits and bowler hats. Gerard was keen for us to attract a crowd and encouraged us to get the musical instruments out. We launched into a hearty rendition of 'The Wild Rover'. This stopped everyone dead in their tracks and a great crowd gathered, spilling off the broad pavement into the street. Motorists also stopped to see what was going on, bringing the traffic to a standstill. Gerard was getting very excited as I introduced our second offering in English but with a heavy German accent, much to the delight of our new-found audience. By the time we'd finished 'The Black Velvet Band' and the police had been persuaded not to charge us with causing an obstruction, Gerard grasped us by the hand. 'Boys, boys,' he cried, jumping up and down. 'Tonight you will be my guest cabaret artists!' And so, after an excellent free dinner and a couple of drinks, we took our instruments to his discotheque cellar and began the very first cabaret performance of our trip. The Procal Turdum had arrived in Austria.

Until we reached Vienna we had been continually on the move, with every night being spent in a different place. Now we were resident for almost two weeks in Camping Wien West 2, a well-appointed campground in a beautiful woodland setting in a valley about half an hour from the city centre by tram. The surrounding tree-lined streets were most attractive, and behind high walls and hedges were concealed many elegant houses. The russet leaves fell gently in the warmth of the golden October sunshine as we spent Sunday settling in and doing our domestic chores between visits from other curious campers, mostly a motley collection of bearded young Australians, all of whom had spent the summer touring Europe on a shoestring. On those evenings when we were not out with the bus, they would call round with large quantities of beer. Our free gallon of Scotch soon disappeared and the evenings quickly degenerated into a haze of alcohol fumes, tobacco smoke – Adrian and I seemed to be the only ones amongst us who didn't smoke – and endless laughter at an unending stream of dirty Antipodean jokes.

It was always late when we crawled upstairs to bed and condensation was proving a problem for those on the top bunks. Clive, Dick and John woke up each morning drenched by the water that continually dripped off the single-skin centre section of the roof. This was partially sorted by purchasing a large roll of polystyrene which John cut to shape and glued to the roof, but the problem was never totally cured.

Our time in Vienna was divided almost equally between being export representatives and attempts to raise some badly needed cash by working for contacts of Herr Lorenz, with Sissy, Hubert and Gunther often on hand to help with our rudimentary German. The Monday following our arrival we visited the British Embassy. True to their word, the Board of Trade had advised them that a sales delegation from Pillock Ltd would be visiting Vienna during the British

Week, so they were expecting us. We were ushered into the impressive office of Mr Major, the Commercial Attaché, a youngish chap with an obvious public school background, who welcomed us warmly. 'Did you have a good flight?' he enquired. We explained that we'd come by road. 'How was the journey?' 'Well, we did hit one bridge on a German autobahn ...', eventually explaining that we were travelling in a twenty-year-old double-decker bus. Mr Major took all this in his stride and by the end of our meeting had given us a lengthy list of people to see. In the course of the next ten days we visited quite a few of them, but getting orders was an almost impossible task. The loud-speaking telephone did not meet the Austrian Telephone Corporation's specifications; the tartan-trousered teddy bears were inferior to and more expensive than the German product already stocked by the stores we visited; interest in the pillow tanks – an emergency storage facility for milk on remote farms – quickly waned once it was discovered that they were designed to be used only once; and a demonstration of the 'Rollergrille', an electric sausage-grilling machine, showed that it only worked effectively with the sort of limp, straight sausages found in Britain. The firmer, curved Austrian sausages passed over the top of the rollers and dropped onto the floor. In any case, they were made to be boiled, not grilled. The only product we were successful in selling was the gramophone styli, from which we obtained a small income. Those of us who thought that being export representatives would give us a degree of prestige and open doors for us were undeterred, but the doubters became increasingly cynical.

The day after our visit to the British Embassy, we started our sales drive in earnest, except that the bus wouldn't start because the batteries were flat again. What was worse, the back wheels had become bogged down in the waste from our sink once more, and the combined efforts of us all, dressed in our business suits, augmented by every available able-bodied Australian and American on the campsite, failed to get it moving. Always ready to rise to a challenge, Bob whipped off his jacket, heaved open the trailer lid and pulled out a large winch and great lengths of steel hawser. Lashing the winch to a convenient tree, Bob attached the other end of the steel rope to the bus, flexed his muscles and wrenched violently on the lever, slowly but surely pulling the bus out of the mire. We arrived at our appointment in town with minutes to spare.

The introductions arranged by Herr Lorenz resulted in a strange variety of jobs for us. As well as being paid, we also received provisions, meals and drinks. Rising at the crack of dawn on Thursday, we collected the Lorenzs and drove to Ohrfandl & Co., reputedly the biggest cash and carry in Austria, and from 8.30 we spent the morning serenading handfuls of astonished customers and workers, for which we were paid 500 schillings and given some tinned meat. At one point The Procal Turdum's efforts were broadcast on the tannoy throughout the entire store, with Herr Lorenz doing commercials for Queen Anne. Alan and I, with the accordion and double bass, found it difficult to play and walk at the same time, so we were loaded onto trolleys and pushed around the cavernous warehouse, surrounded by the others, who sang as they strolled through empty acres of cornflakes and canned goods. It got even more bizarre. It was suggested that we should go outside and be towed around the car park by a forklift truck. Tony and Bob, with a guitar and our giant bottle of Queen Anne to wave around, were put in a large crate on the front and lifted high into the air. The truck then moved jerkily around the car park towing the rest of us balancing precariously in a train of little trolleys. We sang to virtually nobody and were drowned out by the forklift's noisy motor. One result of all this, however, was that we were noticed by one customer, Herr Funk, the owner of the Chattanooga, a bar and nightclub in Graben, the main street in the heart of the city, and he asked us to do a cabaret turn there on the Saturday night.

The next evening, we were invited back to play at Gerard's Bar, where we were also wined and dined. The customers seemed happy enough and were amused by our songs and our bowler hats. This was followed, quite late, by Sissy, Hubert and Gunter taking us to the popular village of Grinzing, to try our hand at singing in one of the wine cellars there. Wearing our bowler hats, we started and, once the audience had got over the initial shock, we were welcomed with open arms. We took the place by storm, mainly because most of the customers were pretty drunk already and it was British Week. We moved around the dimly lit cellars, singing and passing the hat round. Table after table bought us drinks and paid us to sing for them. Hours later we staggered out, and Bob, who had managed to stay sober, drove us back to the campsite. Twice more we returned to the Grinzing wine cellars, but by our third visit, the evening before we left Vienna, the magic had sadly disappeared and we were less well received. British Week was over.

We enjoyed our time in Vienna. The city experienced the best autumn in living memory during our stay and, when we looked back, we would remember it as a warm and generous place. Being businessmen and performers, we were more than just tourists, a pattern that would continue throughout our travels, but we still managed to visit some major tourist sights. Austria's imperial past shone through in the glorious architecture and large open spaces of its capital, making it one of the finest cities in Europe. At its heart St Stephen's Cathedral had been the city's focal point for over 800 years. Almosr completely destroyed by the Germans and the Russsians in 1945, it had undergone a complete and highly sympathetic restoration. 'Choirstall mighty,' was Tim's reaction on being told that the choir stalls were some of the finest in the world. We had performed in two of the city's most important streets, and had frequently driven the bus around the broad and tree-lined Ring, past the State Opera House, the Parliament building, the Burgtheater, and various museums and galleries, all immaculately restored after the ravages of the Second World War.

Having said goodbye to Sissy and Hubert over a drink at Grinzing, and Gunter a day or two earlier, we thanked Herr Lorenz for his help and hospitality and presented his wife with a bouquet of flowers. With fuel and water tanks full, refilled gas bottles and more money in the kitty than we had when we arrived, we headed out of the city towards Graz, the warm sun shining through the trees, their leaves an autumnal yellow and gold, and left the open plains of the Danube, rising gently through beautiful sub-alpine scenery. There were no autobahns here, and our route to Graz, the second-largest city in Austria, followed the old main road which snaked steadily upwards round hairpin bends towards the summit of a steep pass. The Leyland engine never faltered as it took the climb easily, its first major test. Once over the pass we descended to Bruck an der Mur, beyond which we pulled into a lay-by for the night.

Herr Lorenz had phoned his colleague in Graz, Herr Steiner, and must have been fulsome in his praise of us, as a full programme had been organised. We were to meet in the large square in front of the railway station, where Herr Steiner was waiting for us with Herr Hornig, owner of Hornigkaffee, who, fortunately, spoke excellent English. Our job in Graz would be to publicise his coffee, a famous brand locally which was available through an extensive local chain of Hornig cafés, as well as in shops and supermarkets. The press had been alerted and a police motorcycle escort laid on. They took us to Hornig's state-of-the-art factory and coffee-roasting plant, where we would be parking overnight. After we'd cleaned up in the staff washrooms and changed into our suits, we were given a tour of the plant, which housed some extremely sophisticated machines for grading the coffee beans to ensure that only the finest were roasted to make Hornig's excellent coffee. Back at the bus, Herr Hornig's staff had covered the sides with huge banners advertising Hornigkaffee. After posing for a photograph with us, the policeman then took off on his motorbike with siren wailing and blue light flashing, and we followed him all around the town and right into the heart of the old city, narrowly squeezing through the ancient medieval alleyways, finally coming to rest in front of one of Herr Hornig's shops. We completely blocked what we assumed was a pedestrian-only street and, donning our bowlers, stood in front of the bus with our instruments and launched into an enthusiastic rendition of 'The Wild Rover', immediately drawing a large crowd. At this point it began to rain, the first we had seen for weeks. Undaunted, Herr Hornig's staff magically produced several huge umbrellas, all advertising Hornigkaffee. We carried on but, as the rain became heavier and the crowd smaller, Herr Hornig signalled for us to stop and whisked us off to another of his nearby cafés, all chrome and glass, and treated us to a coffee. 'Why can't we play here?' we suggested. Herr Steiner cleared this with the café manager and we began a brief recital, which soon prompted a prosperous-looking gentleman to buy everyone a glass of wine. The manager gave us 100 schillings and as we left, a couple of girls who had taken a fancy to us joined us and eventually stayed all evening, helping the cooks to prepare a huge supper, before joining in as we rehearsed some new songs for the morning. With everyone fed, Herr Steiner produced a bottle of Scharlachberg Brandy, which didn't last long, and we raised a glass to what had been an enjoyable day.

The next day was Saturday and for a fee of 1,000 schillings we spent the morning playing outside five busy supermarkets and shops. Just outside the door of the first, a crowd gathered to hear us, the majority of whom were children – who stood open-mouthed at the wonder of it all. At least that's what we thought, until we discovered that we were blocking the way to a gobstopper machine. Herr Steiner insisted we sing 'She'll Be Coming Round the Mountain' at each stop, and his pretty young wife handed out little Hornig flags to the audience, who waved them in time to the music. At our next stop the press photographers, who were covering all this in force, started yelling at a beautiful blonde who was going into the store. 'Eva, Eva – over here!' they yelled. It was the reigning Miss Austria, Eva Rueber-Staier, who good-humouredly stood alongside us in front of the bus for a couple of numbers and posed with us as everyone took photographs. The following month she became Miss World. The girls from the previous night had caught up with us as we arrived back in the old town. The weather had improved and the acoustics in the little street proved better than anywhere we'd sung before. Our voices echoed along the narrow lanes and attracted huge crowds of young people, Graz being a university town. They clapped, laughed and sang along, and Herr Hornig was delighted. Eventually, to the disappointment of our audience, we played our last song and Herr Hornig and his family took us to a nearby hotel, treating us to a magnificent lunch. We were sorely tempted to stay, but a new deadline was beginning to trouble us. If we didn't cross the high passes in eastern Turkey before the winter snows blocked them, we would be marooned in Europe until spring arrived, and we simply couldn't afford to delay. We said goodbye to all our new-found friends and an hour later were crossing the border into Yugoslavia and a completely new world.

7

Yugoslavian Interlude

We had been worried about crossing the frontier into a Communist country, but the formalities took no time at all and no questions were asked about the height of the bus. At the currency exchange and bar, we came across a coach party from Dewsbury on their way to Greece. A mix of British and Australians of all ages, they were heading for a hotel in Maribor, a few miles down the road. Would they like some free entertainment, I asked, and they immediately said 'yes', so half an hour later we parked at the hotel next to their coach and spent the evening in a function room at the hotel singing to them. It was great having an English-speaking audience who were able to join in all the choruses and obviously enjoyed our performance.

Zagreb was about 90 miles away but, the next morning, to avoid a weight restriction, we made a lengthy detour and found ourselves on an unsurfaced rural road away from the main tourist route. The rear springs were sagging due to the weight of everything on board and the uneven and corrugated track caused the bus to jar and bump, giving a very uncomfortable ride. Bob crawled along at under 10mph, and some of us took our cameras and ran ahead of the bus to photograph it on its first dirt road. The surfaces of Yugoslavia's asphalt roads weren't much better.

By late afternoon we reached Zagreb, the second-largest city in Yugoslavia, where we stopped in a small, leafy public square opposite a garage. They allowed us to fill our water tanks and use their toilet facilities, and it was here that we spent the next four nights. Adrian, Tim and I visited the British Consulate General the next morning, where Miss Rosemary Heyer, an efficient Yugoslav who spoke impeccable English, gave us good advice and made numerous phone calls on our behalf to local 'Enterprises' – workers' cooperatives run by committees, which was how business was structured in Yugoslavia – and organised a series of appointments for us over the next few days. But it was all to no avail. No one we visited could order anything without the agreement of their committee and, although interest was expressed in our oscilloscope trolleys, teddy bears, display units and styli, we would have to come back in a fortnight to get an answer. Some promised to write but they never did.

Meanwhile, Tim had visited the British Council on the floor below the Consulate and was given contact details of a senior director at the local State TV station. We eventually auditioned at the studios of Radiotelevizija Zagreb for the locally celebrated TV personality Mario Bellioni. He was impressed and wanted to record us for his TV show, but his only problem was that no cameras were available. They had all been commandeered by the news department, who had taken them to Banja Luka to cover a big earthquake there. If we could wait a week it would all be possible. We decided we couldn't, and all we came away with was the name of someone high up in the TV headquarters in Belgrade.

Back at the bus we'd had a string of visitors, mostly students, all of whom wanted to improve their English. One of the first to appear was Boris, a bright, high-spirited, dark-haired teenager who made a great impression with his Americanised English and vast vocabulary of English swear words which far surpassed our own. Calling in after their lectures, they drank our instant coffee, declared that it was foul, and asked us about life in England. Many spent their evenings with us and, by the time we left, the local postmen were delivering letters to us from some of them. Boris took a few of us along to his English evening class and tried to pass us off as locals, without success. Instead, an interesting evening was spent talking to the students about Britain and discovering that the main reason so many teenagers wanted to learn English was so that they could understand the words of our pop songs.

I'd intended to bring a Monopoly set with us but, in the rush of our departure, had forgotten. Someone mentioned this to Boris and the next day he breezed onto the bus, greeting us with another colourful expletive. 'Here's a Monopoly set,' he said proudly. It was Italian, and he'd brought along everything except the board. We wondered if they were illegal in a Communist country. Adrian quickly set to work drawing up a Monopoly board and we had our first game. By the end of the evening, we'd decided to copy what Boris had brought along and make our own set, but instead of the streets of Rome, we used the streets of Liphook. I typed up title deed cards, John made the money and Adrian created the board, placing the Longmoor Road, which is where I lived, at the cheap end, and Rectory Lane, which was where he lived, at the most exclusive. The four Liphook garages replaced the stations and the jail became the loo, with an appropriate illustration. Our game was full of local allusions – one of the penalties on the board was 'Bad Debt at Bert's – pay £10,000'. The interesting Community Chest and Chance cards were all products of Adrian's fertile imagination – for example, 'It's Your Birthday: collect £1,000 from each player while they all sing "Why Was He Born So Beautiful"!'

We'd done little sightseeing in Zagreb. The upper town gave views across the terracotta-tiled roofs of the rest of the city, which has a rich history and boasts some fine public buildings. But our desire to move on was great, and so early on Thursday morning, having been unsuccessful either in getting orders for our products or finding work as singers, we hitched on the trailer again and headed out of the city. This was not easy, as a railway line curved around half the city and the bus was too tall to get beneath the bridges under it. Twice we had to turn around, which involved unhitching and manhandling the trailer. A motorcycle policeman, seeing our predicament, offered to find a suitable route and escort us to the main highway. Three more bridges, a level crossing and an hour and a half later he bade us farewell and we were on the road to Belgrade, 250 miles away. Our map showed the road as a motorway, but it was actually a very tired, concrete-slab, single-lane arterial road across the long, flat agricultural plain that lies between Zagreb and Belgrade. The joints in the concrete were uneven, and the bus banged and jarred at each one. We had to slow to 20mph to soften the impact on our weakened springs and it wasn't until the late afternoon of the second day that we reached the only campground in Belgrade that had not closed for the winter. With acres of beautiful trees and situated on a hill high above the city, Košutnjak, a popular local park, took hours to find, as our Belgrade street map bore no relation to the local road network. We parked next to a British Land Rover and minibus carrying a party of twenty-three young people, mainly girls, from London to Sydney.

As dusk fell I decided to have a shower and get cleaned up. It was over a week since we'd left Vienna and in all that time we'd not had the use of any campsite facilities. With the light outside failing, I discovered that the lights in the camp's rather unsavoury toilet and shower block did not work. Undaunted, I turned on the shower, stripped off and stepped into the unlit cubicle. It was in Zagreb that we first noticed that in the Balkans, squat toilets were the norm in most public places, and the toilets in this campsite were of the squat variety. Someone had obviously mistaken the shower for a toilet and in the growing darkness I found myself stepping onto a pile of rather squishy turds. It took me a good half an hour to satisfy myself that my feet were really clean.

After supper, Bob, Alan and Clive went off to the camp restaurant to chat up the girls from the English party, while the rest of us settled down to a game of Liphookopoly. The girls came back to the bus for coffee but, to everyone's dismay, by eleven o'clock the next morning they had all left for Istanbul. It was Sunday, the day set aside for washing, cleaning up, doing repairs and generally lazing about. As many of us did not have the confidence to cook alone, we agreed to cook in alternate pairs in alphabetical order according to our surnames. So Adrian Bird was paired with Bob Hall, Dick Hayes with Tony Hough, and so on. But there were nine of us. John Wilson, who turned out to be a great cake maker, was last alphabetically, so when it came to his turn he paired off with Adrian Bird, and we all shifted back one until the next time round, when the pairing reverted to the original arrangement. After a while, some people expressed a preference to cook alone, which confused things even further, and a complicated rota evolved. Some of us worked hard to keep the place tidy whilst others didn't really care. You could tell who was house-trained, who had been to a boarding school (Adrian, Tony and Tim and, for a short while, me) and those who had mothers who ran round behind them picking up everything. Socks appeared everywhere and were consigned to a sock bag which grew fat on socks that no one was prepared to claim. Nobody won a prize for being the tidiest, but the cup for leaving things strewn all over the place probably went to Alan. Dick was in charge of provisions, kept an inventory of our food stocks and brought in the fresh food we needed such as milk, bread and eggs. Dick had another interest in what we ate, because he was also our medical and first-aid man.

When we weren't on the move, Sunday was also the day when we caught up with letters home and had time to read a book and relax a little. The record player gave sterling service; we had every type of music on board, from Bach to the Rolling Stones, Ella Fitzgerald to Fairport Convention, and Flanagan and Allan to Flatt and Scruggs. More than half the collection belonged to Tim, who bought more records as we went along. Some became firm favourites and quickly began to wear out. We were forever on the lookout for new songs to sing but, as we all needed to agree on what they should be, it took quite a while for our repertoire to expand. Some days we would play a succession of Beethoven symphonies, while at other times it would be a folk or rock 'n' roll day, usually depending on Tim's initial choice of record. Washing lines were strung up between the bus and the nearest tree and our smalls and shirts hung out to dry. We were slowly getting used to living together in a confined space but, as the euphoria of actually leaving England and setting out on our journey dissipated, so the latent tensions between us began to emerge. It would be months before we finally got the measure of each other and lived in reasonable harmony. The lesson that took time for us to learn was that of tolerance, and of accepting people for what they were, not what we would like them to be.

The next day, four of us visited Belgrade's British Embassy where, in contrast to his opposite number in Zagreb, Peter Bull, the Third Secretary (Commercial) gave us little encouragement and was quite negative about our chances of doing any business in the city. Some abortive sales calls later in the morning bore this out. A visit to the TV contact we'd been given found him off sick, and eventually the deputy head of cultural programmes explained that nothing could be arranged at short notice for us. Back at the bus, after a short discussion, it became obvious that unless we were to stay for at least ten days, we would be unlikely to find any paid work. The need to cross the Turkish mountains before the winter set in loomed large again, and reluctantly we decided to move on.

We'd seen hardly anything of Belgrade, which some of us felt was another missed opportunity. It was early afternoon and we drove back down the hill from the park. As we left the city we passed a large railway marshalling yard full of steam engines, whose drivers saluted us by blowing their whistles. In reply I gave them a few bursts on our cow horn and klaxon.

The hilly countryside around Belgrade became drier and more barren and open as we travelled further south. 'One interesting feature,' Tony noted in his diary, 'was the quantity of small brick kilns. They rather resembled an Arab house, except that they had a tiled roof. After the bricks are baked, they knock the walls down and there on hand are about 15,000 bricks.' Wreaths at the roadside marked the site of various crashes and, from the top deck of the bus, rusting hulks of the cars involved could be seen, derelict and forlorn, abandoned deep in the gullies and ravines we passed. The road was quite new, with a good tarmac surface – a vast improvement on the concrete slabs between Zagreb and Belgrade. As we neared Skopje, capital of Macedonia, mountains began to appear on the horizon either side of the flat valley down which we were travelling. Each night we parked on the side of the road, where heavy overnight lorries screamed by us, rocking the bus as they passed. We would start off at daybreak, the distant mountains ahead of us shrouded in early morning mist, and the driver, either Bob or me, would have to get everyone out of bed to bump-start the bus, the interior lights having flattened the batteries the previous evening. Once we were on the move, most would return to bed until the driver found a place to pull up for breakfast a few hours later. Waking one morning, we found we'd parked in a bus stop, and some locals, waiting for their bus, helped us push start ours, so we gave them a lift down the road. The faces of the local people were changing. Those in the west of the country were European in appearance, but here they looked more like Turks or Arabs. South of Skopje, the country became wilder and more rugged as we neared the mountains. The road followed a wide and slow-moving river which ran towards the Aegean Sea through narrow mountain passes and some of the most wild and beautiful scenery we'd seen so far.

We crossed into Greece on the afternoon of 5 November. The bus and trailer were weighed at the border – 12 tons and 1 hundredweight between them. The bus was entered on Tony's passport and if he left Greece without it he would have to pay a heavy import duty. An hour later, we stopped for the night on some open ground away from the highway, and while Tim and John prepared supper, Bob and I built a small bonfire to celebrate Guy Fawkes Night. After supper, we gathered round our small fire. An effigy of Harold Wilson, Britain's Labour Prime Minister, was placed on top before lighting the fire and setting off the one small firework I'd brought from England. This crackled and spluttered, erupting for about thirty seconds, then all was quiet. As we watched the fire, our heads were filled with thoughts of home. We were silent for a few minutes, each in our own private world as we stood staring into the glowing embers. But the spell was soon broken, and we went back to the bus to play Monopoly. The next day, we left the mountains of the border area behind us and soon reached the toll road which would take us the length of mainland Greece south to Athens. It had become warmer, and the craggy outcrops and fertile valleys were spectacular in the bright sunshine. An occasional stone monastery came into view perched atop enormous rocky pinnacles, and now and then the sea could be glimpsed sparkling away to our left, and after another overnight stop by the roadside we arrived in Athens.

8

Athens: The Slough of Despond

The bus had been running flat out for days and we were slowly becoming worried by a change in the engine noise, a slight knocking which seemed to be growing louder. Sorting this out dominated our stay in Athens. Approaching the Greek capital, we came across some Americans we'd met in Vienna, who led us to Camping Attikon, on the Eleusis road about forty minutes by local bus from Athens. We arrived on Friday afternoon and were welcomed with open arms by the owner, Rick Porter-Miles, a bearded, retired BOAC representative who had heard about us from other travellers. He ran the campsite with his Egyptian wife, Daisy, and it was here that we stayed for a couple of weeks. Daisy may once have been a slim, dark beauty, but she was now a large and rather formidable character who, we were warned, sometimes took a fancy to young male campers. The campsite was full of other overland travellers with Land Rovers and VW Campers sign-written with slogans such as 'TransWorld Expedition'. The pluckiest were a couple of English girls, Penny and Carol, who were driving east in an old Land Rover. While Alan and Bob removed the sump cover to check the big ends, which they judged might be worn and the cause of the knocking noise, Tim and I caught a bus into the city to visit the Queen Anne agent and the British Embassy. Here we met the charming and helpful Alexander Zervoudis, the Embassy's Commercial Officer who, having been alerted by London about our visit, had prepared lists of contacts that might be interested in our products. He gave us some useful insights into how business was conducted in Greece; they took long lunches and siestas from noon through the afternoon with working hours extending into the evenings.

Adrian collected our post from the Lloyd's agent in Piraeus. This was only the second batch of mail we'd received since Vienna. We quickly withdrew to various corners of the bus to read our letters and find out all the news from home. The packages also contained the local papers, and in them we read about ourselves in Tim's reports that they'd published, complete with photographs taken with his Polaroid camera. Our parents learned more about our travels from the newspaper stories than they did from our letters. The campsite was pleasant, and the other campers were like-minded travellers and good company. The weather was hot and sunny and the Porter-Miles were happy to have us there. We sang to them all outside in the cool of the evening, and when we expressed doubts about being able to get to Teheran until the spring the Porter-Miles even suggested we might manage the campsite for them while they went away for the winter. Camomile grew around the campsite, and Rick Porter-Miles persuaded us that adding it to our tobacco would make an exceedingly good smoke and that we could double what we had for our pipes and roll-up cigarettes. A camomile-picking expedition was rapidly arranged and the proceeds mixed with dozens of packets of Old Holborn in two large Tupperware containers. Ceremonially, the smokers filled their pipes, rolled their cigarettes and then lit up. To their horror, they found that the camomile/tobacco mixture turned out to be barely smokeable. In their hurry, no one had considered doing a trial mix first, and almost all the tobacco on the bus was ruined in an attempt to make it go further. The non-smokers felt very smug.

On Sunday, apart from Alan and Clive, who carried on dismantling the engine, we all donned suits and travelled to Athens to join the congregation at the little 130-year-old St Paul's Anglican Church for the Remembrance Day service. Inside it was a haven of peace – a little bit of home with the atmosphere of an English parish church. We had to stand at the back as it was packed with well-dressed British diplomats and others from the local English community. When the service was over, we soon found ourselves in conversation with some of the congregation, who were impressed by our turning out in suits and ties, unlike most young overland travellers they were accustomed to meeting. We were invited to drinks with the church's pastor, Canon Crowson, and his wife the following Wednesday, and were then given lifts to the peaceful Phaleron War Cemetery, south-east of the city, to attend a simple English service there. The poignant 'Ode of Remembrance' was read, followed by a Greek Army bugler playing the 'Last Post'. After the two minutes' silence, the British Ambassador, and those of other Commonwealth countries represented in Athens, laid wreaths at the war memorial. Over 2,000 British and Commonwealth servicemen from the Second World War are buried or commemorated there, with almost 600 tombstones carrying the legend, 'A soldier of the 1939–45 war – known unto God'.

New water pump bearings and the replacement big ends had been obtained from the Leyland agent in Athens who, when told we were short of money, gave Tony a large discount and arranged for our water pump to be reconditioned by Evangelos Moros, a large, kindly man in overalls with an open face who spoke no English, whose large engineering business serviced the local Leyland buses. He did this for us without charge. Meanwhile, the sales team were busy, but only managed to sell the record styli. We tried, unsuccessfully, to organise bookings for The Procal Turdum, approaching the Hilton Hotel and an American Forces base. One day the Queen Anne agent, the courteous and hospitable Mr Nicolaidis, and his staff, took us to an upmarket taverna and treated us to a splendid and very lengthy lunch, followed by an extended sightseeing tour, missed only by John and Bob, who were still working back at the campsite. We arranged to take some publicity photos of the bus for Queen Anne with the Parthenon in the background, and once more took cash in lieu of the free gallon of Scotch.

To raise some more money, Bob agreed to rebuild the bodywork on an American Air Force ambulance, based on a Pontiac shooting brake, owned by the Porter-Miles', and enthusiastically set to work with the oxyacetylene gear cutting the roof off and lowering it. One of the VW owners, impressed with the carpentry work on the bus, asked me to build a storage unit between the seats of his camper, which brought in some more cash to bolster our dwindling funds. We had left England with £404 in traveller's cheques. I produced our monthly accounts and statistics. At the end of October we had almost broken even. Our income of £107, mainly from promotional work arranged by the whisky agents, almost met our expenditure of £118, the biggest expenses being fuel (£43), food (£24) and campsite fees (£16). However, in Athens, with the bus off the road and no singing or promotional work in prospect, things did not look too good. Our income during our stay there was only £63, and by the time we left the city we'd spent over £200, just under half of which was on parts for the bus.

After a few days, our Leyland 600 engine was started and roared into life, but after a short test run the knocking seemed louder than ever. Off came the sump again. The standard-sized big ends we'd fitted were slightly too large, so Leyland exchanged them for an undersized set and, a couple of days later, the engine was tested again. This time the knocking noise had disappeared. Delighted to be on our way, we packed everything away, cleaned up where we'd been working and on Thursday 20 November, having wound 'Istanbul' up on the destination blind, received gifts from the Porter-Miles' – including some wine – and posed for photographs in front of the bus, we left. But it was a false start. After an hour, the engine was knocking as loudly as ever and we pulled onto the side of the road for a conference. Should we drive on to Istanbul and, if the knocking noise got worse, work on the engine there – or should we go back to Athens where we could easily get parts and knew people who could help us? 'Well, I'm not going back to Camping Attikon!' said Bob firmly. At first we didn't understand, but then it dawned on us that he must have been propositioned by Daisy. An alternative was to return to Athens and ask Mr Moros if we could work on the engine in his yard. He had some very basic toilets and washrooms there, and all the machinery and equipment we might need. We could live there while the work was taking place, if he would let us. We were likely to feel at home there, too, because, in some respects, it was not unlike the yard and workshops of Three Counties, my family's haulage business, and the army of friendly Greek fitters who worked for Mr Moros reminded us of the cheerful mechanics who worked for my Uncle Arthur. We all agreed that this was the right action to take and so we drove back to the city to see Mr Moros.

Fortunately for us, Mr Moros' English-speaking nephew was there when we arrived. Translating for us, he explained our predicament to his uncle. Mr Moros squeezed into the cab next to me and I drove down the road for him to hear the

noise for himself. He agreed that the wisest thing to do would
be to take the engine out of the bus, dismantle it and check
the crankshaft and bearings. He would allow us to use his
facilities and park the bus in the dusty wasteland just outside
the gates and high walls of his yard. Bob, Alan, John, Dick
and Adrian immediately started to disconnect things from
the engine, and the next day I filmed it being removed from
the bus.

Commerce in Athens, like many of the big cities we visited
in Eastern Europe and Asia, was spread amongst the hidden,
ugly backstreet areas of the city. These districts could be
intimidating if you weren't familiar with them. Each was
devoted exclusively to one kind of activity or another. We were
staying in the commercial motor repair district, with other
areas nearby full of electricians, plumbers, manufacturers
and wholesalers of one kind or another. We were parked on
a filthy, flea-infested, fly-ridden and dusty dead-end piece of
ground which we shared with a derelict truck, four wrecked
cars and heaps of other mechanical junk. We could just see
the Acropolis over the rooftops. Having removed the engine,
Bob then decided to rebuild the rear springs, having found a
cracked leaf in one of them, and add a couple of new leaves.
So he removed them while the engine block, pistons and
crankshaft were taken away to the grinding shop.

My confidence was slowly ebbing away as I began to
doubt our ability to get everything back together again. Our
bus was now up on blocks and with both axles removed.
It had no wheels, no rear springs, no engine, flat batteries and
was totally immovable. Bits of the bus were everywhere. The
inside, despite our best efforts, was like a tip, and we were all
covered in oil and grease and in need of a good bath. Some
took this in their stride, but I was getting more and more
depressed. Then, late on Sunday afternoon, just as we were
about to have supper, a cheery Mr Moros turned up in his

old convertible Cadillac and presented us with a bucket full of small, freshly caught fish and a large bottle of retsina. We invited him, his family and friends to come back later when, to their great amusement and delight, we sang to them for an hour by the light of car headlamps and a small fire under a full moon and starlit sky. The warmth and humanity extended to us by these new friends of ours, even though they spoke no English, cheered me up no end, and I now felt sure that they would do all they could to look after us and see us safely on our way.

By the end of the week the rebuilt engine came back and things slowly began to come together, but the weather was changing. The sun disappeared, the temperature dropped and a threatening bank of billowing dark clouds appeared on the horizon as the rising wind whipped up dust clouds in the gloom. The work on reinstalling the engine continued by floodlights well into the night. Clouds scudded across the moon and just after midnight, as the job neared completion, the skies opened and for the first time since April torrential rain fell. Over the next couple of days, the steady downpour continued, and our dustbowl quickly turned into a muddy swamp as Bob re-set the springs in the yard's machine shop and prepared to bolt them to the chassis once more.

We'd been in Athens for almost a month and had paid several visits to what were some of the most important ancient monuments in the western world, which were scattered around large, open sites throughout the city. Wandering over the Acropolis, we felt uncomfortable when we overheard snatches of commentary given by an English-speaking guide: '... a plaster replica – the best preserved can be seen in the British Museum ...', '... decorative statues, now known as the Elgin Marbles, which can be seen in the British Museum in London.' Nothing was roped off and we could walk through the glorious, perfectly formed but sadly damaged Parthenon, past deep pits and excavations, great walls and broken stairways to the Temple of Athena and the Erechtheion, whose southern portico is famously supported by six carved maidens. On the night of the full moon, some of us returned, and it was easy to imagine the ghosts of the ancients still inhabiting the shadowy temples. We saw the market place of classical Athens, the Agora, and found ourselves standing where Socrates had discussed philosophy almost two-and-a-half thousand years before. We wondered if the present swarthy and volatile Athenians could really be related to the ancient peoples who had created these places. One day, in the warm glow of early evening, we viewed the city from the highest of its hills, Lycabettus, with its cable railway and tiny whitewashed church, and looked out to the sparkling sea in the distance. But we had also got to know another side of Greece away from the tourists, and had experienced the warmth and friendship of ordinary working people, without whose help we would have been unable to get our bus back on the road again. We really didn't deserve the unfailing generosity and helpfulness of all the friends we had made in the commercial motor business, with Evangelos Moros driving hard bargains on our behalf, charging us nothing for the use of his tools and equipment, and accepting with good humour all the disruption we had caused him. We felt very lucky to have met them all.

The rain continued to pour down, and our determination to leave Mr Moros' yard on our second Sunday there was thwarted by a missing bush needed to refit one of the springs, and we had to wait until the following morning to have one specially made for us. Once it was fitted and the spring replaced, the rain stopped, so we were ready to go. We presented Mr Moros with a box of Queen Anne whisky miniatures, took photos of him and his men in front of the bus – looking for all the world like a group of formidable partisans

– and bade our benefactors an emotional farewell. The bus was tow-started and we gently pulled away from the yard but, in less than half a mile, smoke and the smell of burning rubber filled the bus. Quickly pulling into a garage, we found that the inside back tyres were rubbing against the enlarged springs. A handful of cheap washers from a nearby workshop cured the problem, and at last we left Athens behind us. Under a menacing sky, flashes of lightning heralded a magnificent thunderstorm with the air charged with electricity, but the downpour fell elsewhere. As the evening wore on it started to spit with rain, but the windscreen wiper didn't work as we nursed the rebuilt engine on. Bob and I took turns in driving through the night and spent the next 500 miles running the engine in, travelling no faster than 30mph, stopping only for meals, to rest the engine and fix the wiper. We left the main toll highway and continued through the next night splashing through endless puddles along the deteriorating coast road, meeting banks of misty rain as we approached the Turkish border.

As we drove on, all we could hear was the same knocking noise that had caused us to spend several weeks and almost a quarter of our reserves stripping the engine down and putting it back together again. This time we didn't turn back. We never did know whether we'd wasted our time rebuilding the engine in Athens, and by the time we finally reached Istanbul we really didn't care, for by then we had more pressing things to worry about.

9

Travels Through Turkey

'Who are the idiots in the bus?' shrieked the haggard, slightly built, bearded young man with unkempt hair, laughing hysterically as he staggered through the door of the cosy, centrally heated communal mess room at our campsite. 'We are,' we replied. 'You're mad,' he cried, slumping down into a chair. 'You'll never do it!' We stared at him in disbelief. He'd seen the destination blind on the bus, which now read 'Teheran'. 'The roads are covered in snow,' he went on, 'there's ice everywhere. It's been blowing a blizzard for days. Trucks are stuck in snowdrifts 4ft deep. I've just driven through it. Believe me, you'll never get over the mountains in that thing.' His wild eyes were bloodshot after many days and nights behind the wheel. He was an English Jew, hailed from Chester, a graduate, had fought in the Six-Day War for the Israelis and had spent the last eighteen months driving a battered Commer minibus ferrying hikers between Istanbul and Iran. His stories about road conditions in the mountains of Eastern Turkey became more terrifying as the evening wore on. Lorries had been wrecked, he told us. A coach had slid over the side into a deep ravine. There had been several deaths. The gradients were one in four. He said he'd driven buses like ours as a student and we would never get it round the hairpin bends in the high mountains. As he continued, our spirits sank. 'The roads are like footpaths compared to the mountain roads in Switzerland,' he said. 'One slip on the ice and you've had it – there are no guard rails anywhere. The passes are 9,000ft high. You haven't got a hope!' He then told us about the mountain brigands who robbed tourists at gunpoint. We had planned to stay in Istanbul until the following week and this was our second evening at the camp. What on earth were we going to do?

We'd arrived the previous afternoon and hadn't had a proper wash for weeks. The inside of the bus was full of dirty washing, our clothes, sheets and pillows were filthy and damp, and we stank of grease, oil and sweat, so the BP Mocamp just outside Istanbul was a godsend. In its magnificent tiled showers under streams of piping hot water we washed away the accumulated grime and dirt and felt clean for the first time since leaving Camping Attikon. It was the best shower I'd had since Vienna. The rest of the facilities, including the WCs, were equally spotless. We took over the large and very warm common room with tables, chairs, gas rings and sinks for washing up, cooking our meals there to save using the gas on the bus, which we had to keep refilling. The camp's washing machines worked overtime on our dirty clothes, and the big boiler room became full of drying shirts, towels sheets and socks. We'd collected our mail, discovered that the Queen Anne whisky agent had just left for London for a month, and that, according to Mr Spillocchia at the British Embassy, Turkish credit, exchange and import restrictions made the chance of finding importers for our English products extremely remote.

The description of the hair-raising road ahead sparked the inevitable reaction. We all agreed that we'd better get there quickly to see if what we had been told was true. Fanciful ideas about returning to Athens to caretake Camping Attikon, or getting Russian visas to travel through Georgia and Armenia, were decisively quashed, and the next afternoon we completed our washing, packed everything away, washed the bus and headed for the Golden Horn, the famous estuary in the historic centre of Istanbul. It was from here that the car ferries crossed the Bosphorus, for the planned bridge had yet to be built. There had been little time for sightseeing, but the imperative of pressing on overrode everything else.

The queue for the ferries was miles long, and as dusk fell we found ourselves waiting on the roadside next to a railway track watching the sleek blue sleeping cars of the Orient Express slowly starting out on their journey westwards. We watched wistfully as the train disappeared into the darkness, taking its passengers back towards European civilisation while we were heading eastwards into the unknown. Feeling homesick, some of us wished we were on board.

Our 14ft 6in high bus wouldn't fit under the bridge on the ferry. Vehicles drove on at one end of the ferry and off at the other, with the bridge spanning the deck, and as we drew nearer it became clear that the height of the bus would give us problems once more. Amid much confusion, with policemen gesticulating and blowing their whistles at us, we were turned away. They would try to put us on the biggest ferry when it was quieter. It was after midnight when we inched on board, but the low superstructure still barred our way and I had to reverse the bus back onto the quayside. We finally negotiated with the captain of one of the smaller boats that we would reverse onto his ferry, and he would then turn around before other vehicles were loaded. This would line us up to be first off on the other side, thus avoiding passing under his ferry's bridge. The fare was the equivalent of £4 4s. Finally, at 3 a.m. our ferry glided serenely across the smooth waters of the Bosphorus, carrying the nine of us and our bus

steadily away from the lights of Europe and towards new and
unexpected adventures in Asia.

We now had less than £250 in the kitty, which, if we made
good time, we thought would be just enough to cover our
travelling expenses to India. We had another £600 in the
bank in England – sufficient, we guessed, to pay for shipping
the bus and ourselves on a cargo boat from India to Australia.
We anticipated doing this in March, but we didn't really know.
Once in Australia, we would work to earn the money to pay
for our journey back home through the Americas. It was a
simple plan, but its success hinged on our getting to India
as soon as possible and arranging our passage to Australia
before our money ran out.

Once away from Istanbul, I parked at a filling station for
about four hours, and then, with most of the crew still in bed,
set out on a good road across a grassy plain in the direction
of Ankara. As we drove eastwards, the land became hillier
and more desolate, with glowering skies seemingly full of
snow. We decided not to visit Ankara, where there seemed
to be as many horse-drawn vehicles as cars, and stopped for
breakfast after bypassing the city. It was here we that met
a couple of chirpy young Cockneys, Alan and Tom, heading
east in an old Land Rover, and invited them to join us for our
meal. They had set out from England eight days before with
no set plans, encountered snow everywhere and had been
jailed for the night in Hungary for not having visas. They
had met in prison in England, they told us, one an inmate,
the other his jailer and, as a result of this unlikely friendship,
agreed to set out on a road trip once Tom – or was it Alan?
– was released. We talked about the route we were taking,
at which point Tom produced a copy of *Foyle's New School*

Atlas, dating from the 1940s, which was the only map they had with them. It had occurred to us that they might tow our trailer across the mountains for us, but they soon moved on, giving us 5lb of sugar, half a tin of coffee, and the feeling that we might not be the most naive people on the road after all.

We turned north-eastward and, to make up for all the time we had lost in Athens, Bob and I agreed we should drive on into the night once again. We were desperate to see what lay ahead of us. Heeding advice we'd been given about robbers, we agreed that while we were on the road, two of us should stay up every night on guard. As we neared the sea at Samsun, the weather grew milder. All along the Black Sea coast children waved to us on their way to school in their smart black uniforms and white collars, the boys in neatly pressed trousers, the girls in skirts. The gently rolling, tree-clad hills dropped down to quiet sandy beaches, and the bright sky and azure blue sea tempted Bob and Tony to take a swim in the icy waters when we stopped for lunch.

At Trabzon, four nights out from Istanbul, the road turned inland again and headed south to the snow-covered mountains that were already visible on the horizon. Determined to find out as quickly as possible if the passes were blocked by snow, we set off at sun-up, the big Leyland engine easily pulling its 12-ton load in first or second gear up the steep hills into the mountains, the bus barely squeezing through the occasional avalanche shelter. Heavy grey clouds hinted at the potential severity of the weather ahead. However, our fears appeared unfounded for, while there was snow all around, there was none on the road. The bus slowly crawled its way towards the top of the pass, a 600ft vertical drop on one side and a sheer rock face on the other. The gravelled, single-track road had few passing places and, as we'd been warned, there were no roadside barriers. By 11 a.m., I had driven to the summit of the lowest of the four passes we were to encounter, having climbed from the coast to over 6,000ft above sea level. The clouds had dispersed, the sky was blue, and in the clear, fresh mountain air we could see a panorama of snowy mountain peaks which stretched endlessly across the far horizon, which John filmed. The steep road descending the other side of the pass was even trickier; we crawled mile after mile at walking pace, sometimes over large patches of compressed snow, with the engine whining away in second gear acting as a brake around the hairpin bends. Down in the valley the snow had completely disappeared, and when we reached the settlements on the plain it became much warmer. We refuelled at a village garage. The local children, no longer in uniforms, still waved at us with one hand but, once we had passed, slung things at us with the other and a large lump of cow dung hit the cab window about a foot from my head. Bob took over for the next slightly less treacherous pass, which took us high into a vast, unpopulated, white treeless wasteland and, as the sun set behind a distant mountain range far across the snowfields of the high plateau, the temperature plummeted again and the road became icy. We ended the day's journey in the forecourt of a petrol station at Bayburt, and after a welcome hot supper it was Clive and Tony's turn to stand guard through the night.

The next forty-eight hours proved to be the toughest test so far for our 20-year-old bus. It was well below freezing when Tony woke me at 5.30 a.m. to take the first turn at driving. One or two others staggered down, shivering with the cold, and after a warming cup of tea we were on our way. The wide gravel track wound steadily and steeply into a cloudless blue sky, this time taking us to over 8,000ft. There was ice on the road and snow all around, and it took several hours to reach the summit. The view was breathtaking. We were surrounded by snow-covered mountains. The road ahead of us dropped steeply away, winding precipituously below us through a series of sharp hairpin bends, covered with packed snow and ice.We inched our way down in first gear and for the second day running many of us chose to walk in the sun and the bracing mountain air alongside the bus rather than potentially risking sliding over the unguarded edge by staying on board. Instead of keeping to the road, Bob took a shortcut and skipped off down the rock-strewn mountainside towards the road in the valley, far below us. When we eventually reached the valley floor half an hour later, he had completely disappeared and we all looked back up the mountain to find him. Alan and Adrian thought they'd spotted him, climbed back up to give him a piece of their mind for delaying us, but instead found a local peasant cutting wood, who wasn't pleased at being interrupted by two strangers. Was Bob somewhere on the mountain, possibly with a broken leg or worse, or was he ahead of us? We had no way of telling. We waited for him to catch us up, had a snack, and then drove slowly on with everyone scanning the hillside behind us. Our concern was mounting when, after about half a mile, I spotted Bob sitting on the side of the straight, tree-lined road. As he nonchalantly hopped back onto the bus and I picked up speed, tempers were frayed and everyone rounded on him.

By the time we stopped at Erzurum we had all cooled off, and Bob took the wheel as we headed for the final and highest pass of all, the one around which we were told the brigands operated. At Horsan, the main highway crossed a wide river on a concrete bridge. Its overhead struts were lower than the height of the bus, which prevented us from driving across it. Our maps showed an alternative but longer route close to the Russian border, which we decided to follow. The legend on one map indicated that we were heading for 'loose surfaced roads of low standard'. It was late afternoon and, as the road we were on was paved, Bob decided to continue driving into the night. At twilight, we came to a small village at the centre of which was an unsigned road junction where the road divided into three. This was not on any of our maps. We stopped, unsure of which road to choose, and decided to consult some locals who were standing watching us. We were heading for Igdir, a town close to the heavily guarded Russian frontier, and the man we approached, and who fortunately spoke German, was wanting a lift in that direction. He was an army captain returning home on leave, and in return for him guiding us on what he said was a new road built to carry troops to the extreme outposts of our NATO defences – which explained why it did not appear on our map – we offered him a lift. He picked up his bag and a sack and climbed aboard. Whatever was in the sack was alive – it was a chicken he was taking home to his mother. The unmade road was wide, without heavy gradients, and had been blasted through rocks and round mountains. It was unfinished, and the bad corrugations gave us a terrible ride for the next few hours, relieved only by the tarmac in two garrison towns we passed through.

Our passenger and guide left us, and we stopped for the night in the forecourt of a petrol station on the outskirts of Igdir. It was just before midnight and it was my turn to get supper. We eventually ate our meal at 1 a.m. It had been Alan's birthday, and all we'd eaten that day was a small piece of bread each! An hour later, with the exception of the two on watch, we crawled into our bunks. The border with the USSR was not far away, and in the distance searchlights swept across the sky and we could hear guard dogs – or were they wolves? – eerily howling to one another across the void in the otherwise still night.

I was up and in the cab again by 7.15 a.m. and, following the directions given us by the army captain, we headed towards what was the final pass, high across the western shoulder of Mount Ararat, beyond which we would rejoin the main road.

The secondary road we were on was 'unimproved', according to the map, and little better than a track. It grew steeper as we passed small biblical-looking mud hut settlements of sheep and goat herders that could not have changed much in the past thousand years. It was cold, crisp and sunny as we climbed ever upwards beyond the tree line, the back of the bus sometimes grounding on the tight hairpin bends as the engine strained in first gear on the steep gradient. By the time the road reached the sweeping plateau at the top of our climb, I was driving through snowfields, the road ahead thankfully having been recently cleared by a snowplough. We were about 9,000ft above sea level when we stopped at the top for breakfast and played snowballs in the dazzling snowdrifts on either side of the road. It was a gloriously bright day. Away to our left, Mount Ararat, Turkey's highest mountain and the traditional resting place of Noah's Ark, rose some 8,000ft above us and was covered in a blanket of snow which shimmered in the morning sun. Over to the west the land fell away into a deep ravine, with mountains beyond rising sheer from the glistening valley floor. We were soon on the move again and by midday had descended from the plateau, joined the main road at Doğubeyazıt and were driving east across a bleak yet beautiful plain. Flocks of sheep roamed among wild horses against the imposing backdrop of Mount Ararat, which dominated the entire region. As the border with Iran came into sight, so did a British Land Rover, hurtling westwards towards us. It was our two Cockney friends who, unaware that they needed Iranian visas – which did not surprise us – were now driving all the way back to the consulate in Trabzon to get them.

At the border we discovered that what we had been told in Istanbul was true. The week before there had been terrific blizzards. The border post had been cut off for two days, the mountain roads had been blocked by snow and people had been stranded overnight in their vehicles. There had also been many accidents, including some fatalities. It was also rumoured that nine tourists had been shot by bandits earlier in the week on the pass we had avoided because of the impassable bridge.

The paperwork completed, we entered Iran through an archway under the garrison buildings, just managing to scrape beneath a large, illuminated sign saying, in several languages, 'Welcome to Iran'. The road to Teheran was a revelation; wide, smooth, new and with no tight bends. This came as a great relief, and for the first time in a week we were able to cruise at our top speed of 38mph. The next morning, we thought, we would do a bit of sightseeing in Tabriz. We had put the clocks forward by an hour and a half when crossing the border, and it was soon supper time. After yet another meal chosen from the now barely digestible packets of Birds Eye dried food, everyone went to bed – with the exception of the driver (me) and the navigators, Clive and Tony. We continued onwards into the night. Later, over the internal telephone, we agreed to stop for the night just beyond the next small town. It was past midnight as we drove down the empty, brightly lit main street. Arriving at a big roundabout, we saw to our amazement a lone policeman standing at its centre on a grand rostrum. As he watched us pass, I waved. Then the tarmac unexpectedly ran out and we agreed that we were on the wrong road and should go back and ask him for directions. I did a sweeping U-turn and pulled up next to the surprised officer, opened the cab window and shouted, 'Tabriz?' He raised his arm indicating the wide street climbing away from the roundabout to my left. I drove away – to the great surprise of Tony and Clive, who had just stepped off the back platform of the bus and were walking round the trailer to ask the way. They suddenly found themselves standing alone in the silent street being stared at by a very bemused police officer. They were both dressed for bed, Clive with a coat over his pyjamas and Tony in his dressing gown. They watched the tail lights of the bus rapidly disappearing up the hill and then quickly broke into a run in a vain attempt to catch up with it. A mile or two further on, I had pulled off the road for the night. I got out of the cab and went upstairs and was annoyed that Tony and Clive seemed to have already gone to bed. 'You miserable buggers,' I muttered to Tony as I passed his bunk, 'you could've at least said goodnight.' Alan stuck his head out, asking, 'Where are Clive and Tony?' 'In bed!' I replied tetchily. 'No, they're not,' he said. He was right – their bunks were empty. They weren't downstairs either. I was just about to turn the bus around to retrace our steps when they appeared jogging up the road towards us. Alan, Adrian and I had a good laugh but, needless to say, Tony and Clive were not amused.

Next morning we parked in the centre of Tabriz. It was a major centre for heavy industry and internationally famous for its hand-woven rugs, but we saw little of any interest in the short time we were there and were soon on our way to Teheran, speeding along the new highway through wide river valleys alternating with picturesque gorges carved through multi-coloured rocks. At the narrowest points the road pierced the rocky outcrops with short tunnels. Then, with the high mountains far behind us, we emerged onto broad, windswept plains where time and the elements had eroded and rounded off the surrounding hills. Under an overcast sky, distant mud hut villages seemed to grow out of the brown and arid land, and now and then a camel train slowly ambled along the side of the road. One more overnight drive and we would be in Teheran, where some highly unwelcome news was awaiting us.

10

Teheran: Enter 'The Philanderers'

The tallest things at Camping Gol-e-Sahara, the half-finished, heavily walled and gated campsite in the scrub-like semi-desert south of Teheran, were the large, fluorescent street lamps which stayed on all night and towered above the recently planted trees. With Bob at the wheel and most of us asleep, we arrived outside the campsite's locked gates at 4 a.m. on Saturday 13 December and parked for what remained of the night. Then, after checking in and using the camp's unfinished but highly efficient showers – our first after more than a week – Adrian, Tony, Tim and I went into the city, leaving behind the others to check, clean and tidy the bus after what had been a stressful yet very exhilarating journey. The manager had been expecting us and had already allocated a space, as virtually all the other English-speaking campers – including the two Cockneys who had somehow managed to get there ahead of us – had either met us, or heard about us, on their travels. It was also here we picked up the first stories about a Foden steam lorry that always seemed to be on the road ahead of us. Less believable was the rumour about a coachload of young Swedish nuns whom we never did meet!

I felt we had little option but to move on quickly to reach India before our money ran out. Then, suddenly, everything was turned on its head. The post we collected in Teheran included a letter from David Fletcher which gave my self-confidence a resounding jolt. After all the debts we'd left behind us had been settled, he wrote, the £600 in our bank in Liphook – money set aside to pay for our passage to Australia – was now less than £50. On top of this, the money we had with us was now less than £200. The truth was that we were broke, had no real income, and no way of paying to get ourselves and our bus to Australia. Funding our journey needed a radical re-think.

It was in Iran that the relationships between us settled into a pattern which would continue for the rest of our round-the-world journey. Living so closely together in the bus generally seemed to work against the formation of deep individual friendships. We tried to avoid allowing arguments to degenerate into personal attacks but, with little better to do on the long evenings on the road, we debated endlessly about everything, particularly about what we should do next and the petty detail of our organisational arrangements. Despite sometimes heated arguments, we were reasonably tolerant of each other. We were all after the same goal and accepted we could only achieve it if we worked together in harmony. From the start we realised that for us to succeed in our common aim, we needed to agree on everything we did and, as our entire resources were held in common – we had little money of our own individually – everyone should have an equal say in the choices we had to make. By an unspoken consensus, we never once voted on any of the decisions we made, always talking them out endlessly until either the promoters of an idea, or the doubters, were worn down, gave in and everyone agreed. Sometimes this would take days – weeks, even. All for one and one for all was an idealistic concept but one not so easily achieved.

As the instigator of the trip, I had always considered myself our leader, but once we'd left England this didn't sit too well with one or two of the others, notably Alan, who regularly made the point that I was self-appointed. This underlying friction occasionally came to the surface at times of tension. If I had failings, they were that I seemed supremely confident in my own judgement, and was reluctant to delegate because I didn't really trust anyone and thought I could do most things better myself. In our more stressful moments, it was pointed out to me that I was not always right and that sometimes my decisions were flawed. However, the others trusted me to be the chairman of our limited company, hold the funds, keep the books, plan and organise things and act as our spokesman. With some sympathy, Adrian, ever the conciliator amongst us, described me as 'Head of Blame'.

The English language *Teheran Journal* had carried a news story about our impending arrival and the British Embassy's Commercial Section had a large official file for Pillock Ltd. October's *Board of Trade Journal* even contained a short article about us with a photo of us and the bus. However, the commercial officer, Mr Prince, held out little hope of our selling anything, owing to Iranian import restrictions, and our experiences over the coming weeks proved him to be right.

As we walked past a building with a polished brass plate that read 'Iran-America Society', I had a sudden impulse that they might be able to open doors for us and offer us work as singers, and so Adrian, Tony, Tim and I called in and were re-directed to their cultural centre and theatre in another part of town, with an introduction to its director, Dion Anderson. Half an hour later, Mr Anderson, a stylish young American with a neatly trimmed beard, gave us coffee and cakes, listened earnestly to our story, regretted his theatre was already booked and couldn't use us, but immediately telephoned the British Council to arrange a meeting for us with them. He then provided a car to take us to the 'Youth Palace', where he felt sure they would book us. We arrived at a magnificent new £3-million, multi-purpose building with music rooms, café, a large library, concert hall and other meeting rooms, inspired and paid for by the Shah in an attempt to keep the youth of Teheran off the streets. We were so impressed that we offered them a free concert, which was booked for after Christmas.

At the British Council we met someone whose kindness and generosity we would eventually find hard to repay. This was Robin Allan, a cultured, bespectacled, energetic and enthusiastic man in his early thirties. It was Robin who organised and directed our very first television appearance. He also agreed that the British Council could be our contact point in Teheran and arranged for us to give a concert to their students in the Council's main hall. Robin also introduced Tim to a bright-eyed young American journalist, Ellie Cook, from the *Teheran Journal*. Tim persuaded her to visit the bus, which resulted in a full-page article about our exporting and musical endeavours under the heading, 'Nine in a bus try singing for their supper'. 'Pillock from Liphook is here and Teheran may never be the same again,' she wrote, having attempted to interview all nine of us at the same time:

> The crew is a motley one ... Their only real tie is a cheerful collective craziness which seems to prevent them from taking minor difficulties too seriously ... With much good-natured groaning they share cooking, cleaning and selling chores. There is an atmosphere of good music, good talk and continual hilarity. As a business concern Pillock Ltd is efficient and persuasive ... but music is the lifeblood of the fellowship.

It included a description of our bus conversion and a large photograph of us in front of the bus. We were flattered by what she had written, and once it was published we became well known among Teheran's English-speaking communities.

To get to and from the campsite we often used the local bus. These were snub-nosed Mercedes, similar to the post buses of Switzerland. Tim wrote:

> The little bus ... is laden with character, and every time one of the group boards it about half-a-dozen smiling faces say 'Gol-e-Sahara?' enquiringly and laugh. It is particularly pleasing to catch a bus (back) that leaves about 6.30 p.m., for often there is a grizzled old gentleman who stands up, and starts a chant which evinces disciplined responses from the other passengers. This is followed by a long discourse of the works and merits of Mohammed ... Finally he makes a collection. The drivers have connected the internal lights to the brake-light system. In one bus there is a whole festoon of different-coloured lights wired up in this way, and in another, a single light over a picture of Mohammed blazes every time the driver puts his foot on the brake ...

We discovered that, if we arrived at our business calls in the late morning, we would invariably be invited out to lunch, particularly if we were visiting clubs or hotels, and it was a relief to be offered an alternative to our dehydrated suppers. Adrian and I had a splendid lunch with the Queen Anne agent at the exclusive Gorgan International Club. The manager there, a turbaned Sikh, Mr Inderjit Singh, agreed that we should perform at his club and subsequently invited us all to lunch. During a superb meal, he raised the vexed question of our name. He was unhappy with The Procal Turdum. It had already lost us bookings in Athens, and we spent the rest of our expansive lunch discussing different possibilities, ranging from 'The Busmen' and 'Omnibus' to 'Farmhouse Stew' and

'The Piddlers'. Mr Singh then suggested 'The Philanderers'. 'A philanderer is a wanderer,' Mr Singh assured us. It seemed appropriate and had a nice sound, too. It was definitely original, so we quickly agreed and, pleased with his choice, Mr Singh immediately printed the posters for our Boxing Day performance and put it in all the newspapers. Tim had been making a sales call and missed the lunch. When he heard what we'd agreed, he exploded. 'Who was the lunatic who thought that one up? Do you know what a philanderer is?' We repeated what we'd been told, and then consulted the bus' *Pocket Oxford Dictionary*, only to discover that to philander was 'to amuse oneself with love-making'. 'Pure wishful thinking!' was Tim's reaction. But it was too late to change things – and some of us hoped it was an omen of things to come. Meanwhile, Tony, through his grandfather's Ford Motor Company contacts, had wangled an invitation to lunch for us from Ford's Teheran manager, Mr Rowghani, this time at a top nightspot, the Chattanooga. Whilst there we persuaded the management to give us an audition, as did the Teheran Hilton, who also became interested in us. 'The Philanderers' were beginning to make an impression, and were booked to give performances at some of Teheran's most exclusive venues.

Our first Christmas away from home soon came round, and we decided to organise a big Christmas lunch for everyone at the campsite. We'd brought with us a range of Christmas decorations, including a small, artificial Christmas tree complete with lights, and we festooned the bus with these. Dick bought two magnificent turkeys, commandeered the camp's new kitchens and restaurant, and set about gathering all the ingredients of the festive season together. The English girls we'd met in Athens, Carol and Penny, arrived and helped Dick and Bob, with sporadic assistance from the rest of us, to prepare everything.

Christmas Eve saw us all, for the second night running, at parties in the British Embassy compound. The previous evening, alongside Embassy staff, we had sung carols, and were guests of Jack Burridge, the man responsible for the Embassy's transport, at a riotous party fuelled by endless beers and gin and tonics. We eventually sang to the partygoers and ended up parking in the Embassy grounds overnight. Mr and Mrs Wilson from the Embassy were our generous hosts on Christmas Eve, feeding us well, after which – while the others took the bus back to the campsite – the majority of us attended a traditional English midnight carol service at Teheran's St Paul's Anglican Church. This gave cause for reflection about the nature of our adventure together and, as we returned to the camp by taxi, Tim and I talked frankly about resolving the rather fractious relationship that had developed between us. The Christmas spirit worked its magic, and a more mellow fellowship began to develop between us all.

Christmas Day dawned and the turkeys were in the ovens on the bus and in the camp's kitchen. The vegetables were on the stoves, bunting was discovered by the camp manager, the restaurant decorated and tables arranged and laid out for a sumptuous Christmas banquet. The meal was scheduled for early afternoon, but then disaster struck. The turkey in the campsite oven was barely cooked at all, even though it was at maximum heat. John tested the oven and found the gas pipe was blocked. Because it was a sealed unit, it couldn't be cleared. It seemed that our meal was doomed, but Dick rose to the occasion and, with an inspiration born of necessity, sliced the half-cooked bird and fried the pieces. It was dark by the time twenty-five of us eventually sat down to a fabulous four-course Christmas dinner. Soup was followed by turkey with all the the vegetables you could ask for, then Christmas pudding with custard and cream, accompanied by the wine from Camping Attikon and dozens of bottles of beer, with our little Christmas tree the centrepiece of the table and crackers and festive hats for everyone. It was all a great success, thanks largely to the initiative and imagination of Dick and Bob. The evening was rounded off with huge quantities of cheap vodka, cigars and coffee, enjoyed with music from the LP collection. As the only girls present, Penny and Carol were danced off their feet!

The next day, we made an enormous turkey and vegetable broth from the leftovers, after which Dick put the turkey remains into a large saucepan and put the lid on. A couple of days later, Tony and Clive decided to use this as the basis for a stew but, removing the lid, they found that the contents had turned a yellowy-green colour with an unfortunate odour which they disguised by adding vinegar, tomato ketchup, pepper and mustard powder. This successfully masked the smell, but gave it an unusual and rather metallic taste. Alan refused to eat it, but the rest of us did – luckily with no ill effects. What was left remained in the saucepan for weeks, with the idea of making more soup from it. Thankfully, no one did, and we eventually buried the remains by the side of the road.

The round of parties, lunches and performances by the newly named Philanderers continued well into the New Year, involving us singing in front of audiences ranging from a few dozen up to several hundred people. New Year's Eve was a particularly busy time, from recording a half-hour TV performance for Robin Allan in the morning, to a celebratory supper and in seeing the New Year playing Auld Lang Syne at the crowded Gorgan International Club, then on to perform at La Cheminee, the most expensive club in Teheran and one frequented by the Shah and his entourage. It was a delightful dimly lit place full of tipsy Iranians, with beams and brick columns and an enormous fireplace and chimney as it's centrepiece. This was followed by our late arrival at a Hogmanay party given by Dr and Mrs Wright at the Embassy. We really were burning the candle at both ends.

Teheran was a new city, but with a growing dichotomy between the wealthy, westernised members of its society, and the poor, many of whom found solace in the teachings of Mohammed. The seeds of the revolution that was to rock the country ten years later were already sown and, for all his good intentions, Shah Pahlavi's attempts to modernise Iranian society were continually thwarted by those who saw this as going against the teachings of the Koran, or who had become rich by having their hands in the till. Sitting on the steps of Teheran's imposing General Post Office, licking the delightfully lemony-biscuity-flavoured stamps and sticking them on our letters home, Adrian found himself next to a friendly Iranian Hindu who told him in a confidential, almost conspiratorial manner that the regime was corrupt and that revolution was coming, concluding that he supposed he was being watched. On the surface, though, Teheran was a prosperous enough place, full of broad and charming tree-lined avenues. Fast-flowing streams of crystal-clear water ran in gullies along the main north–south avenues and modern buses and cars, many of which were Iranian-built Hillman Hunters, filled the streets. There were many modern glass and concrete buildings but, like our campsite, many of them seemed unfinished. Snow-capped mountains rose to the north of the city, providing an attractive backdrop for the well-off who lived there, but to the south, where our campsite was located, the underlying poverty was more visible.

Between Christmas and New Year, Robin Allan invited us home to Sunday lunch, where we met his charming and heavily pregnant wife, Janet, and their two delightful little girls, Katherine and Clare. Their hospitality was overwhelming and, grabbing my toilet bag and clean clothes from the bus outside, I scrounged the best bath I'd had in months. Refreshed, I joined the others for generous pre-lunch drinks and the most perfect roast lamb any of us had tasted since leaving home. Robin's house was crammed with books about film and the theatre, and he and I found we shared a passion for cinema and, in particular, the work of Walt Disney. We all talked for hours as the meal settled, and Janet told us about the problems they were having with their plumbing. John chivalrously offered his services, and two days later appeared with a bag of tools and spent the best part of a week digging up their bathroom floor and walls in search of various leaks.

Our frenetic lifestyle was beginning to affect me. I'd not felt well since before Christmas when, after being dosed up by Dick, I was eventually packed off by Robin in a British Council car to see their doctor, a highly professional Iranian woman. She put me on the scales. I'd lost almost two stone since leaving England and was now well under ten stone. She prescribed cough mixture and pills and told me to take it easy. It was now early into the New Year and I was feeling even worse. We'd parked for the night outside the home of Mr MacDonald, the Director of the British Council, and his wife, having played at a big party there. Tony wrote in his diary:

> ... a voice croaked my name. Turning, I saw a weak hand flap up and down and realised that Richard wanted me. I peered into his bunk and he ... gasped for some cough mixture and lay back on his pillow. I obediently staggered downstairs and returned with mixture and spoon. He managed to prop himself up on one elbow and I spoon-fed him some mixture, after which he sank into troubled slumber.

When Dick took my temperature the next morning it was 104°F. He swiftly decreed that I needed medical attention, went to see Robin and arranged an immediate appointment with the British Council doctor, who diagnosed influenza, dosed me up and prescribed bed rest. 'Like angels of mercy,' Tim wrote, 'the Allans immediately offered their spare bedroom as a sick room, despite the chaos being caused by John, who was knocking part of the bathroom wall away.' For the first time in over three months I crept, grateful and exhausted, into a proper bed, and immediately fell into a deep sleep between crisp, clean sheets. For the remainder of our stay in Teheran, I was Robin and Janet's house guest, with the others visiting me or checking up on John, usually around mealtimes, when they knew there was every possibility of them being fed. Janet slowly nursed me back to health and I became extremely grateful to them both. Less than two weeks later, Janet gave birth to a baby boy called Frank, I became his godfather, and we all remained lifelong friends.

The crowning achievement of our visit to Teheran occurred a couple of days before we left. My illness had delayed our departure and, while I lay in bed, and John was tearing up the floor and ripping out the toilet in the Allans' bathroom, trying to find the cause of wet patches there and on the ceiling below, Clive had been seeking a booking at the Abberle Ski Resort in the mountains north of the city. He had met a Mr Amirali, who arranged the entertainment for the state-owned hotel and resort chain, and was also the director of the charitable Pahlavi Foundation, established by the Shah. He immediately arranged an audition at the Vanak Hotel. Clive hurriedly got everyone together, dragged me from my sick bed, and at 6 p.m. we were rehearsing before the genial, well-dressed Mr Amirali, who appeared sufficiently satisfied to offer us $100 US to perform at a private function the following day. He told us little, asking us to meet him at the Pahlavi Foundation building the next evening. We arrived in the bus and were asked to follow a couple of large, black,

American limousines which led us deep into the exclusive residential enclave north of the city, eventually stopping outside a high wall with an impressive gateway flanked by armed sentries. Our guides seemed nervous, told us to stay on the bus, produced a bottle of Scotch and some nuts, and said that this was the palace of the Royal Minister of Court, and that the Shah himself was present. This came as a shock. We poured ourselves a drink, while outside armed guards were patrolling the grounds. A couple of security men thoroughly but rather ineffectually searched us and our instruments, after which we were hurried through the gates and into a large room, which was full of Iranian entertainers, inside the luxurious palace. Dancers were limbering up, comedians nervously rehearsed their jokes and jugglers dropped clubs everywhere. We were liberally supplied with food and drink while, one by one, the others were ushered out of the room to perform. Then it was our turn. Suitably fortified, we walked through the door with our instruments and strode confidently into the centre of the palace's magnificent reception hall. Our audience was the cream of Iranian society. Seated slightly to one side was a dignified grey-haired man instantly recognisable as the Shah of Iran, with the Empress Farah sitting next to him. Tim described our performance:

> Never before had Richard introduced a performance more thoroughly engagingly, quietly introducing the group from England on a world tour. The guests were delighted when he said 'and as we're a group from England we'll start with an American song', introducing 'Worried Man Blues', to which the audience immediately started to clap along, followed by 'Toe Tapper', the risqué West Country song, which produced a smile from His Majesty. Introducing 'Chastity Belt', Richard talked of the crusades 'where

our ancestors may well have met your ancestors'. This was followed by 'Farmer's Boy', the earthiest song in the repertoire full of animal noises – 'We were expecting to play in a rather larger hotel than this' – and this number His Majesty really enjoyed, exchanging the fixed benevolent smile for out and out laughter. The final number was '500 Miles', and the applause from the small and select group of guests was generous as the Philanderers, faintly dazed, left the floor.

Mr Amarali told us that they were so pleased with our performance that our fee would be doubled to $200, and the Royal Minister of Court, the Shah's cousin, came to thank us. It was one of the most remarkable experiences of our entire journey.

A couple of days later, in bright sunshine, the bus pulled out of Camping Gol-e-Sahara for the last time and drove to the Allans', where John had finally restored the bathroom and kitchen, having sorted out the elusive leaks. Robin and Janet presented us with a box full of luxuries – sweets, canned sausages, baked beans, whisky and cigarettes – and late in the afternoon we finally departed. Dick had already stocked up the bus with staples such as Turkish coffee, sugar, beans, a sack of potatoes, flour and rice. Our income in Teheran was little short of £400, but we needed a lot more than that to get to Australia. We were heading for Afghanistan, having obtained visas during our stay in Teheran, and as night fell we climbed the northern foothills towards the Caspian Sea, the city lights twinkling below us. We were leaving behind some good friends but taking with us many happy memories.

11

The Road to Kabul: The Freezing International Highway

The highest mountain peaks north of Teheran rise to over 18,000ft, and the main road east, grandly named the Asian International Highway, climbed high into the range and took us into broad snowfields. We spent a cold night in the mountains parked outside a police outpost, where the officers on duty were rather impressed by the bus, allowed us to use their facilities and donated some paraffin for the Tilley lamp and heater that Clive had bought in Teheran. We soon adjusted to our usual routine when on the road, starting off just after sun-up with the majority still asleep and breakfasting – brunching, really – well into the morning once everyone was up. The smooth tarmac highway, well maintained and cleared of snow, gently descended to the Caspian plain and we were surprised to find ourselves entering a lush, green landscape with prosperous-looking houses hidden amongst small copses of fresh green trees. We were taken with the unexpected beauty of it all in the light, misty rain.

The next morning, we found a small town where Alan, Adrian and I bought some provisions. We returned, jubilant that we had found some fresh eggs, as well as supplies of milk, onions, oranges and what we thought was a cabbage but was actually a lettuce. We eagerly awaited a 'full house' breakfast, with the eggs, enough for two each, being a special treat. Tins of sausages and baked beans were opened, potatoes chipped and fried, and the pan made ready to fry the eggs, only to find out, amongst groans of disappointment, that they were all hard-boiled. We fried them anyway.

The drizzle continued as the Asian International Highway degenerated from tarmac to mud and gravel and, as we slowly bumped and crashed our way forward across a bleak plain, it soon dawned on us that the road was still under construction, the way ahead becoming completely blocked by heaps of rubble, unfinished culverts and a gang of roadbuilders. Having buckled the rear body panels by grounding the back of the bus a couple of times, Bob followed the example of some trucks and turned the bus around. We retraced our steps until we could join the old road, which wound away towards the hills to the south and parted company with the unfinished highway, which carried on eastwards into the misty rain. The bus was slowly becoming covered in mud. Later, as we neared the hills, the sun broke through, the scenery changed, and we found ourselves entering a beautiful national park. The unsurfaced track passed through several wide, shallow fords and I found myself driving through an enchanted valley. We headed towards the high plateau, the trees became snow-covered, the sun set, and it became noticeably colder. The frozen mud on the road gave way to snow and ice and, with the trees now far behind us, we finally left the milder influence of the Caspian Sea. With the road still climbing, I drove cautiously into the freezing, snowy darkness, the road slippery with ice, until we reached what was obviously an overnight stopping place for trucks and coaches with a café and filling station, seemingly miles from anywhere. Here we cooked supper and, taking the advice of truck drivers who said it would be foolish to continue, stopped for the night. Having eaten, we huddled together listening to the wistful singing of Mary Hopkins on a pirated LP that Tim had bought in Teheran, thinking longingly of our warm homes far away.

We'd brought with us a pair of old snow chains for the rear wheels, and had purchased another set in Teheran for the front. Bob, Tony and John fitted them after we'd stopped, and a kindly Iranian sorted out a problem with the leather straps on our pair, which kept snapping in the freezing cold. The next morning we set off with the chains clanking, the ride being unexpectedly improved by the compacted snow on the road. However, with the road slowly descending and the temperature rising, the surface began to turn back to grit and mud, which forced us to remove the chains to prevent damage to our tyres. We stopped for more provisions. Tony wrote in his diary:

> As usual, we attracted a small crowd of inquisitive adults and a majority of children, all shouting 'Allo, Meester.' I had also learned hair-raising stories of these people being vicious and the most terrible thieves, but I and the others found them gay, cheerful, a slight nuisance, perhaps, but no real trouble and often willing to help, if possible.

After lunch, we spent the afternoon slowly rattling along towards Quechan, the road gently climbing into bare, snow-covered hills. The downstairs windows, now caked with mud, were completely opaque.

The clear, bright sun drew closer to the horizon, throwing long shadows in front of us as we came round a bend and found our way ahead completely blocked by a Leyland truck, immovably stuck on rising ground the other side of a dip in the undulating road. Its springs had given way and the overloaded body was resting on the back wheels. Two local buses at the bottom of the hill had disgorged their passengers, who were highly amused when an old British double-decker pulled up behind them. Other vehicles had bypassed the blockage by driving off the road and up the bank next to the broken-down truck, but the track they had made looked steep and muddy, and a further complication was a ditch at the foot of the hill. Piling out to inspect the terrain, we watched the empty coaches struggle up the slope, only just making it to the top of the hill – their passengers running alongside.

While Adrian and Tony set off to see if there was an alternative route along the new highway works nearby, the rest of us, with the help of some locals, started collecting rocks and used shovels from the trailer to fill in the ditch, currently impassable because of our low ground clearance. When the work was done, Bob jumped into the cab and drove flat out across the ditch and up the hill ahead, only to slow to a halt three-quarters of the way up, as the rear wheels started slipping on the mud. We were well and truly stuck – The Asian International Highway was completely blocked. It was getting dark and, as we stood around hopelessly trying to decide what to do next, a huge Mack truck appeared over the brow of the hill ahead of us. Quickly taking in the situation, the driver agreed to attempt to pull us up the hill, using his winch. It only took a few moments for the powerful American lorry to haul all 12 tons of the bus and trailer off the muddy slope and, to our great relief, back onto the highway. As we loaded our gear into the trailer, I produced packets of Wilkinson Sword razorblades from the vast stocks we'd been given in England and handed them out as a gift to the lorry driver and those others who had helped us, creating a stampede of every Iranian within sight. Some thought they were sweets and I mimed shaving until they understood what they were.

With snow chains on, Bob drove on to Quechan where, at 11.30 p.m., we stopped for our evening meal. In temperatures of -14°C, Bob and some of the others changed a punctured trailer tyre. The four burners on the stove warmed things up a little as I cooked vegetables and simmered the dehydrated farmhouse stew, but there was a steep temperature gradient; at floor level it was still below zero, while towards the ceiling, the thermometer registered 12°C. Our feet froze, and we sat on the backs of the seats with our feet on the tables where it was warmer. We kept the sack of potatoes under the sink. A leaky paraffin container had been placed on top of them and every potato tasted of paraffin. Having looked at the steaming supper, Tony stepped outside to help Bob and the condensation on his glasses immediately froze – he couldn't see a thing. Upstairs, the heater only added to the condensation, but the moisture permanently froze, creating icicles on the walls inside the bus. When we were on the move, the front windows continually froze over and had to be regularly cleared. On the top bunks, Clive, John and Dick's damp blankets were stiff with frost and stuck to the roof. Our water tanks were kept empty, as the frozen water would have split them.

We decided to carry on through what was the coldest night of our entire journey, and it was my turn to drive. By now, the engine had been running almost continuously since we left Teheran to prevent the oil and water freezing, but the cab heater we'd fitted had stopped working back in Europe and the cab temperature was well below zero. I dressed for a freezing cold night, with pyjamas under my jeans, two pairs of socks, a vest, shirt, two sweaters, an anorak, thick driving gloves and an old flying helmet on my head covering my ears. Blankets draped over my knees and, with little hope of success, were stuffed into all the areas where draughts entered the cab, which was just about everywhere. The only source of heat was a small but ineffective paraffin engine warmer alight under the driver's seat. We left Quechan at 1 a.m., grinding along in third gear on a snow-covered road with snow chains clanking and the temperature below -15°C. Tony and Adrian stood watch upstairs, while the others tried to get warm and find some sleep in their bunks. Getting steadily colder, I continually swore to myself, ran out of swear words and began, for some reason, to mutter 'naft', the Farsi for paraffin. The sky was full of stars. Then the bitter night slowly ended and at 6.30 a.m. the sun gently rose over the horizon ahead of us and, growing into a giant, warming, red ball, climbed into the sky. After stopping for breakfast on hot porridge, tea, toast and marmalade, we arrived in Mashed.

To our surprise, Mashed turned out to be a well-planned city of attractive, tree-lined streets, the edges piled with melting snow, and modern buildings that dazzled in the bright sunshine reflecting off the snow. We found it to be full of hospitable, helpful people, too. A religious centre, it had a celebrated mosque with a splendid turquoise dome that glistened in the sunlight, while the prophet's tomb boasted a dome of burnished gold.

Students wishing to practise their English offered to show us around and, as some of them helped Tony and Bob seek out a decent set of snow chains to replace the now broken leather-strapped ones, the rest of us were taken on a short sightseeing tour, which included visits to the bazaar and various establishments where semi-precious stones were processed, polished and sold. But it was a fleeting visit and, with the fuel tanks refilled and more water taken on board, we left the city in the early afternoon and headed towards the border with Afghanistan.

It was my turn at the wheel again, and very soon the tarmac ended and snow and ice on the muddy track thickened in the deepening twilight. We were now on the embankment of an unfinished part of the new Asian International highway and, with the wheels beginning to slip on the ice, I stopped the bus to fit the snow chains. Getting out of the cab I suddenly realised that the bus was slowly sliding on the ice towards the side of the road. I grabbed at some stones but they were frozen to the ground and it took a while to dislodge them. Bob, coming round the back of the trailer with the snow chains, also saw what was happening and flung them under the rear wheels while I chucked some stones underneath the front tyres. To our great relief the bus stopped moving, dangerously close to the edge of the embankment. By mid-evening, the temperature outside the bus was almost as cold as the previous night. The fuel line connecting the main and auxiliary tanks had already frozen, even though we had been adding petrol and paraffin to the diesel to reduce its freezing point, but the engine stopped because the line from the tank to the engine had also frozen. As resourceful as ever, Bob had rigged up a five-gallon tank on the wing, connected it to the pump and filled it with fuel from the reserve tank. Tim reported:

> Bob drove on through the night, but at about 3.30 accumulated tiredness born of three days of wrestling with chains and blockages in the bitter cold overcame him, and he decided to stop for the night. Three hours later Richard was back in the cab, and driving on to the border town of Taibat.

'The town is at your disposition,' said the Mayor of Taibat warmly. Adrian and I had taken all the passports to the Passport Control Office to have them stamped, when we were approached by an official who informed us that the mayor wished to see us. An earnest and smartly dressed man in his early thirties, he had read in the press about our exploits in Teheran. It seemed that the English singing group and their double-decker bus were now famous in Iran. Wishing to extend to us the hospitality of his town, he invited us to take breakfast with him at the local café in the town's wide gravel and mud main street. This was a substantial affair, with hot, hard-boiled eggs, cheese, bread, nuts, butter, soft drinks and coffee. Replete, we were then taken to see the town's 500-year-old mosque, of which they were particularly proud, and which was being restored, then on to the town's freezing-cold cinema with its massive antique carbon-arc projector, where it was suggested that we might consider giving them a concert that evening. However, we had been on the road for five days and were all looking scruffy and in need of a good shower. The bus was even worse, being completely covered in mud. We asked if they had somewhere to wash the bus and clean ourselves up. The bus-washing facility turned out to be a tap in the street with a hosepipe attached and a tall ladder and, as Adrian and Bob hosed the bus down, the rest of us were ferried in relays to a spotlessly clean public bath-house, where we enjoyed a welcome hot shower, washing away the dirt and grime accumulated on our gruelling 750-mile journey from Teheran. By now it was late in the afternoon and we were wondering how we could possibly get out of playing in sub-zero temperatures in their unheated cinema. Our dilemma was resolved by one of the mayor's helpful minions, who advised us that, as our passports had already been stamped with that day's date, we would be required to report to the border that night. We refuelled, and, as we said our farewells, a car sped towards us and out jumped the bath-house manager, clutching a wristwatch that one of us had left there. It was dark as we thanked them all for their kindness and hospitality and, with regrets that we had to leave, I hopped into the cab and started off down the brightly lit main street, made a sweeping U-turn to get back to the main road and brushed against some overhead electricity cables. Suddenly there was a series of violent, lightning-like blue flashes and all the lights in the town went out – we must have blown the fuse at the main power station. Feeling a little guilty, but with no time to stop, we hurried on our way and made for the border some 10 miles away.

Our papers were in good order and we left Iran, crossing into no man's land between the two countries, the border posts being about 5 miles apart. A smooth, paved highway approached the Afghan border. Tony described our arrival in his diary:

> My first impression was of a neat little post spaced out with trees and gardens but, after walking through mud to the police checkpoint and entering a dingy, dirty and empty hollow-sounding building, my ideas quickly faded. We were told to go to the customs by an incredibly badly dressed and scruffy soldier. We entered another empty, uninviting-looking building through an incredibly tatty door, and heard tremendous shouting ... In one corner, two Afghans were having the most violent argument, with a small group chipping in, making matters worse. We crept into a dingy office and waited. As there are no uniforms it was impossible to tell who was who as the shouting match turned to screaming. Eventually the argument died down, with the official coming into the office. After asking us what we wanted, he said the post was closed, come back at 10 a.m. the next morning. After seeing the worst of his temper, we hastily agreed and left to have supper and bed.

We awoke the next morning to find everywhere shrouded in a thick fog. It was cold and damp as we started to prepare breakfast, when, through the mist, we noticed that a heavily modified British Ford Cortina, covered in writing just visible through layers of mud, had parked not far behind us. Sleeping inside it were two young English mechanics from Ipswich who were bearing greetings from their home town to the cities of Ipswich in Australia and America. We invited them to join us for breakfast and found that one of the drivers, John Summers, knew Tony's uncle. Then, with the mist slowly clearing, we completed the lengthy passport and customs formalities and were free to enter Afghanistan. As the sun broke through, the sky turned a hazy blue and our spirits lifted. We headed east to Herat on a beautiful modern road, built with Russian aid, across a wide, dry plain with distant mountains to either side. We met up with the Cortina a couple of times during the morning and they agreed to help us film the bus on the move, giving us an opportunity to gain some tracking shots, something we'd not done before.

Filming our journey had never been easy. Our Bell & Howell Filmo camera would take no more than forty seconds of film before the clockwork motor required rewinding, and our thirty spools of 16mm Kodachrome, with two-and-a-half minutes of running time each, were very precious. To film the bus passing at full speed, the camera crew had to walk at least half a mile down the road to enable the bus to pick up speed before passing the camera. It had taken over an hour to get a shot from a German autobahn bridge, for example. Stopping half a mile before the bridge, John and Tony walked down the road, climbed the bridge and set up the tripod and camera. With no walkie-talkies, they waved to us when they were ready. We then drove the bus flat out so that we reached our top speed of 38mph by the time we got to the bridge. We counted the seconds for half a minute to allow the camera's clockwork motor to unwind, and then pulled into the side of the road. With the shot 'in the can', John and Tony then walked three-quarters of a mile to where the bus had stopped. Every shot taken of the bus on the road required a similar exercise. Setting a shot up sometimes took hours and, as a result, filming our journey was not a popular activity. As each spool was completed, it was posted back to England for processing and it was months before we saw the results of our efforts. Here, we could film the bus from another vehicle, and John wedged himself tightly into the spare wheel bolted to the Cortina's boot and the bus and car moved off together, which achieved some splendid tracking shots of the bus at full speed on Afghanistan's excellent modern highway.

We bade the Cortina farewell and it sped off ahead of us. Dirty fuel was clogging our fuel filters and the freezing conditions in Iran hadn't helped. The weather was warmer now, so Bob dismantled the temporary tank on the wing, cleaned the filters and reconnected the main tanks again. We refuelled in Herat, where we drove past wild and exotically dressed horsemen riding around the dusty wasteland outside the town, some of whom, when they saw us, raced the bus along the highway. We thought this might be an Afghan equivalent of the Liphook Donkey Derby, but they were probably there for the sport of Buzkashi (translated as '*dragging of goat*'), described by the official Afghan Tourist Organisation as:

a remarkable feat of horsemanship performed by opposing teams of hardy riders ... A beheaded calf is placed in a circle, the contestants riding swift nimble horses rush to pick up the carcass from the ground and carry it to the end of the field ... and bring it back to the goal. The ensuing struggle, snatching and pulling the calf from each other, is a thrilling sight.

The road was full of horse-drawn tongas, the first we had seen, which were ferrying the spectators back to town. We didn't spot the headless calf.

Paddy Garrow Fisher had started his 'Indianman' overland bus operation in the late 1950s and his Kingston-based company, Garrow Fisher Tours, had published a primitive booklet which we carried with us and which described our route in detail. In it he mentioned the lack of refuelling facilities in Iran and Afghanistan, and we had taken this to heart and fitted a reserve fuel tank. If there were no filling stations between Herat and Kandahar, which is what his book told us, we would need both tanks to complete the journey. With Bob at the wheel, we were barrelling along at top speed on the new highway when I decided to make a pot of tea. Coming down the stairs, I could see through the back window what looked like a trail of water on the road behind us and, thinking it might be a leak from the radiator, I asked Bob to pull over. It was in fact diesel, draining out of the half-open stopcock on our reserve fuel tank. We turned the tap tightly shut, but both tanks were by now less than half full and Kandahar was still over 300 miles away. Should we turn round and drive the 90 miles back to Herat to refill them, or should we carry on in the hope of finding more fuel this side of Kandahar? We had a further five gallons in a jerry can, but at 10 miles per gallon this wouldn't get us very far. The map we'd acquired in Teheran showed several settlements near the new highway, and so we decided to chance it and press on. Next morning a strange mirage slowly appeared in the desert in front of us – an American-style service area, complete with high canopy, modern fuel pumps and a shop and coffee bar, right in the middle of nowhere. We'd seen nothing like this since Europe, and with great relief we swung onto the forecourt and refilled our empty tanks.

We had been driving across a spectacular arid plain with a backdrop of jagged mountains rising high in the distance to the east, the far ones bright with snow which shimmered in the sunlight. To the south and west, the flat, sandy plains disappeared into infinity and an indistinct horizon. Another trailer tyre blowout gave us some extra shopping to do in Kandahar, and Bob and Adrian looked for a replacement. We parked for the night at a local hotel, reminiscent of Kipling at his eeriest, which had facilities we could use. Kandahar had a distinctly medieval feel to it, with more horse-drawn vehicles, donkeys and other animals in the streets than lorries or cars. It was no bigger than a small English market town, and recent rain had left the streets awash with mud, which added to the illusion of another time. We changed money in the bazaar, where we got a much better rate than at a bank, bought some provisions and by midday were back on the road. Speeding towards Kabul at a steady 38mph, we were surprised to find a number of complete concrete bridges, several spans long, standing tall in the desert some distance from, and parallel to, the new road we were on. They had been built as part of a highway project by German engineers, we were told, who had underestimated the power of the melting floodwater – the approach embankments had been washed away by the annual spring rains many years before. The Americans, who had financed, designed and built the road we were on, had overcome this by substituting concrete floodways for bridges; even so, for some days each spring our road would be made impassable by floodwaters from the mountains. We stopped for the night in open country. Kabul was only a few hours ahead of us.

12

Kabul: The Secret of Our Success

We drove to the British Embassy in Kabul, where the walls still bore scars from when the building had been held siege and under fire earlier in the century, to ask if they had any ideas about where we might park while we were in the city. It was now 112 days since we had left England and at the Embassy gates the mileometer clicked round to 31,114 miles. We'd covered 7,787 miles since leaving the Deers Hut in September. It was early afternoon and we'd driven all over the city trying – unsuccessfully – to find somewhere to stay. Embassy official Bill Beck suggested we speak to the Consul, Edith Urquhart, a marvellous Scottish lady celebrated in diplomatic circles for her work in getting penniless hippies back home. We could find nowhere that was a secure resting place, we told her, noting the Embassy's enormous park-like walled and gated compound, which contained the ambassador's residence and also houses for most of the senior staff, but she insisted the bus remain outside the gates and that for us to park inside was a decision that could only be made by the ambassador. Meanwhile, would we all like to have baths and clean up? Jumping at the chance, I spent a splendid half an hour soaking in Miss Urquhart's piping-hot bath. We offered to give a free concert that night for the Embassy staff, some of whom, we discovered, had already heard about us from their colleagues in Teheran. Liking this idea, Miss Urquhart immediately sent messages inviting them to congregate in the Embassy clubroom at 8 p.m. to hear us play – and told us we could park inside the gates, just for the night.

The evening was a wonderful success. We were heavily plied with drink and sang for two hours, much to the amusement of all, including the ambassador, Sir Peers Carter, who joined in the singing and celebratory atmosphere. By the end of the evening, we seemed to have endeared ourselves to the whole company. Then, to our great relief, the ambassador generously set protocol aside and, breaking all the rules, told us he would be delighted to have us stay in the Embassy grounds as his personal guests while we were in Kabul. As far as I'm aware, we are the only group of overland travellers who have ever been granted this privilege. We parked the bus outside the second secretary's house, which was unoccupied. And so our weeks in Kabul became an unending social round as we became sought-after supper guests of members of the tightly knit Western diplomatic community, whose warm hospitality we greatly enjoyed. They took in all our washing, too.

Six thousand feet up in the Hindu Kush, on a large plain surrounded by mountains and spread along the banks of the Kabul River, the capital of Afghanistan was home to just under half a million people. The 56-year-old King, Zahir Shah, had been on the throne since 1933 and headed a benignly autocratic regime which paid lip service to democracy but was slowly allowing greater political freedoms. Russia and America vied with each other to exert their influence, pouring aid into the country, the stability of which was growing increasingly fragile. Initially, prospects for us as export salesmen seemed better than anticipated. Esmond Hoyle, the Embassy's assistant commercial attaché, shepherded us around Kabul, and with his help we did a certain amount of business. The Afghan International Trade Agency arranged meetings for us to discuss the importation of Tony's father's pitch fibre pipes and Chichester stainless steel tableware, which seemed to interest some of the army generals. We later discovered that they were intending to smuggle it into Pakistan, circumventing that country's stringent import restrictions, rather than using it to grace the tables of the officers' mess. We worked hard at selling the telephones and gramophone styli – more candidates for the smuggling trade, perhaps – but the styli faced stiff competition from Japanese products on which importers avoided paying duty by smuggling them in, we were told, inside imported radios. Unsurprisingly, there was no market for teddy bears or sausage-grilling machines.

We needed to earn some immediate cash. At the end of January, we had just over £300 in the kitty, a marked improvement on the £200 we had with us when we arrived in Teheran, but we needed much more. We had become friendly with the Hoyles, who invited us to supper soon after our arrival, and it was in front of their log fire that I worked on our accounts and wrote to David Fletcher back in England, using Esmond's typewriter, about negotiating a bank overdraft to cover the shortfall on the costs of reaching Australia. Our monthly accounts showed that our income in January exceeded our expenditure by just over £1! All my errors were concealed by 'adjustments for exchange rate conversions'.

The best hotel in town was the newly opened seven-storey Intercontinental, built by Taylor Woodrow. Set on a hillside north-west of the city centre with views of the Summer Palace and the peaks of the majestic Pamir mountains beyond, it had 200 bedrooms and a ballroom that seated 500, and we badly wanted to play there. Tony, Tim and

I met the hotel's general manager, Mr Khaliffe, a Lebanese gentleman, and after a couple of visits he finally agreed that we should hold a concert the following Saturday and receive a percentage of the takings. This was a prestigious booking but, sadly, the hotel did little to promote our appearance. The big advertisement in the *Kabul Times*, which had already run a story about our arrival in town, read: 'They're Famous, They're Talented, They're The Philanderers', but this only appeared on the afternoon of our performance. Having been well fed in the hotel restaurant, we moved to the ballroom, where 400 seats had been laid out, and were dismayed to find only ten people sitting on them. The start of the concert was promptly delayed for half an hour, by which time the audience had swelled to twenty. Undeterred, we gave our all in a two-hour performance that our sparse audience, which included the Indian ambassador, seemed to enjoy. Our cut of the takings amounted to just under £5, but at least the management consoled us with drinks afterwards and gave us a marvellous reference, saying what excellent entertainers we were. A financial flop at Intercontinental was worth several well-paid bookings at less well-known places, thought Tim.

Our concert at the Embassy had been attended by Ken Pearson from the British Council, who invited us to supper the following evening. Here, plans were made and a stringent rehearsal undertaken late into the evening for a performance at the Council the following Sunday, for which we would be paid £30. Meanwhile, Alan had visited Kabul's UN Club and Hostel, meeting the vivacious young English manageress, Pat Jessell, and had come away with a booking for the following Monday, when we would be given supper and the whole door take, which turned out to be more than £50. We gave another performance there a week later and raised another £55. Two performances in the coffee lounge at the Spinzar Hotel netted us a further £23 and an appearance in front of a hoard of enthusiastic teenagers at the American School towards the end of our stay gained us a fee of $50 US. By the time we left Kabul, we had added just under £200 to our coffers.

On our third evening in Kabul, we were invited to take part in an informal theatrical evening at the British Council by the Kabul Amateur Dramatic Society. Here we met a range of interesting characters, many of whom we saw on a regular basis over the coming weeks. One was Freddy Learoyd, a mature English teacher with a powerful stage voice and strong dramatic presence whom we'd met at the Pearsons' the night before, who sang 'Have Some Madeira, M'Dear'. Others recited Shakespeare, and a talented Austrian classical guitarist, Erich Edlinger, played a couple of Spanish compositions. There was a Czech ballet dancer and others performing their own party pieces and, when they involved the audience, we enthusiastically joined in. Then Tim stepped forward and recited his own poetry. This was received with great acclaim, he thought, and thereafter he was regularly requested to recite more – usually, he said, in the most ludicrously inappropriate places. The Philanderers had opened and closed both halves of the show and were very warmly received. We were now working together more effectively as a team. When appearing in public, being interviewed or just meeting people, we were starting, as a group, to do a passable impression of the early Beatles. Several of us saw ourselves taking on the Paul McCartney persona, while Alan's personality matched the humanity, humour, honesty and sometimes barely concealed shoulder-chipped cutting edge of John Lennon. Clive, Alan's younger brother, with his fair hair, blue eyes and an impressive guitar and banjo style, was the front-line star the women swooned over. Our shared experiences over the previous four months had drawn us all together, and our personalities blended well.

We seemed to spark positively off each other in a good-humoured way, bringing out amusing traits in each of us, and this came through not only in our stage performances but also when meeting people as a group. Tony wrote to his parents: 'Actually we get on very well and seem to create a good impression wherever we go, which is also partly to do with our singing.'

Television had yet to reach Afghanistan and in Kabul we made our first radio broadcast as The Philanderers. Through a contact of the influential Mr Sayir, the friendly manager of the Spinzar – arguably the top hotel in Kabul until the Intercontinental opened – Tim lined up a recording session on nothing more than Mr Sayir's recommendation. Each evening at 10.15 p.m., Radio Afghanistan broadcast forty minutes of Western music, and we would be recorded for this slot. It was a Saturday morning when we rolled up at the studios and were ushered into the radio station's large music studio. There was an immediate problem. As we had noticed in the 'Afghan Room' at the Spinzar Hotel, where Mr Sayir had invited everyone attending a large dinner party at which we'd been guests to listen to some traditional ethnic music, Afghan musicians always sat on the floor. As a result, all the microphone stands in the studio were no more than knee-high, and there were no stands for musicians who performed standing up. Tables had to be brought in and the microphones on short stands placed on top of them. It took some time to sort everything out, but at last we were ready. In all, we recorded nine songs, starting with 'Wild Rover' and concluding with 'Goodnight Irene', which were all broadcast as a radio concert the following evening. We didn't get paid for this, but the professional quality tape of our performance was of great value to us and made the effort really worthwhile.

Only seven of us were well enough to perform on the recordings. Several of our number had succumbed to the flu. Bob and Adrian were both suffering badly and had been confined to their bunks all day when the bus arrived outside the house of Kate Farah, the young English widow of a wealthy Afghan doctor, once the King's physician, who had invited us to dinner with some of the other locals we had become friendly with. We had met Kate when we were dinner guests of Gwynne Howes, whose company we had enjoyed at supper at the Pearsons' the previous week. 'You can't stay on the bus like that, you'll only get worse,' was Kate's immediate reaction, and Bob and Adrian were quickly spirited away into comfortable beds in Kate's centrally heated house, where she and her elderly maid nursed them for five days until they were better.

For our show at the British Council, we had been encouraged to improve our image by wearing dark trousers and coloured shirts. Clive, Alan and I stood in front, wearing what used to be white shirts, now dyed a deep shade of yellow in the bazaar, arranged by Dick through Mrs Hoyle, whilst the others, standing behind, wore blue shirts from their existing wardrobe. Previously we had all been a bit cavalier about the costumes we wore on stage. In Teheran, Robin Allan had insisted on us wearing suits and bowlers for our British Council work, but back in England, as The Procal Turdum, we usually wore an outlandish mixture of outfits, from Edwardian bathing suits and agricultural waistcoats and gaiters to exotic dress uniforms, top hats and tails, with most wearing trilbies and other felt hats reshaped with a point on top by pouring boiling water into them. We had brought some of this gear with us and wore it to rather poor effect when we played in some of the nightclubs of Teheran. Taking our music more seriously now, we decided that an improved stage image would give us a better group identity and help our performance. With the little spending money we'd allowed ourselves, Alan had purchased a colourful Afghan waistcoat in the Green Door bazaar which caught everyone's fancy, so we all trooped off to buy a waistcoat each.

Kabul was a strange place, quite unlike anywhere we had been before. Bizarrely, it boasted a Marks & Spencer outlet, which traded as the St Michael's Shop, named after their clothes and underwear brand. But if you turned off the modern avenues, where plodding camel caravans still plied their trade between colourfully decorated lorries, buses and modern cars, you quickly found yourself in an ancient world of crooked little passageways tightly squeezed between higgledy-piggledy old houses and mud huts, the only form of transportation there being pack donkeys carrying goods to the bazaars of the 'old city'. Here the shops on the narrow muddy alleys were like Aladdin's caves with the owners beckoning you in to inspect their marvellous treasures. Although the sun shone warmly most days, it barely penetrated this labyrinth of pathways, and heaps of dirty compacted snow were everywhere. Here we bought the embroidered waistcoats which we would wear on stage, together with other souvenirs; Afghan clay and skin drums, native hats, camel-skin coats – which eventually rotted and stank due to being inadequately cured – and other knick-knacks. Tony bought an antique British Army rifle dated 1868. We were all sure it was a fake, but he put his faith in a Certificate of Authenticity, which the rest of us were certain was forged.

Towards the end of our third week in Kabul, the latent wanderlust and desire to see beyond the next mountain range was growing and we were beginning to feel that it was time for us to move on. Almost every night we had dined out, gone to parties, given concerts and been guests of some of the most hospitable people we had come across so far on our trip. Back in England, the Luffs had told us about an English girl they knew who was travelling the world on a motorcycle. Relaxing after a large dinner given by Glen Bowersog, the Director of the Asia Foundation, and having sung with a group of American ex-pats who had formed a barbershop group, 'The Kabulaires', we discovered that Mr Bowersog's secretary, Mary Seivier, was the person we'd been told about. We'd got to know her when we arrived in Kabul – she belonged to the drama group, and had arranged our invitation to Glen's dinner. Adrian then found that he'd been given her name and address before leaving home, and had it in his pocket. She had ridden all the way to Kabul on an old BSA motorbike, using the same route that we had taken – a remarkable solo achievement that made our own efforts seem very tame – and was planning to continue her journey once she had saved enough money. We wondered if we might meet her again on our travels.

My 27th birthday was celebrated with a party at the UN Club arranged by Pat Jessell, who had become a great supporter of ours. The club's bar was the nearest thing to an English pub that we'd come across since leaving Liphook and was somewhere we felt at home. An iced cake appeared, crowned with six candles and a small plastic double-decker bus, and my health was toasted in champagne. Many of our new friends had joined us and I felt suitably honoured. We then played to everyone for the rest of the evening.

The day of our departure eventually came, and the bus drove through the Embassy gates for what we thought would be the last time. We hadn't gone far when the faint rumbling sensation we had felt through the lower deck floorboards over the past few days slowly rose to a great crescendo, becoming an insistent drumming that caused the whole bus to vibrate. Limping back to the Embassy, Bob investigated and announced that the cause was a universal joint on the prop-shaft. He removed it to reveal a fractured and broken prop-shaft end. To buy a replacement part in Kabul was impossible, and to air freight one from the UK would be fantastically expensive. Esmond Hoyle came to our rescue, saying that he thought one could be made cheaply at a friendly engineering works he knew in the bazaar. Taking the shattered remains of the cone-shaped prop-shaft end with them, Bob, Clive and Esmond found that the cheerful Afghan engineer, who had served his apprenticeship in Birmingham and was very pro-British – he even spoke English with a Brummie accent – could make a duplicate part from an old Chevrolet half-shaft on his British-built lathes. It would take a few days, though, which delayed our departure for another week. In the end he charged us less than a tenner.

One of the lessons we were learning was that it took time to arrange bookings for us to play anywhere, particularly in the bigger hotels, and so Tim volunteered to travel on ahead to Rawalpindi, the next important town on our route, hoping that he could get some advance publicity and arrange a cabaret season for us in a big hotel there. Early each Thursday, an Embassy vehicle, an Albion that was a cross between a small bus and a van, set out for Peshawar to collect supplies for the commissary. Tim could cadge a lift and catch a local bus to Rawalpindi from there. We wished him luck and he disappeared off into the unknown.

Meanwhile, the enforced delay allowed us to spring-clean the bus. Miss Urquhart lent us her vacuum cleaner, and carpets and upholstery were cleaned, curtains washed, internal paintwork scrubbed, outside bodywork repaired, touched up and polished, a broken window replaced, a new tyre for the trailer sourced and many small, outstanding mechanical jobs attended to. Then Esmond and I collected the repaired prop-shaft and Bob fitted it back in place under the bus. The Ambassador and his wife also paid us a social call to look over the bus – they had a Land Rover converted as a camper which sparked their interest – and to wish us bon voyage. They narrowly avoided being covered in cooking fat by Tony, who was making our breakfast at the time. Mary Seivier invited us to supper one night, when we listened to the Beatles' new *Abbey Road* album. We heard it again the following night, our last in Kabul, at dinner with the Loddenjaards, who worked for the US Aid Administration.

It was Friday 13 February when we finally left Kabul. We thanked the ambassador for his kindness, said goodbye to everyone, from the smiling Gurkha guards at the gates to the Hoyles, Miss Urquhart, and all the other friends we had made at the Embassy, and they all waved us off. We then drove round to the UN Club, which had become a second home to many of us, to say goodbye to Pat Jessell. She was surprised to see us and quite stunned when we told her that we were leaving immediately, to such an extent that she couldn't speak for at least five minutes. She herded us into the bar and gave us all a stiff farewell drink. We owed her a lot, as more than half the money we had earned in Kabul had come from appearances at her club. Mary Seivier, Gwynne Howes and Kate Farah soon arrived and tearful farewells were exchanged as we trooped outside and posed for photographs in front of the bus. Eventually we moved off and, after refuelling and having refilled the water tanks, we pulled away from Kabul for the last time. We were looking forward to new adventures, and set course for the Kabul Gorge and the Khyber Pass, wondering all the while what Tim had managed to achieve for us in Rawalpindi.

13

Pakistan

We headed towards the impenetrable-looking wall of mountains across the high, flat plain east of Kabul but, on reaching the steep, rocky foothills, the road, instead of climbing, followed the Kabul River through a cleft in the rocks and plunged headlong into the most spectacular gorge any of us had ever seen. It was here that an entire British army and its followers were annihilated while retreating from Kabul in 1842, the first of three successive failures of British India to occupy Afghanistan. Parting company with the river, which tumbles more than 2,000ft through a series of waterfalls, the new highway, wide enough for two trucks or buses to pass, snaked down the side of the gorge through a series of giddy hairpin bends high above the river, which raced along the floor of this narrow gash in the mountains. Grabbing the camera, John scrambled down towards the road by the river far below to film the bus's descent. In low gear, and with the brakes smoking, Bob nursed the bus gently down the gorge. The road tunnelled through small shoulders of the mountain high above the river, which had been dammed in several places to provide hydro-electricity. One tunnel was too low for us but, fortunately, we could by-pass it on the precarious old track cut into the rocks overhanging the rushing river. It was early afternoon, but the deep, narrow gorge was in perpetual shadow. Brightly painted trucks and the occasional bus or car vied for road space with lines of camels slowly plodding their way in both directions, bearing their loads with an aloof dignity. As the gorge widened and the river slowed, Bob pulled over to let the brakes cool off. Leaving the ravine, the rugged rocks of the mountains were replaced by great mounds of pebbles held together by banks of mud – dune-like, soft and undulating. At this lower, warmer altitude the country opened out to reveal lakes, rice paddies and an altogether greener countryside, still with a distant backdrop of the snowy Hindu Kush mountains. Kabul is less than 150 miles from the Pakistani border at Torkham and fewer than 100 from Jalalabad, which we reached at the end of the afternoon. We were surprised by the town's modern appearance, and the large number of young girls in Western-style clothes, laughing and waving to us as we passed – a big contrast from the women of Kabul and southern Afghanistan, where many wore the Islamic 'chadri', an all-covering outer garment and meshed face mask which made the wearer look like a medieval ghost. We parked on the outskirts of a small village and Tony, Dick and Adrian spent the night playing Liphookopoly, on watch for unwelcome visitors.

For some unknown reason, large loudspeakers were blasting out 'Tara's Theme' from *Gone with the Wind* as we arrived at Pakistan's border post the following morning. Our permits in order, we crossed the valley on the narrow road that climbs slowly towards the infamous Khyber Pass through mud-walled villages, passing women balancing water jars on their heads and laughing children waving and shouting at us. The roadside was littered with the skeletons of trucks that had been involved in head-on collisions. The Afghans drive on the right and the Pakistanis on the left and, near the border, trucks approached each other at speed in the centre of the road. The drivers, often tired or high on drugs, would pull aside at the last minute to the same side of the road and smash into each other like two rutting stags.

The tribal areas on the border were famous for their lawlessness, and we had been warned not to stop or take photographs. In the Pass itself, badges of famous British regiments that had been stationed here in years gone by were carved into the rock walls, and modern pillboxes and tank traps stood deserted alongside earlier fortifications, but there were no signs of any troops. The setting was less spectacular than the Kabul Gorge, and we were surprised to find a railway line running parallel with us, crossing and re-crossing the road and tunnelling through the rocky outcrops around which our road snaked. It was often only wide enough for one vehicle, and had an unprotected sheer drop away from the rock face. We were never sure whether we might have to turn back, our way blocked by a low rail bridge or rock arch. It was a beautiful, sunny morning, the air fresh and warm and, as we crested the top of the rugged pass, we saw in front of us the vast valley of the River Indus and the road ahead weaving its way steeply down the hillside to the distant plain over a thousand feet below. We pulled over to admire the magnificent view, and no sooner had we put the kettle on than the bus became surrounded by the tribesmen we had been warned about, some of whom carried old rifles with cartridge belts slung over their shoulders. We did what we had done many times before and invited the leaders, a couple of bearded, fierce-looking Pathans, to look round the bus and have a cup of tea with us. To our surprise they both spoke English. 'I don't suppose you see many British double-decker buses up here?' I asked. 'Oh no,' came the reply, 'but my cousin, he drives one of these in Coventry!'

Approaching Peshawar was like driving into the military town at Aldershot. The barracks, the 'lines' and the parade grounds all had the atmosphere of a British military camp – not surprising, perhaps, because twenty-five years before, this is exactly what it was – with its sandy soil, shady trees, tarmac roads and brick buildings. Rows of British Bedford army trucks and soldiers in British-style army uniforms reinforced just how much like England parts of Pakistan appeared to us. The roads were full of old Morris Minor taxis, but mixed in with camels, bullock carts and horses pulling two-wheeled pony-traps decorated with bells. It was as if we'd stumbled across a parallel universe, where life had gone off at a slightly different tangent to life in England. It all had an oddly familiar feeling to it. Unlike Iran and Afghanistan, the garages sold branded petrol and Esso garages were plastered with: 'put a tiger in your tank'. Old-style British road signs were in English and cigarette packets were of the familiar pre-war British designs and, while everything appeared spick and span, it all seemed rather quaint. Peshawar's crowded bazaar had more of an oriental flavour, and there, in the warm, hazy, perfumed air, stirred by a light breeze, with birds singing above a cacophony of chatter and other sounds, I bought a set of nine brass goblets as a souvenir of our visit.

We were following the Grand Trunk Road, the 1,600-mile highway to Calcutta that crosses Pakistan and India and is one of Asia's longest and oldest roads – a trade route that has existed for more than 2,000 years. It was rather like driving through a gently undulating golf course of green and brown grass studded with willowy trees, which also lined the highway. The present route was built by the Mughal Emperor Sher Shah Suri in the sixteenth century and the road reconstructed, and improved by the British 300 years later. In his novel *Kim*, Kipling described the Grand Trunk Road as 'such a river of life as nowhere else exists in the world'. It was certainly very colourful and busy, and dangerous too, as the buses and trucks we passed seemed to be driven by suicidal maniacs. We had a further 100 miles to travel before we reached Rawalpindi and having crossed the mighty River

Indus at the impressive and strategically important Attock Bridge ('No Photographs. Strategic Military Target'), we stopped for the night on the forecourt of a garage. The next morning we found our way blocked by a low railway bridge just beyond Lawrencepur, and were forced to follow a minor road north towards the site of the Tarbela Dam, an ambitious international project to harness the Indus to provide irrigation and power, control the flood plain and increase the amount of fertile agricultural land. Reaching the dam site and its vast work camps, the road narrowed, climbed eastwards away from the river and wound through fields yellow with spring flowers, eventually becoming a tree-lined lane of elm, poplar and oak. We could have been in England. We reached a main road and turned south again, our detour adding three hours and a further 70 miles to our journey.

In Rawalpindi, Tim, who was staying at the cheap and highly undesirable Empire Hotel, had had little success in finding bookings. We arrived at The Mall, parked outside the tourist office and found Tim in the *Pakistan Times* office just above it. He'd arranged for us to use the tourist office facilities and it was here that we spent our first night in Rawalpindi. For the rest of our stay we parked overnight in the grounds of the Pindi Club, a splendid colonial building in a park-like setting with many mature trees. Founded by four British Army captains in 1882, it had maintained its traditions continuously ever since, the only noticeable difference being the changing faces of the polo team in the photographs along the club's panelled corridors. In 1948, the year after independence from Britain, Pakistani officers replaced the British ones. The *Pakistan Times* carried an article telling our story that day under the headline 'Singers' Group in City'. We all headed off to see what work we could find as entertainers and, just as we were beginning to think we should move on to

Lahore, having received mainly negative responses, Clive and Alan returned from visiting the local American school with a confirmed booking for Friday worth $50 US. We decided to stay.

Many curious passers-by called on us, and the clothing manufacturer over the road, Mr Aziz, wanted us to represent him on the rest of our tour. But it was a visit by two gracious Pakistani ladies, beautifully attired in saris and silk shawls, that completely changed our life in Rawalpindi. They invited us to supper. Tony wrote home:

> We gladly accepted and quite suddenly stepped into the high society of Rawalpindi ... The house belonged to the President's sister, the President's aide-de-camp was also there, plus the Commander in Chief of the Pakistani Royal Signals. They were great fun and we passed an enjoyable evening. Of course the subject of washing came up and today, to our amusement, an army ambulance drew up, two uniformed orderlies got out, came to the bus, picked up our washing, bundled it into the ambulance and drove off, to the astonishment of passers-by, and ourselves.

The invitation, issued by Grace Phillips, a divorced Pakistani Christian, and her friend Martha from Karachi, was to join them for supper at the spacious home of Phyllis Thalia in the old cantonment. There we met two old sisters, both doctors, one of whom reminded us all of our grandmothers and was universally known as 'Tantie'. 'Another attraction was Grace's 18-year-old and beautiful daughter Tina,' Tim wrote, 'and for the first time since Germany, the group spent an evening being entertained by the nationals of the country they were visiting.' From then on 'Tantie' took a grandmotherly interest in our welfare, opening an account for us at a local grocer's with instructions that the bill should be sent to her. We were too embarrassed to take up this generous offer and, discovering this, 'Tantie' arrived at the bus with a hamper full of food, including nine steaks. They also arranged for us to have cholera booster jabs. We returned a couple of nights later to a larger and more lavish dinner party at which we entertained all the friends we had made earlier. This time the company included several high-ranking army officers, who joined us in getting pleasantly tight on the free-flowing booze.

Our Pakistani friends arranged introductions for us, and offered us baths, food, drink and somewhere to relax. We were their guests at lunches, teas and dinners for the remainder of our two weeks in Rawalpindi. One of Phyllis's guests, Madame Azuri, was an adviser at Pakistani Television and introduced us to a producer there, which resulted in our being offered twenty-five minutes on the following Friday's live peak-hour music programme. The studios were in an old army barracks. Here we met Gareth Gwenlan, a BBC producer/director sent to Pakistan by the Foreign Office to help set up the new State Television Service. Gareth, who went on to become BBC Television's Head of Comedy, rehearsed us – using the skill he'd honed directing *Top of the Pops* – for what was one of Rawalpindi's most popular TV shows. The day of our live TV performance came round and, after another run-through and a visit to make-up, we stood around growing nervous while an old episode of *Perry Mason* was transmitted. Then it was 8.25 p.m. and, with heavy rain drumming on the studio's tin roof and great banks of dazzling lights shining in our faces, the floor manager counted us in and we launched into 'The Wild Rover'. All went well except that the tin roof leaked and, in the middle of what was our most poignant and subdued number – one we had recently learned called 'The Butcher's Boy' – water found its way onto one of the big lamps right above our heads, which exploded with a loud bang and showered us all with glass. With unaccustomed professionalism, we carried on as if nothing had happened. The show finished and we were heartily congratulated by all as we crunched our way through the broken glass to the studio door and headed off to a celebratory supper with our new-found supporters at the home of Begum Idris, the sister of a high-ranking army officer. Everyone there had seen the show and all were highly complimentary.

'Colourful Philanderers Thrill Audience' read the headline reporting our afternoon concert at Rawalpindi's Gordon College, one of the oldest academic institutions in Pakistan, where students enjoyed a reputation for rioting and disorder. We had been warned that they would be a very rude audience. The newspaper article continued:

> Sadly enough, as has become habitual with our audiences, there was an unappreciative section of listeners who managed to keep up a constant echo of rowdyism in the packed hall. A contemporary poetry-reading by Timothy Palmer, one of the group, had been planned. He writes his own poetry ... However, due to misbehaviour from some members of the audience, he refused to read and walked off the stage.

We all thought Tim was very brave to have attempted this, as shouts, whistling and booing had accompanied our opening numbers and, after attempting to sing a couple more songs, I told the audience we were stopping due to their rudeness and we left the stage fuming. Tony wrote in his diary:

> We sat in the wings, but had a surprise visit from the organisers, who had managed to clear the louts from the hall ... those who remained wished to hear us again. This time to a well-behaved audience we sang away, plus Tim and his poems, until 6 p.m. with no trouble.

John was really wound up by this bad behaviour and had returned to the bus, where he was accosted by some students wanting their money back. He turned, jabbing his finger at them, and gave them a big piece of his mind. He would have physically assaulted them if they hadn't taken fright and run off. By contrast, our concert at the American school in Islamabad the previous week had been a delight. We performed outside in the well of a small amphitheatre with a wildly appreciative audience of parents, staff and children, all of whom loved our songs and jostled for our autographs.

We toured Islamabad, just a few miles north of Rawalpindi. Adrian, our architect, wanted to see Pakistan's new capital, but was disappointed in what he found. He judged the Secretariat building – one of the few completed and operational – to be a mess. Apart from its newness, there didn't seem to be anything modern about it. Much of the city had yet to be built. Seen from the viewpoint on a low hill just above the new city, it was obvious that there was much still to do. We also visited Taxila, probably the most important archaeological site in Pakistan, containing some of the country's earliest ruins, dating from the sixth-century BC. These, together with later settlements and Buddhist stupas, were spread over a wide, undulating site in a pleasant valley, with sensitive areas fenced off, padlocked, and opened for visitors by a resident caretaker who lived in a nearby tent. Goats and cattle grazed the area, and we were pestered by tiny, barefooted tots all yelling for 'baksheesh' as we walked to the top of a rise from which we could survey the whole site. The museum was full of interesting artefacts, but the whole place seemed grossly underfunded, and had a quiet, low-key, almost neglected air that belied its historical significance. A polite and ingratiating local man insisted on becoming our guide, shepherding us around the whole site, but when it was time for us to leave he became rather difficult to shake off, making himself useful around the bus, clearing out the rubbish, washing up dirty cups and dishes and generally tidying up, before offering to come with us as our servant. Not a good idea, we thought, and gave him 2 rupees, Alan's old jeans and an ancient sweater of Tony's, with which he seemed delighted as he waved us goodbye.

We all had a splendid time in Rawalpindi. Our smokers, now at the end of the camomile tobacco mix, were delighted when representatives of the Pakistan Tobacco Company called on us one morning, offering us 400 cigarettes each in exchange for posing for publicity photos for their house magazine. As successors to The Imperial Tobacco Company, they still produced all the old British brands, from Woodbines to Player's Navy Cut and Capstan Medium. The boss of the company, Mr Habibullah, had a connection with us, as his children, Moneesa and Nashaba, were pupils of Adrian's girlfriend's mother back in England. Some of us enjoyed a concert in Islamabad by the Munich Chamber Orchestra, to which we'd been invited, and Bob, John and Tony spent a happy afternoon racing sailboats on a reservoir near Islamabad with staff from the High Commission, with Tony falling into the water and getting soaking wet. We also went to the cinema to see a dreadful musical called *Honeymoon*, the Pakistani hit of the year, as the guests of Begum Idris. Tony had ill-advisedly traded his watch for a couple of semi-precious stones and, as soon as she heard about this, Grace Phillips took them to her jeweller, who declared them worthless. Tony, enraged, charged back to the shop where he'd bought them, mentioned Brigadier Idris' name, and was immediately given his watch back. We'd had a couple of broken windows on the bus repaired, and I finally made the long-threatened Spam pie, to which I added the tinned meats we'd been given in Austria. We dined with the Adairs, English Canadians whom we'd met at the American school, and sang at an evening supper at the Pilkingtons', the only British employees at the UN mission in Islamabad, where we met other UN staff stationed there. Mr Pilkington had organised a whip-round and, the following morning, Tony was surprised to find the equivalent of £30 in various currencies stuffed into his jacket pocket. We made many good Pakistani friends and on our last night entertained them all at a special concert we'd arranged to give at the Pindi Club, of which our army officer friends were members. Our all-Pakistani audience genuinely enjoyed our music. We sincerely regretted leaving, wished them a fond farewell, and expressed our grateful thanks for their endless hospitality, before eventually retiring to bed for the night, or what was left of it. It was a fitting end to two memorable weeks in Rawalpindi.

14

Famous Penny

Tony frantically pressed the bell-push, and Bob slammed on the brakes. We used the bell system in the same way as when the bus was in service: two buzzes, to tell the driver to pull away, and one to tell him to stop. Tony, dozing quietly, had been awakened by a rather nasty screaking noise and found that the trailer drawbar had fractured and buckled, and the trailer had tipped backwards and had been scraping along the road in a shower of sparks. Bob wanted to dismantle the trailer completely, stick the contents inside the lower deck, remove the trailer's suspension units and wheels, and strap the base onto the back of the bus – as he'd designed it to do. The drawbars needed reinforcing and arc-welding, and the trailer couldn't be towed until that had happened. Alan thought we could patch things up using our oxyacetylene and continue to tow the trailer, emptied of heavier items, to Lahore, where a proper weld could be effected. After a short debate, the rest of us agreed with Alan, Bob shrugged his shoulders and Alan set about making the temporary repair. We stopped where we were for the night and moved the trailer's contents into the bus the next morning,

Before all this happened, we'd already had one adventure. We were beginning to doubt the honesty of people who told us about fording wide rivers in Pakistan but, during the morning not long after we'd left Rawalpindi, we found ourselves diverted off the road down an embankment, and driving through the sluggish waters of the Jhelum River, fording a wide riverbed several feet deep where a road bridge had been washed out on the Grand Trunk Road.

It was the end of February and the speedo read 31,881 miles. We had now travelled 8,544 miles, and Tony's fuel statistics showed an average consumption of 8 miles per gallon. Since leaving Istanbul, where we had around £250 between the nine of us, we had earned just under £600 – £281 in Teheran, £194 in Kabul, and a further £123 in Rawalpindi. Our expenses over the past three months had totalled £410. This was all complicated by varying exchange rates. You could buy 24 rupees for a pound in Kabul but the official rate was 11.35 to the pound, although you couldn't change them for sterling or dollars at a bank, or buy sterling or dollar traveller's cheques with them. For the purpose of our accounts, we set an arbitrary exchange rate of 20 rupees to the pound. We now had 771 rupees in the cash box in the safe upstairs, together with $812 US and £135 in sterling, having cashed all of our remaining traveller's cheques. Changing money on the black market in Pakistan was punishable by fourteen years' imprisonment. We still needed to earn a lot more money and have it in convertible currencies.

Arriving in Lahore and taking down an overhead wire up a side street – the wire coiling itself round a surprised pedestrian's feet – we finally came to rest outside the tourist office on The Mall. By the end of that day the press, television, High Commission, the Gymkhana and Commercial Gymkhana clubs, Punjab Club, big hotels and the American school had all been contacted. We'd pushed the trailer to a nearby welding shop where a repair was soon effected. We parked overnight in the grounds of the Commercial Gymkhana Club, where most of us enjoyed an evening in the bar drinking at the invitation of a Pakistani official from the High Commission. We were also running very low on propane gas and Bob spent the following day driving around Lahore unsuccessfully searching for a refill. Without gas we couldn't cook, and our refrigerator would stop working. Our two large cylinders under the stairs were empty, and we were now using our smaller reserve one.

Lahore, once known as the Paris of the Orient, was probably the most cosmopolitan and attractive city in Pakistan, with broad avenues and majestic old buildings. The old city was steeped in antiquity and was once a Mughal capital. More recently the British had created wide and shady tree-lined avenues and parks radiating from The Mall, which was by far the nicest area of the city and where the best hotels were located. By chance we had arrived in Lahore at the start of the National Horse and Cattle Show week, a major event in the country's calendar, and all the hotels were busy. Faletti's, a venerable and highly regarded colonial hotel, the oldest in Lahore and second only to the recently built Intercontinental, offered us a cabaret 'season'. We would get 7 rupees for every diner in their 250-seat night club, free breakfasts, evening meals at staff rates, and the use of toilets and showers, while sleeping on the bus in their grounds. For this we would play after dinner every night for a week. A full house would earn us a lot of money, we thought.

The Intercontinental offered us 150–200 rupees a night, subject to an audition, which we were unable to give because the bus was still running around town looking for a gas refill. So we decided to accept the Faletti's deal – 'You'll find they'll have nearer 20 than 200 people in their nightclub,' the manager of the Intercontinental warned us – but, with our gas running out, a source of cheap, good-quality meals suddenly became a deciding factor. Returning to Faletti's, this time with the bus, we shook hands on the arrangement and quickly settled in for the next seven days. The Intercontinental manager's prediction was right, however, and at the end of the week Faletti's paid us 900 rupees, worth less than £45. Following our complaints about indifferent meals and poor service, and to compensate for our intense disappointment, Mr Kahn, the manager, agreed not to charge us for supper.

The large advert in the next morning's *Pakistan Times* read: 'Faletti's Hotel Proudly Presents, for Seven Days Only, The Philanderers, England's Famous Group Of Cabaret Artists. Also Famous Penny and Exotic Nelofar...' 'Famous Penny' was Nadia Bismillah, a 22-year-old English Muslim girl and the singer with the hotel's four-piece band. In South Africa, she had recently married an African Asian and had been expelled from the country five days later for breaking their draconian immorality laws. Bossy, slightly built, rather plain, somewhat naïve, but well-meaning and kind-hearted, she regaled us with tales of her career as an airline manager with PIA, Pakistan's national airline, and as a singer in various European and international cities, and generally frightened us all by her determination to rule our lives. Apparently from a good English family, her natural talent for telling people what to do was turned on us and we were regimented around Lahore on sightseeing trips, commanded to appear in her room every day at 5 p.m. for tea, taught a violent card game called Cheat, and could use her bathroom whenever we wanted. Uninvited, she supervised our salad lunches each day and insisted on our taking coffee in her room after the show, but it was all well-intended and good-natured, and she was in reality very kind to us, befriending us and offering assistance when we really needed it. After our first supper at the hotel – a rather indifferent meal made worse by the poor service given by the hotel 'bearers' or waiters – she treated us to a beer as we settled down in the almost deserted 'Kashmir Room' restaurant to listen to her singing. This turned out to be pretty awful. Then, 'Exotic Nelofar' – a dumpy, heavily painted, unappealing little girl in national costume with rings on her fingers and bells on her ankles, whom Adrian rechristened 'Neophart' – tripped onto the floor in front of the band and stumbled through a couple of what we supposed were intended to be exotic folk dances. When it was over, the handful of dinner guests, most of whom had ignored everything, hardly applauded at all, and we wondered what on earth we were letting ourselves in for.

Temperatures were now in the high 20s, and during the day Faletti's was a peaceful place. Set in its own walled and park-like grounds, the hotel's rooms were mainly on the ground floor and opened onto cool cloisters. The bus was parked in a corner shaded by trees and we could sit in the sun and catch up with reading and correspondence. Our cabaret spots were scheduled for late in the evening, and on our opening night we were disappointed by the low number of guests – at 7 rupees each they hardly covered the cost of our supper. However, by the weekend things were looking up, and the large crowd on Saturday cheered us on and shouted for more when the second of our two twenty-minute spots ended.

We had managed to wangle free tickets to the VIP stand at the Horse and Cattle Show, a comfortable spot from which to watch the arena events. The highlights were tent-pegging, where horsemen in handsome costumes rode at breakneck speed to lift pegs from the ground with their sword or lance, and a splendid display of trick motorcycling by the Military Police, which culminated in a great mobile pyramid of precariously balanced policemen moving slowly along, propelled by several wobbly motorbikes. There was also an exhibition of award-winning cattle and, in the afternoon, the Shah of Iran, on a state visit, presented prizes in the arena not far from where we were sitting. I doubt if he would have expected to see us there, but our TV friend Gareth Gwenlan, helping to supervise coverage of the show, was most surprised to find The Philanderers in the VIP stand.

We returned in the evening to witness the floodlit tattoo. This time, a high-ranking military officer, a friend of Nadia's, had procured tickets for us. Tony wrote:

> The Tattoo was fantastic. The whole stadium was plunged into darkness and one searchlight picked out a lone bandsman dressed in white. He slowly marched forward while bagpipes and drums were playing away unseen. Then quite suddenly the lights blazed on, revealing 2,000 pipes and drums. They marched in impressive formations while playing, which continued for half an hour before they marched off to thunderous applause. The band was followed by displays of drill without orders, the climax of which was the shape of a fort formed by men. The lights went out, they fired their guns one by one and then marched out. There was folk dancing by wild Pathans, a body of men holding flaming torches and forming interesting patterns and spelling out 'welcome' in Urdu.

It was an amazing show that we were very lucky to see.

Nadia decreed that we should go sightseeing on Sunday, and we spent the morning visiting the Lahore Fort. Dating back to antiquity, it took its current form in the sixteenth century when Mughal Emperor Akbar created the present fortified palace. The buildings and ruins were very impressive, with little gardens, charming pavilions and a maze of rooms and corridors. We then crossed the road to the Badshahi Mosque, the city's most iconic building. Built in the 1670s, it is one of the world's largest mosques, with space for over 100,000 worshippers in its vast courtyard. Climbing to the top of one of the 200ft-tall minarets, we had an excellent view over the city. Next, we visited the recently completed Pakistan Monument, a distinctive 200ft-high concrete tower celebrating the creation of Pakistan as a separate homeland for Indian Muslims, and afterwards spent the afternoon in the Shalimar Gardens, which we reached by an interesting ride in two tongas through some of the poorest parts of Lahore, places not usually visited by tourists but somewhere that Nadia wanted us to see. Nadia provided a running commentary throughout the day on the background and history of the things we were seeing, and we arrived back at the hotel happy but exhausted.

In the following day's *Pakistan Times*, the Lahore Notebook page carried a lengthy article headed 'The Festival Week', almost half of which was taken up with extolling our virtues as enterprising young British businessmen. Having described our journey from the UK, the writer continued:

> Hairy Pillock 2 has, however, not brought in any tourists. It has brought here nine young conservatives who may call themselves Philanderers ... They are not on any wild goose chase impulsively; they are company directors on a business tour travelling comfortably in a bus well converted to each and every facility they may require on the way ... They seek engagement as a group of folk-song-cabaret artists in the best hotels where they are likely to meet important businessmen at their most relaxed moments.

The export department of Pillock Ltd had not been very successful in Pakistan, and Mr Freeman, the commercial officer at the British High Commission in Lahore, had been highly pessimistic. Shortly after our arrival, however, he had invited us to join him and a number of British and local businessmen for cocktails, where we made some contacts, but no business had resulted.

Meanwhile, Bob had been racing around Lahore trying to find other singing engagements for us, but had discovered that the holy month of Muharram was about to commence, during which devout Muslims fast and avoid enjoyment and most places of entertainment close, so nobody was prepared to book us. With only one booking at the American school left to fulfil, we decided to move on towards India. On our last night, 'Exotic Nelofar' was replaced by a different girl – much more attractive and a better dancer – who, much to our amusement, suggestively threw a floral garland around Bob's neck at the end of her final number. Our American school concert was another great success, earning us a further $50. Returning to Faletti's for the last time, we hitched up the repaired trailer, collected our fee from Mr Kahn, said goodbye to Nadia, and headed for the border some 25 miles away.

We were sorry to leave Pakistan. It was a country full of friendly people, many of whom had taken us into their homes and made us feel so welcome. The Pakistanis seemed to respect the British and there was a nostalgia for the certainty and stability of the British Raj among some of the older and better-off people that we met. Between Rawalpindi and Lahore we stopped at an army officers' mess and had a drink with a group of officers, all of whom assured us that the Pathans, the frontier peoples, were never beaten fully by the British. 'Not like the Indians, whom the British really suppressed. We drove the British out many times,' I was told as they handed me another drink. What they really wanted to do, it appeared, was to have another crack at the Indian Army after the inconclusive war of 1965 and gain for Pakistan the disputed province of Kashmir, but they didn't say so. At 3 p.m. on Tuesday, 10 March, we pulled up at the Pakistani frontier post and had our passports stamped. As we drove across the 200 yards of 'no man's land' we wondered what would happen next.

15

India: Philandering in Delhi

Arriving at the Hussainiwala Gate, the only crossing point open between West Pakistan and India, we were subjected to the most rigorous border inspection we had ever encountered. Never before had we been asked to open the trailer, and the female Indian customs officer wanted to see all over the bus, looking in vain for the hashish she assumed we must be carrying. Getting increasingly frustrated, she finally admitted defeat and, after endless form-filling, we were just about to be released when she and her boss unexpectedly invited us to join them for tea. We enjoyed a pleasant half an hour chatting and being told how refreshing it was to meet nine such promising chaps, and that we would find no anti-British feeling in India. Sending us on our way, the superintendent wrote in our visitor's book above his official stamp:

I had an opportunity to cast a glance inside the double-decker bus. It is so nicely arranged that one finds an atmosphere of a house. I am sure a passenger travelling by this bus shall never suffer from home sickness. The youngsters travelling by this bus also appear full of life

and I wish them all happy and comfortable journey.
With best wishes from Indian Customs. V.D. Chaudhaigr,
Superintendent.

It was a nice start to our time in India.

We made a detour to visit Chandīgarh, passing through
a now familiar warm, dusty landscape, with camels slowly
plodding in circles, powering water wheels which irrigated
small fields of green corn amid gnarled and stunted trees,
small ravines and patches of salt desert. Overhanging
branches and lumbering bullock carts piled high with hay
slowed our progress. Chandīgarh, the new state capital of the
Indian part of the Punjab – divided in two at independence in
1947, the mainly Hindu area in the east going to India and
the predominantly Muslim area in the west becoming part of
Pakistan – was being built to the masterplan of the French
architect Le Corbusier, who had also designed some of the
futuristic public buildings, which Adrian was keen to see.
Like Islamabad, it was only partially completed, with weeds
already growing between the cracks in the pavements.
On the whole, Adrian found it impressive, and compared it
favourably to what we had seen of Islamabad. We were near
the foothills of the Himalayas, and saw distant, white-capped
mountains for the last time before turning south towards
New Delhi.

Our plan was simple. We would drive directly to the best
hotel in town – in this case the Oberoi Intercontinental
in Wellesley Road – ask for the general manager, give an
audition and, hopefully, be offered work as cabaret artists.
We drove up the approach road of the ten-storey-high
modern slab of a hotel and parked on the forecourt. However,
the manager, George DeKiss, a Hungarian American,
wouldn't be there until after lunch. As soon as he returned, I
went to see him, taking with me glowing references from the

Kabul Intercontinental and Faletti's, photographs, and the tape we'd made for Radio Afghanistan. He agreed to give us an audition and kept the tape. As I walked back through the lobby, I suddenly found myself listening to The Philanderers playing 'Wild Rover' over the hotel's canned music system. It was being played in all the public areas, including the washrooms and the lifts. An hour later, we assembled in the 'Chinois Room' on the roof of the hotel for a rigorous audition in front of the diminutive Mr Bakkelund, the hotel's hard-to-satisfy banqueting manager. This was followed by tea on the balcony, with its magnificent view across the whole of New Delhi, a green sward stretching west into the hazy distance in the late afternoon sun, sprinkled with imposing, imperial-style buildings just showing above a canopy of beautiful trees. In the nineteenth century the British ruled India from Calcutta. During the newly crowned George V's visit to India in 1911 to attend the Durbar, a gathering of all the maharajas and Indian rulers held in Delhi to celebrate his accession, he announced that a new city would be built here which would become the capital of British India. Sir Edwin Lutyens led a team of British arhcitects and created what was to become one of the world's great Imperial cities, designing some of the most imposing public buildings of the twentieth century. We were highly impressed by this great British legacy, with its massive India Arch, a memorial to the Indian dead of the First World War and its aftermath, and the many acres of green parkland and mature trees, with wide, arrow-straight roads radiating out from several hubs, the main ones being the India Arch and Connaught Circus, New Delhi's main commercial centre. The central spine is Raj Path, a broad mall which leads from the India Arch to the majestic Presidential Palace, a building radiating power and authority, originally designed to house the Viceroy. It was enormous, set in 330 acres of manicured grounds, with its central brass dome in the shape of a 'stupa', the large stone burial mounds of the Buddhists. Raj Path passes the huge, circular Parliament House with 144 sandstone columns, and then between the two enormous Secretariat buildings which mirror each other either side of the ceremonial highway. At the centre of the large roundabout on which the India Arch sits is a tall plinth, now empty, under a sandstone cupola. On it once stood a statue of George V, but this was quietly removed in the mid-1960s. We were greatly impressed by India's capital city.

The hotel only really wanted us to perform at a couple of big parties, Mr Bakkelund told me, but there would be no decision until the next day. The bus could stay where it was until then. During the morning, we had contacted the press, radio, TV, the British Council, the American school, and other clubs and institutions. BBC's India correspondent, Mark Tully, appeared and interviewed me for the *Today* programme on Radio 4. He copied our Radio Afghanistan tape to use in the broadcast, and told us that a lengthier version would also be aired on Radio Solent, our local BBC station. Dick and I then recorded a piece for All-India Radio for their youth service. *The Statesman* newspaper sent a journalist and photographer to cover our arrival and a glowing report was published the next morning, complete with a large photo of us and the bus, with the headline: 'The Enterprising Nine'. I went to see Mr DeKiss with the paper under my arm and, after some hard bargaining, was offered an initial ten-day season, to include free meals in the hotel's executive staff dining room, use of the showers in the assistant manager's locker room, a secure parking place at the back of the hotel where we would sleep, and the use of all the hotel's facilities except – much to Alan's disgust, as he was dying to have a swim to cool off – the hotel's 'club' swimming pool. We would earn 260 rupees a night, which was somewhere between £10 and £15, depending on whose exchange rate you used. Tim summed it up as '... ten glorious days lounging in one of the finest hotels in Asia, set in one of Asia's most beautiful cities'.

Our first performance was at the re-opening of the hotel's main restaurant, 'The Taj', which had just been refurbished. Late that afternoon, we ran through a few numbers for a soundcheck with the resident band, led from the piano by the cheerful, charming and slightly chubby Benny. The room was so big that we were asked to use microphones, something we were not used to. Then we changed, had our supper in the executive dining room, and waited for our cue. Tim wrote:

> The band blew a fanfare, the lights dimmed, Alan played the intro to 'Wild Rover', the spotlights came up and we were on. Suddenly it struck one that this was actually the Philanderers – The Procal Turdum from the George Folk Club and the biggest confidence trick on the South Coast folk circuit, which was seen through by everybody – playing to a big international nightclub audience in one of the top hotels in Asia – and being taken seriously. It was a shattering moment ...

And so began our cabaret season in New Delhi. Even though some of the diners seemed more interested in their food than in the entertainment, Mr DeKiss was delighted and, when I told our audience that it was Clive's birthday, he signalled the head waiter and, as we finished our spot, a birthday cake with one candle on it appeared and the band played 'Happy Birthday'. Our first night had been a success, and each evening afterwards was a slight improvement on the last.

Mr Bakkelund was highly sensitive about the way we looked on stage and, in the interval on our first night, he pointedly sent us brushes and a tin of polish, and told us to do something about our shoes. Coming to the bus on Monday, he wanted to take our trousers and have them cleaned and our black shoes properly polished. He insisted that we should all wear black trousers, white shirts and identical ties with our Afghan waistcoats. We frantically went through our wardrobes to find black trousers for everyone, while Tony dashed off to buy nine black ties. We also gave our hair a trim, and that night looked impressively smart in our Afghan waistcoats with cleaned and pressed trousers, laundered white shirts, new ties, and highly polished shoes – and continued to do so for the rest of our season. Mr Bakkelund also told us that the hotel would be arranging a special 'Philanderers' Night' the following Saturday, a ticket-only barbecue dinner by the ornamental pool at the front of the hotel. It would be 'our' evening. The next day's newspapers carried advertisements: 'Listen to the beautiful ballads and fabulous folksongs of the enchanting folk singers – THE PHILANDERERS! at The Nishat Lake under the stars ... Dance to the romantic strains of shimmering music under the silvery moon.' Big posters were put up all over town, and by Saturday hundreds of tickets had been sold.

By now, temperatures at midday were in the low 30s and Alan was still highly indignant that we were not allowed to use the hotel pool. We eventually arranged to use the pool at the British High Commission, one of the biggest British diplomatic establishments in the world and, each day, when we weren't doing other things, we could be found lazing around the High Commissioner's swimming pool in New Delhi's leafy diplomatic quarter. Our sleep was becoming disturbed by mosquitoes, even though the area behind the hotel where we parked had been heavily sprayed with insecticide, and we all spent sleepless nights swatting blood-filled insects against the underside of the bunk above. We were kept awake not only by mosquitoes, but also by the regular thumps of others as they squashed yet another one, followed by a triumphant 'Got you, you bastard!' We all kept individual tallies. Many of us succumbed to attacks of Delhi belly. John was in bed for two days with such severe gut problems that he missed our first night. We looked to the High Commission for help but, as it was the weekend, we were unsuccessful and ended up taking him to the hotel's doctor, who prescribed some medicine and put him on a strict diet of clear soup, grilled fish and dry toast. 'You seem miserable and emaciated,' the doctor told him, but he seemed his usual self to the rest of us!

Two days after our arrival in New Delhi, we recorded a twenty-minute broadcast for All-India Television including interviews and several songs. A few days later, we recorded a half-hour music programme for All-India Radio. Bob had been energetically trying to find other cultural or educational bookings for us and, as a result of his efforts, we gave concerts to appreciative audiences at the New Delhi Municipal Town Hall, and at Miranda House, Delhi University's exclusive girls' residential college. Here we met some nice Indian girls whose company some of us enjoyed for the rest of our stay in the city. The following Sunday, Bob, Tony, John, Alan and Clive took seven of our new female friends to Okhla Lake, formed behind a barrage across the Yamuna River south of New Delhi, and spent an enjoyable afternoon splashing about in rowing boats. Tony and Bob went for a swim to cool off and discovered later that the lake was full of water snakes and a poisonous chemical which had killed off thousands of fish a few weeks before. They both survived without ill effects. Earlier, the High Commission had torn Tim off a strip for his indiscreet remarks about Pakistan's attitude to India that had been published in *The Statesman*. 'Pakistan military officers, it seemed to me, are quite keen to have another bash at India – they seem to want to fight again,' he was quoted as saying. 'I hope you're proud of yourself,' said Alan to Tim bitterly, thrusting into his hand a small gutter newspaper a couple of days after this was published. Its screaming banner headline read 'Pakistan Plans Fresh Attack!' above a story in which Tim's casual remarks had been twisted and inflated to back up the inflammatory headline. It identified us and the bus as its source and taught us a salutary lesson.

Pillock Ltd was not doing too well. Indian import restrictions were so tight that the High Commission suggested that we might only be successful with the Agriplan Building System, where we would be selling know-how, and possibly Temple Tubes pitch fibre pipes, but we'd almost given up any idea of making money through sales commissions. We were also disappointed not to be booked by the American School. It seemed they had used up their entire budget sponsoring a concert by Ravi Shankar. We managed to get hold of the highly sought-after tickets for this, and found ourselves sitting on the floor in the school's music room a few feet in front of the world-famous sitar player and his entourage. Witnessing a virtuoso performance at such close quarters was spellbinding, particularly for Alan, who had just bought himself a sitar from the same shop that supplied instruments to The Beatles, and he sat mesmerised at the master's feet. For some of us it was the highlight of our visit to India's capital city.

When we were in Kabul, a friend of Clive's, John Storey, who was travelling overland to India, had said he would try to get us some advance publicity in India, and we had given him some of our press releases and a photo or two. We thought nothing more of this until a young journalist, Ravi Narula, working for the *Junior Statesman*, a popular weekly magazine for young people published by *The Statesman* newspaper, called and presented us with the current week's copy, inside which was a full-page spread telling our story, complete with photograph. Headed 'The Philanderers Are

Now Here', it read: 'Yes! The Capital will soon encounter The Philanderers! Look not askance, for they are only a harmless singing group.' The photo was captioned, 'The Pied Pipers of Liphook'. Ravi wanted to do a second big photo feature about us. Asking about his friend, Clive was told that he was now in jail serving a two-year sentence for drug smuggling offences. We thanked our lucky stars that we'd been sensible enough to avoid all that. Ravi interviewed us and then organised his cameraman to photograph our cabaret turn that evening, and we ended up with a good set of photos of us performing. Ravi and the photographer came back to take some more photos of us a few days later, this time dressed in our suits and bowlers, and we spent a good hour posing in various luxurious settings throughout the hotel.

The bus was in front of the hotel for 'The Philanderers' Night', and the trees round the little artificial lake were festooned with hundreds of coloured lights. Microphones were set up, a soundcheck performed and we were ready for our audience. Little stalls covered the grass around the lake, behind which chefs barbecued the most delicious-looking kebabs and other delicacies. The area soon filled with diners strolling around the lake and taking their food to tables and chairs that had been set out around the garden. We performed on the dance area, a raised, marble-floored platform built over the centre of the lake, and at 9.30 p.m. we were on. The audience included tourists, members of the diplomatic and business community and India's high society, including the hotel chain's owner, Biki Oberoi, and his party. Ravi Narula described the evening in the *Junior Statesman*:

Under the starry sky, the Philanderers came out with their best numbers. The first half of the performance was full of Irish rural melodies. In the second half, geared in supposedly English farm labourers' clothes, they went wild

with the audience presenting a dramatic selection of rural
English songs. Swinging high in one of their action songs
'Farmer's Boy', Bob and Dick tossed Tony into the lake ...
To the delight of the audience Bob jumped in voluntarily
to his rescue while Adrian, a pole in hand, mimed fishing
them out.

The evening was an undoubted success and we celebrated
with rum and cokes on the bus with Benny and the band.

Meanwhile, we were finding it hard to get quotes for
shipping the bus to Australia in New Delhi. It was even more
difficult to establish whether we could sail on the same boat.
The following Monday, Mr DeKiss paid us 2,600 rupees for
our first ten days. 'We will terminate your agreement on
Saturday as you are in a hurry to get to Bombay,' he told
Adrian and me, agreeing to us remaining at the hotel until we
left New Delhi, probably early the following week. None of us
were quite sure whether this was a great relief or a shattering
blow – Tim thought it was 'DeKiss of Death' – but at least it
spurred some of us on to do some sightseeing. Before we
left the city, Peter Moss, Robin Allan's friend and opposite
number at the British Council in New Delhi, spent a day with
us filming the bus driving along Raj Path past the impressive
state buildings and around Connaught Circus. Then, after
lunch at his house, we drove through the crowded streets of
Chandni Chowk and the twisting lanes of Old Delhi to film
there, taking the opportunity to visit the Red Fort, Delhi's
seventeenth-century Mughal strongold and place, which was
similar to the fort in Lahore.

Each night our performances in the Taj Restaurant taught
us something different. We learned not to do 'requests' if we
didn't really know them, having made a complete hash of
'The Gypsy Rover', after struggling to recall the words during
the interval. One night we were asked if we could include

a French song, so I said 'Farmer's Boy' had been brought over by the Normans, which impressed Mr DeKiss as an inventive piece of quick thinking. Our last night came round. It was a Saturday and we had a full house, and at the end of the first half something happened that touched us deeply. Tony wrote:

> The maître d' came forward with a gaily wrapped box. He said a few words about how much those of the Taj Restaurant had enjoyed our stay and how sorry they were to see us go, after which he presented Richard with the parcel, amidst applause from the surprised audience. When we came on the second time, Richard showed the audience our present, a beaten brass peacock, which looked very beautiful in the spotlights ...

Before we left, we gave them a return gift of a brass horn to use when urging on the restaurant team in the inter-staff football tournament. On our last night in New Delhi, visiting the Taj Restaurant to say goodbye to everyone, we were coerced into doing a final rendition of 'Farmer's Boy' and were joined by almost the entire restaurant staff, who performed it alongside us.

It was the last day of March when we bade a sad farewell to all our friends at the hotel and headed up Wellesley Road towards Connaught Circus for the last time. Our last encounter in New Delhi was with the Indian banking system. We had some cheques to cash, payment to myself and Dick for the interview we had given on All-India Radio and another for the music programme we'd recorded. They could only be cashed at the issuing branch of the National Bank of India. We arrived to find it packed. Enquiries directed us to window 23 at the back of a queue of thirty-five people, most of whom were paid to wait in bank queues. The man in front said that we wouldn't reach the window for at least an hour. As we'd been invited to lunch by a friend of Tony's father, we just couldn't wait that long, so I explained to the rest of the queue that we were a group of desperate folk singers on our way to an engagement and they all generously moved aside. At the window the red tape seemed endless – the cheques had to be endorsed and then verified, and we should take the tokens we'd been given to window 50 to await the passage of the cheques through the system. This time there were only seven or eight people in front of us, but they were all withdrawing thousands of banknotes, everything being carefully counted twice. The man in front here told us that we would probably be there for four or five hours as it was not only the end of the month but also the end of the financial year. He suggested that we should see the assistant manager who, on hearing our plight, short-circuited everything and eventually gave us our 150 rupees, worth about £8. All this had taken a couple of hours, and it was well after midday when we drove away from India's capital city.

We were beginning to regret that we hadn't taken a proper look at the countries we had been travelling through, and were determined to see as much of India as we could on our way to Bombay. For the next couple of weeks at least, we would become proper tourists and, after being cosseted in the finest air-conditioned international hotel in New Delhi, we were looking forward to experiencing the 'real' India.

16

Tourists

'That's all gone up on women's heads,' declared Mr Ingham, our host and a business acquaintance of Tony's father, gesturing with pride towards the large, half-finished concrete factory. We were 10 miles south of New Delhi and he had invited us to lunch, in order to photograph the bus in front of his new building. He stayed at the Oberoi Intercontinental, was a regular diner in the Taj Restaurant, and had treated four of us to supper at the hotel a few nights before. He now provided a superb curry lunch and quantities of beer. 'They've only got four concrete mixers,' he said, telling us that the factory had been built in a quarter of the time it would have taken in England, due mainly to the effective use of female labour. We'd stopped on our way to Agra, and after lunch drove the 120 miles south on a good tarmac road, rolling into Agra after dusk. I slowly manoeuvred the bus through the narrow, twisty streets full of bullock carts, bicycles and bicycle rickshaws, all without lights, bringing down several low telegraph wires. We parked for the night at the Circuit Rest House, half a mile from the Taj Mahal.

Built by the Mughal Emperor Shah Jahan as a memorial and tomb for his favourite wife, Mumtag Mahal, who died giving birth to his fourteenth child, the Taj Mahal stands on the banks of the Yamuna River, rising like a mirage in white marble on a high marble platform with slender minarets at each corner. It is one of the world's most easily recognised buildings. Craftsmen were brought from Persia, France and italy to help with its construction. It had taken 20,000 labourers twenty-two years to build in the first half of the seventeenth century. Set in restful walled gardens with fountains, trees and trickling waterways, the first view the visitor gets of the Taj Mahal is framed through a single gateway, and the beautiful monument radiates an air of serenity and peace. It left a deep impression on all of us. In contrast, the Red Fort, close by and also on the river, was a vast, impregnable fortress filled with barracks, palaces and gardens, the palaces containing some beautiful rooms and delicate pavilions. We were shown round by an ancient guide, who interpreted the building for us in eccentric English. He described the outer fortifications: 'First moat, crocodiles. Second moat, elephant and tiger – fighting!' He showed us the room in which Shah Jahan died. He had been imprisoned there by his sons, partly to prevent him bankrupting the state by building a second, black mausoleum for himself on the opposite bank. From his window, overlooking the river, we could see the Taj Mahal silhouetted sharply against the hot midday sky. He was buried in the Taj Mahal, next to his wife.

Leaving Agra in the mid-afternoon, it took us about three hours to cover the 75 miles to Gwalior. On the road we met several vast herds of cattle, shepherded by thin, dark, turbaned cowmen who, when we decided to film the bus passing their cows, all stood to attention in front of the camera. To get the shots we wanted, we had to point the camera in the opposite direction and then, once they'd all posed, quickly swing the camera round to film the bus and the cattle before they repositioned themselves in front of us again. Arriving at sunset, we stayed the night at Gwalior's Public Works Department Rest House, larger and more geared up for tourists than our previous night's resting place. Here we met some government food inspectors, who took some of us on a tour of the town. We ended up at a market in the busy main square, where we were treated by our hosts to interesting local snacks cooked out in the open at the many stalls, which were lit by strings of gaily coloured lightbulbs. At one end of the square, was what seemed in the darkness to be a large statue of Queen Victoria, looking not at all amused and very regal in ceremonial robes, glowering imperially over the crowds at a more modern statue at the opposite end of a highly emaciated Ghandi, dressed only in a loin cloth. It was a hot evening and we were offered a deliciously refreshing drink made from freshly squeezed sugar cane, chilled by chunks of ice. A small urchin appeared and topped up the big glass ice container as we took our first sips and looked for somewhere to sit. At the edge of the square, next to the pavement behind the stalls, we saw the little boy again, this time sitting cross-legged on a sack on a huge lump of ice, chipping pieces off with a small axe. They fell into the rather smelly gutter and, when he'd done enough, he scooped them up into a container, took them to the front of the stall and tipped them into the glass bowl. The whole process was completely ignored by our food inspector friends. We looked at the ice in our glasses and wondered if we should prepare to die. We were still alive when we woke the next day and suffered no ill effects.

Gwalior is dominated by a magnificent fort, which completely covers a high sandstone outcrop standing 300ft above the plain. It was once India's most invincible fortress, and the grandeur of the fifteenth-century palace which, with its six towers, forms the fort's sheer eastern wall, is one of the most impressive sights in India. We spent the whole morning exploring the site, with its intricately carved Jain and Hindu temples from an earlier period and a great number of statues, large and small, all carved from the rock of the hill. Miles of battlements were decorated with pinnacles, balconies and turrets and, in one place, a strange archway carrying a plaque stating that the gate had been constructed by a British Army major in 1895 from pillars and an arch found on the site, under the command of another officer. This quite amused us, causing Tim and Adrian to imagine a conversation which went: 'Sir, I've found assorted pillars and an arch on the site. Permission to build a gate, Sir.' 'Carry on, Major. And, Major – jolly good show.'

Tony had been unwell since leaving Agra, and for the next few days had what Alan described as a sad case of the 'galloping runs', causing us to stop the bus regularly for him to dash to a large boulder, bush or tree behind which to relieve himself. This was not as easy as it might seem, for even in the most remote places here people would spring up from nowhere, and Tony quite often found that the rock or tree he was heading for was already 'occupied'.

We left Gwalior on the tree-lined roads of Madhya Pradesh. Usually, they consisted of a one-vehicle-wide strip of corrugated tarmac in the centre, on both sides of which were bumpy and uneven hard shoulders onto which vehicles have to drive to pass each other. Each time we did this, clouds of dust and dirt filled the interior of the bus, and the shelves and cupboards on our bunks continually collapsed due to the constant jolts and vibrations, shedding their contents on our beds and across the gangway. Indian truck drivers, usually behind the wheel of the ubiquitous 1956 Mercedes lorries still built in India by Tata Motors, would drive straight at us at high speed, moving to one side at the last minute. Bob enjoyed playing 'chicken' with them, but it gave us a most uncomfortable ride. We were driving south-east in the bright, hot afternoon sun towards Khajuraho to see the amazing temples there. Tim wrote:

The bus rode on through villages where beautiful small children run naked, gazing on the world with big dark serious eyes, as they have done for centuries, their parents living out their restless, often nomadic lives, almost untouched and scarcely aware of the vast nation of which they are all citizens.

We turned north off the main road and eventually arrived at the Public Works Department Rest House in the small village of Khajuraho, where we spent a peaceful evening in the village's open-air café, sitting under a spreading tree drinking iced Coca-Cola. The nights were much hotter now, and the heat inside the bus was so oppressive that some of us had taken to sleeping outside on the lid of the trailer. The next day we were up early to see the temples in the cool of the early morning.

The temples at Khajuraho were built by the powerful Chandella rulers in the tenth and eleventh centuries, and the sculptures covering the walls depict a multitude of people at work and play. In a beautiful, garden-like setting with newly planted trees, the temples are built on high platforms and are shaped rather like a boot, with the entrance at the toe, rising through several peaks to a final pinnacle at the rear. The Hindus of Khajuraho who built and decorated these temples lived without shame, and they celebrated this in their carvings, the best-known of which depict human warmth with complete frankness, showing couples in a variety of positions for making love, the more acrobatic ones needing the help of others, who modestly look away. These exuberant sculptures cover every external face of the temples. Voluptuous women are depicted washing, arranging their hair, dancing joyously, coyly displaying their charms, and embracing and fondling their partners. Less than 5 per cent of the sculptures depict erotic pleasures, though, the rest illustrating forms of human activity, all shown in exquisite detail in the beautifully carved sandstone. They represent possibly the finest examples of

Central Indian temple architecture that exists today, and their remoteness deep in the central Indian plain is probably what saved them from later destruction by the Muslims.

Some of us rode back to the bus on an elephant. Since leaving The Deers Hut, we had been sending things back to Bert, the landlord, including a home-made Christmas card, a joke Pillock Ltd 1970 calendar, both devised by Adrian, and an April Fools' joke from New Delhi in the form of a letter from the Oberoi Intercontinental Hotel saying that Bert was held responsible for our unpaid bar bill there. Our letters to him were full of insults, which he always took in good part, and Alan's, dated 'Middle of India 3rd April', addressed Bert as 'Dear Bald-Headed, Brainless old Berk'. 'Adrian, Richard, Clive and I had a ride on an elephant today,' he continued, 'and looking down from the platform we saw that it had a bald head with a few hairs poking out, just like you.' We all harangued Bert in our letters for his failure to write to us, and I was surprised that he ever did, considering how rude we were to him.

After breakfast we left for Sagar, 125 miles to the south. It was a hot afternoon and the sky was overcast as we drove across the plain on a long, straight road, overtaking a lengthy column of bullock carts carrying swarthy-looking tinker and gypsy families. Changing gear at the top of a small hill, the gear lever suddenly became slack and stopped working. We glided to a halt and Bob whipped the top off the trailer, got his toolbox and crawled underneath while I worried about the gypsies catching us up and nicking things from the trailer before we could move on. A bolt from the gear lever linkage had fallen out and caused the problem, and Bob quickly replaced it. Now surrounded by inquisitive locals, we quickly repacked the trailer and were on our way before the gypsy procession arrived. We stayed that night at the Circuit House at Sagar, an imposing building dating from the 1890s which overlooked the town's attractive lake, and Bob generously bought supper for us there. The temperature inside the bus was over 37°C now, which made for an uncomfortable night. The next morning, we left early and crossed the Tropic of Cancer while driving the 90 miles to Sanchi, where we planned to visit the celebrated Buddhist Stupas. It was Sunday and we pulled into the Sanchi Tourist Lodge where Tony ordered breakfast for everyone, which ended up by being a substantial vegetable curry. After we'd eaten, we climbed the hill to the imposing Buddhist Stupas in the midday heat. The first of these stone burial mounds was built around 200 BC, and the largest and most impressive was 45ft high and topped off by what looked like a stone umbrella and surrounded by a stone stockade with four vigorously carved gateways. Quietly situated on a hill overlooking the hot, dry Indian plain, we could see in the shimmering distance long freight trains making their leisurely progress across the far horizon. After I had filmed the others photographing the gateways, we returned to the Tourist Lodge for a cooling drink before leaving for Bhopal.

We soon reached the nearby town of Raisen. There had been a market there that day, and I found myself driving against crowds that were flooding back into the countryside. In the main square, I was frantically waved down by an insistent policeman who animatedly addressed us in Hindi. A passer-by who spoke English explained that he was telling us that we'd left our cine camera back at the Rest House. A little while later, the Tourist Lodge's official white Hindustan Motors Ambassador – actually a 1957 Series 3 Morris Oxford that is built in India – screeched to a halt next to the bus, returning the camera to us. By now the district police superintendent had appeared. We had punctured one of the front tyres on the bus earlier in the day and were running on the spare, and he kindly offered to get it repaired. As it was getting late, he generously arranged for us to stay the night at the local Government Rest House. The town was at the foot of a sandstone hill crowned by a massive abandoned fort which John was keen to explore. A guide was provided, and Tony, Tim, Adrian and Alan joined him clambering up to the extensive ruins. Meanwhile, I was invited home by the police superintendent to wash and have tea. The 'bathroom' was an outdoor shed with a hole in the floor and no running water. I was presented with a large bowl of water and a tin mug, shiny from heavy use, and proceeded to rinse myself down. After changing into fresh clothes, I joined him for tea, served by his wife, who quickly withdrew and to whom I was not introduced. He had served in the North African desert in the Second World War and, as with many Indians we met, had a strong affection for the British. His favourite author was Thomas Hardy. 'Tell me,' he said, 'is England really as it is portrayed in Hardy's books?' I replied that he would recognise much of what Hardy had described. The Controller of Development for the area then called by and the three of us had an interesting and positive talk about the future of India. I returned to the bus for supper and, well after sunset, the others appeared from the fort, having had an exciting scramble down the hillside in the dark.

Further south, the flat plains gave way to drier, hillier country, wilder and less pastoral, scrubby and with fewer trees on its high plateaus. We passed through Bhopal, and on the road the next day encountered fourteen overland travellers in a scruffy-looking but brightly painted Australian double-decker bus, just out from Bombay on the fourth day of their journey towards England, led by an Englishman from Gosport, Chris Guy. They picked our brains about routes and obstacles and we lent them some of our annotated maps while they extravagantly filmed everything with a very professional-looking camera.

Two days later we arrived at the Buddhist cave temples at Ajanta. They had been cut into the rock walls of a remote, horseshoe-shaped canyon by Buddhist monks who came to the area in the second-century BC. Over the next 900 years they created a series of sanctuaries and monasteries which they adorned with brilliantly coloured paintings and frescoes illustrating scenes from the life of Buddha. Years of visitors had taken their toll, and a team of artists from the National Archive in New Delhi was now painstakingly restoring the paintings and making full-sized copies for display in the national museum. The thirty or more caves had been forgotten for over a thousand years until a British hunting party stumbled across them in 1819. The interiors were a marvel, with every part of them, from columns and huge statues of the Buddha, to beds and benches, all being sculpted from the solid rock.

After suffering a series of punctures to our trailer tyres, we stopped at Aurangabad, the next big town, to have them repaired, and then drove on to spend the night at Khuldabad, a small, historic walled settlement on a ridge not far from Ellora, our next destination. The bus squeezed through the old walled town's narrow gateways, arriving at the Rest House just as the sun was setting. Here we took a couple of rooms, as most of us had decided to sleep in the cool, high-ceilinged Victorian building. We sat outside with refreshing drinks, watching the sun slowly sinking behind the hills across the plain below us, the sky glowing orange, gold and red, finally turning the deepest shade of blue before being claimed by the darkness of the night. Then the moon appeared, lying on its back like a thin silver saucer just above the horizon, accompanied by the evening star. It was a sublime moment as we reflected on the timelessness of this magical land steeped in so much history, in which our own countrymen had played only a small part. We were becoming rather fond of these Rest Houses, where, for a couple of rupees, we could find a safe haven and friendly welcome, washing and toilet facilities and a cool bed for the night. Tony wrote in his diary:

We enjoyed the quiet evenings at rest-houses and the breathtaking view from a high fort at sunset. I found in all these small villages that the natives, as soon as one has made a move towards being friendly, would fall over themselves to help and it was quite touching.

Early the next day, Dick took what became one of the most iconic photographs of the whole trip – the bus emerging into the bright early morning sun from Khuldabad's main gateway. Fifteen minutes later, we arrived at Ellora. Here the temples were carved into the western side of a gentle hill, from which the plain stretched away into the distance. The earliest were cave temples created by Buddhist monks in the seventh century AD, but Buddhism was then already in decline, and the most impressive, bursting with energy and inventiveness, were the work of Hindus a century or more later, being completely free standing buildings carved from a solid block of rock and each dedicated to a different Hindu god. There are over thirty Buddhist, Hindu and Jain temples at the site, the most amazing of which is the great Kailasa Temple, named after the God Shiva's home in the Himalayas. A stone bridge leads to a courtyard where statues of elephants and enormous pillars flank a massive two-storey temple and pavilion. Every statue and all of the structure were created from the rock of the hillside. Shrines are cut into the side walls, where the rock was quarried to create the space around this amazing building, which covers the same area as the Parthenon and is the biggest monolithic structure in the world. There can be few wonders of the world that can compare with this magnificent temple. Over 1,000 years old, even today it would be an almost unimaginable undertaking.

Leaving Ellora, we drove south to visit the fort at Daulatabad. During the fourteenth century, the slightly deranged Sultan of Delhi, Muhammad Tughluq, decided to move his court and, indeed, the entire population of Delhi, to Daulatabad, where he intended establishing his new capital. Thousands died on this lunatic march, after which he changed his mind and marched them all back to Delhi again. The fort survives, standing on a huge pyramid of rock 600ft above the flat, arid countryside. From the gate in the old city walls, a guide took us through passages and spiralling tunnels, spectacularly lighting our way with a flaming torch as we climbed our way to the summit. The fort was virtually impregnable, and boiling pitch could be poured onto invaders through the many shafts which pierced the tunnels, should they try to force their way to the top. After descending in 37°C heat, we were pleased to find a refreshment stall across the road, delightfully named 'The Rock and Feathers Snack Shop'. The advertising read: 'Don't forget to stop for a really cold drink. Homemade cakes, cookies, biscuits etc. also available. Proprietor Mrs N.A. Mitchell, Retired Manager of the Aurangabad Railway Hotel.' Mrs Mitchell greeted us as we approached. An Englishwoman, probably in her sixties, she had been born in India and 'stayed on' when India had become an independent nation twenty-three years before. She generously gave us all a free iced Coke and chilled melons grown in her own garden. Trade was not good, she told us, as the Indian tourists preferred to patronise their own native establishments further up the road. The British who had remained in India were now few and far between, and she was the first one we had actually met. Feeling refreshed, we set off on the 165-mile drive to Poona. Arriving there at dusk, we managed to smash the nearside upper-deck front window when turning into the gateway of the Rest House, here labelled 'The Inspection Bungalow'. Bombay was just over 100 miles away and our time as tourists was almost over. We would soon find out just how difficult it would be for us to get ourselves and our bus to Australia.

17

Bombay Bombshell: The End of an Idyll

The road from Poona to Bombay wound steeply down the Western Ghats to the coastal plain, and we were in bottom gear for most of the descent. Trucks and cars that had come to grief littered the bottom of the ravine through which the road passed. Once on the plain, the scenery changed, with more open and cultivated countryside, and the road became an 'expressway'. Those upstairs had an exhilarating journey due to the breeze through the missing front window, and the upper deck got a much-needed airing. Tony wrote:

> Our spirits rose at our first sight of the sea since Istanbul, but the smell on the wide motorway leading into Bombay was a little overpowering. Not only that, the poverty was sickening; thousands of people living in large encampments with shelters made out of every type of material, but there was always the smell, with large pools of stagnant water surely breeding some disease-carrying insect.

We arrived at the Taj Hotel, opposite the Gateway of India, but the general manager was away at a conference for the weekend and nobody else there would make a decision about booking us. It was noon, and the heat and humidity was like a steam bath. Tony had a letter of introduction to the Ford agents, so he and I grabbed a taxi and went to see them. We needed a secure place for the bus and trailer in this teeming city of almost six million people, and although they offered us a guarded compound there were no proper washing facilities. I had another hunch, and decided to call on the Ritz Hotel, not far from the Taj, where I explained our predicament to Mr Mario, the hotel's Italian manager. 'I might be able to help,' he said. 'Come back at the end of the afternoon.' When Tony and I returned, he told us he would happily help us, and if we weren't wanted by the Taj we could work for him. We could park alongside their sister hotel, The Airlines, just over the road, he would put us up in en-suite, air-conditioned bedrooms there, and would give us meals there as well. We moved the bus and settled in, then – showered and changed – we went down to the dining room, where we were served an excellent four-course dinner. We couldn't believe our luck, retiring to bed between clean sheets in air-conditioned luxury before enjoying the most comfortable night's sleep we'd had in a long while. Things might be working out after all.

The next day, while Adrian visited the shipping line contacts given him by Mr Joshi, the Lloyd's agent, Tony and I returned to the Taj to discover that the manager had cabled to say that he couldn't see how he could use us in the immediate future. As we were leaving, we were taken aside by his wife, who told us that she would see that he gave us an audition on his return. Back at the Airlines Hotel, though, we all agreed to offer our services as cabaret artists to Mr Mario. We could start on Monday in the hotel's 'Little Hut' nightclub for a trial week's engagement, he said, subject to gaining permission for us to perform from the authorities and other minor details. Meanwhile, we would be his guests, and on the following Monday move into a spacious, three-bedroomed apartment next to the Airlines Hotel, which was about to close.

On Monday, Adrian and I continued sounding out the shipping contacts we'd been given and learned that three cargo ships were due to sail to Australia in the next few weeks but that there was no way that we could accompany the bus. The only realistic way for us to reach Australia was to fly, we were told. In the afternoon, we moved into the flat which, to our surprise, came with two servants. That evening The Philanderers entertained a handful of people in the nightclub for the first time, all of whom seemed to enjoy our performance.

Conversations with the British India shipping line suggested that the SS *Bankura*, sailing at the end of April, could take the bus for £250, which would leave us with around £500 to get ourselves to Australia – nowhere near enough to buy air tickets. We talked about working our passage to Australia as entertainers on a passenger liner, but none called at Bombay. We could take a train to Madras, a boat to Singapore, and another from Singapore to Australia, someone suggested, but this would take three to four weeks and cost over £1,000. Our debates about this became quite heated. Could we charter a plane? A visit to the airport closed that door. Mr Mario had contacts with Alitalia, but they were lukewarm about arranging heavily discounted tickets for us. As the week wore on, the arguments continued. Mr Mario agreed to extend our season for a further nine days, giving us more time to agree about what to do next. Our performances in 'The Little Hut' were beginning to attract an audience, following a large advert in the *Bombay Evening News*, which also carried a lengthy story about us. We thought about renting Clive out to the Bombay film industry which, we were told, were always on the lookout for handsome, fair-haired young men. None of the rest of us qualified. Alan and Clive contacted Bombay Radio, but the schedules for the next six weeks were already agreed. Meanwhile, the bus was taken to the Ford depot for the broken front window to be replaced. It had travelled 10,863 miles since leaving Liphook, of which, according to Adrian, 7,920 were spent 'on the road' – with almost 3,000 miles clocked up driving around the cities we'd visited.

Then, on Friday, the bombshell hit. Mr Mario had been contacted by the State Home Office. They had refused his application for us, as foreign nationals, to work in his hotel. The only performances we were allowed to give in Bombay had to be either 'cultural' or 'charitable' and, as neither of those two categories applied to what we were doing in his nightclub, Saturday would have to be our last night. Formal notice of this was received from the Maharashtra State Legislature on Saturday. Mr Mario was very sorry. We could stay in the apartment until Monday, but after that we were on our own. Our audiences in the 'Little Hut' had been increasing, though, and customers had been warming to our act. On Saturday, our last night, they had the highest number of customers for four months, and Mr Mario seemed genuinely upset to see us go. So were we, as our main source of income – performing as an internationally famous cabaret folk group – had evaporated, together with our free meals and accommodation.

The heat and humidity in Bombay were now intense. To fly to Australia, we would have to borrow money for the fare, I thought. Dick told me of a 'fly now, pay later' scheme he'd heard about that was operated by BOAC. 'With this scheme we would pay 10 per cent for the flights now and the rest when we've earned it in Australia,' I explained to the others. 'We won't actually be borrowing any money at all.' 'Bullshit!' ranted Alan. 'We don't want to be in debt to anyone; it's against the spirit of the trip.' 'Have you got another option?' I asked. 'Yes. We'll stay here until we've earned enough to pay for everything.' 'That could take years,' I replied.'We've been stopped from working here, and even if we did earn anything it would all be in rupees, which the airlines won't take anyway!' Tempers were frayed, and the temperature and humidity didn't help. I had worked for days checking prices and had produced ten pages of calculations investigating every possible option. It seemed obvious to me, but not to everyone else, that we had to get to Australia immediately and start earning some real money there, although I fully understood Alan's argument. On Sunday morning, Tony and I went to see BOAC's Bombay manager and, yes, they did have such a scheme and, yes, there were seats available on a flight on Tuesday. This would mean that we wouldn't be borrowing any money and would be using an established method of deferring payment to the airline. To secure the tickets, though, we would have to name referees who would act as guarantors and be legally responsible should we default on our debt. I proposed Pillock Ltd's bankers, Midland Bank, and my father, and Tony put forward his grandfather, Sir Patrick Hennessy. The Bombay office then sent a telex to London asking them to confirm this arrangement, naming the referees, who would be contacted, and we provisionally booked seats on Tuesday's flight. Back at the hotel, Mr Mario agreed to let us stay a further night while we sorted things out. We bought some cheap suitcases and started to pack, sweating heavily in the steaming humidity of the bus – just a few minutes in the stifling heat and we were wringing wet! Sadly, we had to cancel bookings that Bob and others had arranged for the next week or so. All we were waiting for now was confirmation from BOAC, which made for a troubled night's sleep in our apartment.

There was no quick way of explaining our predicament to those back home. International telephone calls had to be booked days in advance and were prohibitively expensive, as were telegrams, and it would be difficult to explain everything in a few words. Tony and I had painted a bleak picture to BOAC to get them to act swiftly, but the telex to the UK remained unanswered. Then, on Tuesday morning, Tony received a telegram from his grandfather which read: 'MR KING AND I HAVE RECEIVED REQUEST FROM BOAC FOR GUARANTEE APPROX. £1,500 PASSAGE TO SYDNEY BUT HAVE NOT HEARD FROM YOU – PLEASE REPLY.' We responded at once: 'PLEASE CONFIRM GUARANTEE WITH BOAC IMMEDIATELY ...' I sent my father a similar telegram and shot round to the BOAC office to explain what had happened. Anticipating a telex from London, the manager confirmed our seats on the evening flight to Colombo and an onward flight to Singapore, and tickets were prepared. Tuesday lunchtime we moved out of the flat. At the end of the afternoon, Tony and I returned to the BOAC office to find that they had received a cryptic telex which said that The Philanderers had guaranteed to pay £1,500 by 1 July. Sir Patrick Hennessy had guaranteed the account and we needed to advise the names of the members in the party and the group leader contact in UK. We telexed BOAC London giving our names and my father as the UK contact, asking for urgent confirmation of the invoice reference number, without which the tickets couldn't be issued. We returned to the Ritz for our final dinner there, still uncertain where we would be sleeping that night. Tony and Adrian had agreed to remain in Bombay to organise shipping the bus and had some basic accommodation arranged through the Ford agents. We said goodbye to Mr Mario, who paid us 1,000 rupees for our performances – he was now faced with a fine for employing us without a permit – and headed, with our luggage, for the BOAC office.

There was still no news. The plane was scheduled to leave at 11.20 p.m. and we needed to leave the BOAC office at 9.20 p.m. to allow time for the formalities at the airport. The deadline came and went. We tried to contact BOAC's Bombay manager at home and get his authority to issue our tickets, but he was out. We tried to talk the staff into giving us the tickets on the strength of the earlier telex, but this was impossible because the tickets had to include the London invoice reference number. The clerk said that if we left before 10 p.m. we might still catch our plane. I paced up and down in the telex room watching meaningless messages being hammered out by the machine. At 9.40 p.m., the operator was explaining to me how the machine worked when a message came in from Hong Kong – it was a relay of one from London. I watched as the keys typed out, 'Nine Philanderers confirmed for Bombay/Sydney. Invoice 90 per cent cost, number ...' It was the sort of thing that only occurred in films, I thought – a real-life cliffhanger. In my whole life, I'd never cut things this fine before. We were issued with the tickets, already made out and waiting for the magic number, and bundled into a fleet of taxis which raced to the airport. Tony and Adrian came along, too. The flight was being called as we arrived. The formalities were short and informal, and within half an hour we were walking across the tarmac to a Trident of Air Ceylon, with Adrian and Tony waving us goodbye. We settled into our seats for the two-and-a-half-hour flight to Colombo and roared off into the clouds. Our overland adventure had come to an abrupt end, and new, different and more difficult challenges lay ahead.

18

Down and Out Down Under

'Just like bloody Manchester,' said Tim dejectedly as the large station wagon, its windscreen wipers fighting the lashing rain, carried seven of us from Sydney's Kingsford Smith Airport through grey, damp inner suburbs to the YMCA. It was 8 a.m. and we were told we couldn't book in until 10 a.m. I then discovered that the cheapest accommodation in town was at 'The People's Palace', the Salvation Army's hostel in Pitt Street, near Central Station. It was Thursday 23 April and we'd not had a proper night's sleep since Monday. We trudged wearily down the dismal street in the chilly downpour, the gutters flooding with water, checked in and crashed out. We were exhausted both physically and mentally. Less than a week before, we'd been happily performing in a nightclub in a very hot Bombay and now we were in Australia, virtually penniless, cold and wet, with no bus, and a £1,500 debt hanging over our heads. Most of us slept through until Friday morning.

Flying across India, looking down at the little pinpricks of light, each a small rural town like those we had stayed in on our way to Bombay, some of us wished we'd never left. After four hours' sleep in the Galle Face Hotel, Colombo, where palm trees rustled in the breeze through the open window and the Indian Ocean crashed on the beach in front of the hotel, we'd boarded BOAC's VC10 for Singapore, where we'd planned to stay for several days. Wearing a lightweight suit and carrying a briefcase, I quickly cleared immigration. Alan and John followed, wearing jeans and bearded, Alan carrying his accordion case and John a banjo. When asked how much money they had, they said that I held the money for all seven of us. The immigration officer beckoned me. 'Come here, please,' she said. 'Exactly how much money do you have?' 'Four hundred and ten American dollars and fifteen pounds sterling.' 'Not enough! You may all only stay two days – give me your passport.' I handed it over and she put two lines through the transit pass she'd just stamped in it and wrote 'cancelled' across it. But when we tried to book our onward flight, we discovered that all the flights to Australia in the next few days were full, except for one leaving in an hour's time. With no other option, tickets were issued and we reluctantly checked in our baggage and headed for the departure lounge. Approaching us along the corridor were some British soldiers, who greeted us warmly. 'Well, fancy that!' they said. 'What are you lot doing here?' They were young officers from Longmoor Camp now stationed in Singapore – and occasional drinking companions of ours from 'The Deers Hut'. Had we met them an hour earlier, things might have worked out completely differently. As it was, we said goodbye and boarded BOAC's Boeing 707 bound for Sydney. To me it was a relief, as Singapore wasn't cheap and we could ill afford any unnecessary expense.

'We've gotta get out of this place,' said Alan desperately on Saturday morning, 'it's a flaming nut-house!' 'The People's Palace' was full of ageing, poverty-stricken folk visiting from the Outback who wandered around in a semi-trance wearing wide-brimmed bush hats. There were also a number of semi-senile permanent residents who added to the depressing institutional atmosphere of the place. Anyway, at $13 a night each, it placed too big a drain on our meagre resources. Clive and I scanned the *Sydney Morning Herald* for somewhere to rent and found the middle third of a shabbily furnished bungalow at 23 Stanley Street in the run-down suburb of Bondi Junction, 4 miles from the city centre. The owner, an unshaven, balding, squat little man in a string vest who boasted never to have been further than 13 miles from Sydney, inspected us, took $100 as a deposit and the first week's rent, which included gas and electricity, and handed over the keys. We moved into what was to become our home for the next four months. That evening, Clive and I took a look at Bondi Junction for somewhere that we might be able to play. Along Oxford Street we came to a bar – 'Chez Ivy'. In the dimly lit interior we were served by a rather beefy barmaid. I got into conversation with a buxom blonde while Clive started talking to a chap next to him at the bar. 'Got nothing like this in Newcastle,' the man said. 'Oh no?' Clive responded. 'It's easy to see what's going on here,' the man continued. 'What, you mean drugs?' Clive looked taken aback. 'No, no it's all sexual deviation, isn't it? They're all blokes in drag.' Clive looked around the bar and then took a good look at the barmaid and realised she was a man. Clive nudged me. 'Richard!' he hissed, but I was busy chatting up the blonde. 'Let's get out of here,' he whispered urgently, 'they're all blokes in drag.' I looked at Clive, then at the barmaid, then at the blonde, and we both headed for the door as fast as we could. Afterwards, whenever I told this story, it was Clive chatting up the blonde and not me.

Our bungalow was clean but basic, the furniture old and shabby and the floors covered with linoleum. It had three bedrooms – triple, double and single – plus a shower room and toilet, all off one side of a hall which led to a good-sized kitchen with an ancient gas cooker and an antique water heater. Off this was a lean-to with a small sitting room with a paraffin heater and a fourth single bedroom. The beds had all seen better days, with mattresses that should have been consigned to the tip years before. There was no bed linen. We couldn't afford to buy any, and slept on bare mattresses, with no cases on the pillows, under thin, grey blankets. We'd exchanged our currency for $356 Australian, and by the end of the second week, after buying food, fares into the city, giving ourselves a one-off payment of $10 each as a living allowance and paying the next week's rent, we had less than $50 left. We studied the newspapers in search of jobs. Alan visited the Commonwealth Employment Service and got a job as a fitter. Clive started work as a quantity surveyor with CITRA, a French civil engineering consultancy, and John found employment with a builder's merchants. Dick became a storeman and Tim a packer with the same motor spares firm, and Bob gained the appropriate licence and started driving a bus between Bondi Beach and the city. Everyone worked as much overtime as they could, paying all their wages into the company kitty, from which we paid our rent, travel expenses and food bills. Later, we gave ourselves a $5 weekly allowance, but for the moment our finances really were on a knife-edge. On 25 April, the Australians celebrated what was probably their most important national occasion, ANZAC Day, which honours the Australian servicemen who served in two World Wars and other conflicts, the date being that of the first landings at Gallipoli in 1915. Then there was the bicentennial celebration of the first landing in Australia of Captain Cook at Botany Bay, where a re-enactment took place, complete with aboriginal protestors, in the presence of the Queen, who was making a state visit, but we were too concerned with our own problems to pay much attention.

We'd been in Sydney less than a week when a cryptic telex arrived for us at the Lloyd's Agents, Joint Cargo Services, who received our mail: 'BANKURA 1200 POUNDS GUESS

FINAL 800 ALTERNATIVE WAIT MONTH 700 MAXIMUM DECISION TUESDAY – ADRIAN.' In Bombay, Tony and Adrian had £250 in cash and traveller's cheques to pay for shipping the bus, plus 2,254 rupees to cover their living costs. The British-India agreement to ship the bus on SS *Bankura* for £250 was subject to formal approval from London, who, it seemed, were not prepared to do this and now wanted £1,200, the standard rate – money we just didn't have. However, The Shipping Corporation of India's 'Vishva Vikas', sailing in early June, would take the bus for £650. But we would have to send Tony and Adrian £400 before it sailed, to cover the additional cost. I walked in a daze down to Circular Quay, wondering how on earth we would manage, and then headed back to Bondi Junction to tell the others.

Huddled in our depressing little sitting room around the paraffin stove, we had another long discussion. If we all worked hard and spent as little as possible, we might just be able to send the extra £400 to Bombay by the end of May, we thought, but if we did this we would be unable to pay BOAC by their July deadline. Worse still, my calculations of our earning potential had relied on nine of us going out to work, but Tony and Adrian wouldn't be here for at least six weeks. So, to settle the BOAC debt by our 1 July deadline, we needed to find an Australian sponsor who would pay us sufficient by the end of June to cover it. After a reasonably good-tempered debate, we all agreed that, instead of going out to work, I should look for a sponsor. We wrote to Tony and Adrian telling them we would try to send them £400 by the end of May, and I wrote home asking if BOAC could be persuaded to accept staged payments through to September. Meanwhile, knowing nothing of this and unknown to us, Tony and Adrian made contingency plans for their parents to send them the additional money if needed; their cabled code word to trigger this was 'SPONGE'!

We spent the next few weeks in absolute poverty. By the middle of May we'd scraped enough together to send Tony and Adrian $250. Our cash book showed that on 20 May we had no money at all other than a £5 postal order. On 22 May, with more wage packets in, we cabled them a further $220, leaving us nothing for the rent. That Saturday morning we hid from the landlord! Finally, on 4 June, just three days before the boat sailed, we cabled them another $435, which left us with only $56 in the kitty. In all, we'd transferred £415 from Australia to India in less than a month, which, added to the £250 Tony and Adrian already had, was more than enough to pay for shipping the bus. And we had done it all without borrowing a penny. Now we had to sort out paying what we owed to BOAC.

I spent hours in Sydney's central library, compiling long lists of companies and advertising agencies from business reference books there, followed by days sitting in a phone booth in the General Post Office in Martin Place armed with a pile of 5-cent coins, phoning for appointments. I tried petrol companies, tobacco companies, airlines, tyre companies, banks, and anyone else who might listen. My spirits soared when I got encouraging signs, only to be dashed a few days later by a polite brush-off. By mid-May I'd visited over fifty potential sponsors, all of whom eventually said 'No'. I switched to targeting advertising agencies. Most people were helpful. Arthur Holland of Young & Rubicam, one of the leading agencies, gave me some friendly advice:

Whether you like it or not, you're in business and you've got to approach the agencies on their levels. Do your homework. Find out which agency handles which account and have outline schemes for each class of product, and then make your proposition. You should be paying me for all this information!

He mentioned a book, published by *Broadcast* magazine, which listed all the agencies and the accounts they handled. I found it in the library and studied it.

Then a letter from Adrian contained the sad news that he wouldn't be joining us in Australia. The delay had forced him to change his plans, and he wanted to visit Expo '70 in Japan and the USA before returning to his post-graduate studies at Cambridge. We'd known that Adrian would be leaving sometime but, when we hurriedly parted company in Bombay, we were sure we would see him again within a couple of weeks. I was sorry to lose his calming influence, his usually sober judgements and his off-the-wall sense of humour. His was the voice of reason, and his role as a peacemaker would be sorely missed.

A few days later, Bob announced that he had been offered a much better-paid job that he'd applied for, working for three months with a geophysical survey team servicing Land Rovers and helicopters in the Outback in South Australia. The job was 'all found', including flights to and from Sydney, and we would collect his salary direct in Sydney each week. He could break the contract at any time and would return for a week's leave once every six weeks. He decided to accept the offer and, a couple of days later, flew off to Adelaide. Now there were only six of us and we wondered wistfully when we would see him again.

Then a letter arrived from BOAC's Sydney office. It was our first direct contact with the airline concerning our debt, and I quickly arranged to see their young accounts manager, a Mr King. After a couple of meetings, he agreed to our paying off our debt at $200 a week, subject to Head Office approval, with the final payment due in September. I opened a bank account with the ANZ Bank, deposited $210 in cash from our wages and on 11 June paid BOAC a cheque for $200 for our first instalment. At last the way ahead seemed clearer. The bus was on its way and Tony would be joining us, giving us another weekly wage packet. If everyone kept working, we could easily afford the payments I'd agreed with BOAC, and I might still find a sponsorship deal. Life in our rather squalid little flat became less stressful and we allowed ourselves $5 a week each spending money. Our hand-to-mouth existence eased as we began to accumulate some cash in reserve.

Saturday was the day of the 'big shop'. Several of us would walk to the shops in Bondi Junction and buy everything we needed for the coming week, except for milk, which was delivered to our doorstep. We would then call into the pub on the corner for a lunchtime drink before returning to the flat. This was a typical Sydney pub, the interior designed to facilitate the 'six o'clock swill'. Until 1966, pubs in Australia stopped serving at 6 p.m., a 'temporary' measure introduced during the First World War, and at 'knocking-off' time men would head straight for the bar and line up several beers just before closing time, downing them all in the fifteen minutes' 'drinking-up' time allowed. Hand pumps had given way to hosepipes, which refilled the glasses of the great scrum of drinkers really quickly. The bars were tiled, enabling them to be hosed down after the drinkers had staggered off home, often throwing up in the street – 'chundering' in Australian parlance. English comedian and satirist Willie Rushton christened these pubs 'green-tiled puking parlours'. Bars were the province of men, women being relegated to a 'ladies bar', and our Bondi Junction 'local' was one such pub, its only redeeming feature being a blazing log fire, very welcome in the surprisingly chilly Sydney winter. Beer was served in pint glasses called 'schooners', half pints in 'middys'. I enjoyed cider, though, and soon found that Australian cider, quite colourless by British standards but just as strong, was considered to be a woman's drink. The pub refused to serve it by the glass, but would sell me quart bottles in the 'off sales' shop, which I then carried to the bar and ask for a 'schooner' glass to drink it from. John enjoyed stout and cider, so a second 'schooner' would be half-filled with stout and topped up with cider. All this was being watched in astonishment by the locals, who started by taking the mickey out of us 'Pommies', but soon grew used to our strange ways and enjoyed hearing tall tales about our adventures with a bus. This was the sum total of our social contact with Australians.

Our one indulgence was the TV set we'd rented. We spent our evenings watching hours of old films, ancient British and American TV series and dire Australian entertainment shows on the four available channels. Our main amusement came from the imaginative commercials. Warren Mitchell, in his Alf Garnett persona, advertised Rosella tinned soup – promoted as 'soup you could eat with a fork' – by saying 'Ere, wot's this muck?!', and Methodist minister and media cleric, Roger Bush, told us with a mild speech impediment that 'the offers at Norman Woss discounts were guenuine – I wouldn't do their commercials if they weren't!' We had few callers. Brinsley Smith, who had emigrated from Liphook to Australia eighteen months before with his wife Natalie and two daughters, appeared on our doorstep one day and was an occasional visitor, and another Liphook YC, Mick Harris, a steward on the P&O liner *Oriana*, would drop by with a taxi full of beer whenever he docked in Sydney and treat us to meals on board his ship.

My days were filled with visits to dozens of advertising agencies and potential sponsors. Sydney's biggest shopping centre, Roselands, offered us $1,000 to appear in a big promotion they were organising later in the year, but it wasn't the sponsorship deal we badly needed. My appointments were beginning to look like a roll call of every major advertising agency in Australia. I'd contacted over fifty of them, followed them up with visits and, although I was praised for my presentations, I was still waiting for somebody to say yes. The press cuttings we'd accumulated, the photographs of us at the Oberoi Intercontinental and the Radio Afghanistan tape were all useful sales tools, and I spent hours on Tim's typewriter concocting sales pitches.

Early one Wednesday morning in the middle of June, Tony arrived after a four-day stopover in Hong Kong. He'd left Bombay before the bus was loaded onto the Vishva Vikas and Adrian had stayed until the bus was on board and the ship sailed. A couple of days later, a letter arrived from Adrian confirming that the bus was on its way, secure in the hold, and describing in detail the traumas involved in getting the bus onto the ship, which he had filmed. His letter concluded:

> Well, it's been nice knowing you boys. I even miss you sometimes, which is disgusting. It's had its ups and downs but definitely a worthwhile trip. On the other hand, it's nice to be a free agent again ... Have fun. A.

Tony got a job humping meat around at Grace Brothers' Bondi Junction store, and over the next few days filled us in on their adventures. After seeing us off, they had spent the night on the pavement next to the bus in the side road opposite the Ritz, and the next day moved the bus into the compound at Ford's and took up residence with Mr Fernandez, a retired chief security officer at Ford's, and his extended family and lodgers, twenty in total, in the neighbouring old church hall. For over a month they slept on a balcony overlooking the busy street just off Queens Road at Charni Station. They met John Compton of the British Council, who invited them to a party where an Indian lady, Madge Mukerjee, befriended them. She introduced them to the Calcutta-based editor of the *Junior Statesman*, a well-known Indian-born English journalist, Desmond Doig, who was visiting Bombay. She suggested he use the bus to promote his magazine, in which we'd already featured a couple of times. On meeting Tony and Adrian, he agreed, but first thought they needed a holiday. So the *Junior Statesman* paid for their first-class travel to Ootacamund, a popular hill station in Southern India, and gave them 500 rupees to cover other expenses. After two nights in a first-class sleeper compartment on the train from Bombay, and a journey on the little steam-hauled rack and pinion railway that climbed into the Nilgiri Hills, they checked into the Sir Ratan Tata Officers Holiday Home for five relaxing nights. Returning to Bombay, the 'Magical Mystery Tour' promotion, organised by the *Junior Statesman* and Polydor, involved the bus being plastered with colourful stick-on flowers, psychedelic posters and huge banners advertising Polydor records. With Adrian driving, the bus, loaded with goodies, PR people and some attractive Indian models, visited several nightclubs where crowds of young people were waiting, ending up at the Juhu Beach Hotel, where Tony and Adrian chose 'The Girl They Would Most Like to Go Around the World With'.

Then the monsoon broke, and back in the compound they prepared the bus for its long sea journey. They gave all the remaining food and other stuff to the Fernandez family, emptied the trailer, dismantled it completely and, at the docks, removed the wheels and suspension units and strapped the base of the trailer under the bus. Delays at the docks meant that Tony had to leave before the bus was loaded. Finally, having filmed the bus being lifted on board, Adrian handed over the cine camera to the ship's captain and waved the bus goodbye. They had overcome immense difficulties and in the process had had some memorable adventures.

By the end of June, I had almost exhausted my list of potential sponsors in Sydney. However, almost 40 per cent of the big agencies had their headquarters in Melbourne, so I argued that I should go and seek a sponsor there. At first I met some resistance from the others, as it would cost at least $50 and my experience in Sydney gave them little hope that I would do any better in Melbourne. But I was determined to go and, on Saturday 27 June, John accompanied me to the station, where I spent $20 on a return train ticket and, with $30 in my pocket, boarded *The Spirit of Progress* for the overnight journey to Melbourne. This was a long shot, the last throw of the dice, and if I didn't succeed we were likely to be stuck in Australia for years.

19

'Buy One — Get One Free!'

It had been a long and uncomfortable night, sitting upright in the unheated train. All the other passengers, mostly soldiers, had brought blankets with them, but I soon grew cold in my lightweight suit. After thirteen hours and 596 miles, we pulled into Spencer Street Station at breakfast time on a grey Sunday morning. I knew nobody in Melbourne and had one phone number – an old friend of my girlfriend Gale's mother, Nairne Butchart. I found a phone booth and rang him, secretly hoping that he might ask me to stay. 'I've heard all about your travels,' he said, 'but I thought you were in Turkey ... Where are you now?' 'I'm at Spencer Street Station,' I replied, adding that all I had was $30 and didn't know where I should stay. 'Well, we can't leave you there. I'll come and pick you up,' he said. Twenty minutes later, I was in Nairne's brand-new Renault 16 heading towards Grange Road, Toorak, one of the most respectable addresses in Melbourne. Nairne was in his fifties. A tall, lanky, delightfully gentle and charming man whose ancestors had settled in Melbourne at the start of the colony in the 1840s, he had met Gale's parents during the Second World War when they offered troops stationed near their home in Hemel Hempstead tea and a bath. He had kept in touch with Gale's mother ever since. In 1939, he had been cycling around Europe. As war threatened, he headed for London and was in Downing Street when Chamberlain broadcast that war had been declared. He immediately joined the British Army and ended the war skippering a schooner in the Eastern Mediterranean running supplies to Greek partisans. Now he made beautiful and much sought-after spinning wheels in a workshop at the bottom of his garden, forging the steel parts as well as working the wood himself. Nairne lived with his 82-year-old mother and their ancient terrier 'Twinkle' in a delightful old colonial cottage set in a mature and leafy garden. 'Of course you must stay with us,' they insisted, and I spent a wonderful week in their company and was made to feel most welcome. Mrs Butchart ran a well-ordered and comfortable household, doing all the cooking and insisting on treating me as if I was totally incapable of doing anything for myself. With tea and cakes at 4.30 p.m., sherry before dinner and brandy afterwards, I felt pleasantly at home, although it took a little time to get used to the possums landing with a crash on the cottage's corrugated iron roof in the middle of the night. It was such a peaceful and civilised change from the upside-down life in our flat that I felt in a different world and grew heavily nostalgic for life back in England.

After a relaxing Sunday, I started out looking for a sponsor. I spent the week phoning advertising agencies and going to appointments, getting around on Melbourne's splendid tramway system with its beautiful antique trams and traditionally uniformed drivers and conductors, taking the No. 8 tram back to Toorak each evening. It was winter, dull and overcast with squally rain showers and a strong winter wind blowing in from the Antarctic. I wasn't dressed for this sort of weather. I started with the biggest of the agencies and by Friday had telephoned forty-two and visited fourteen of them. I was met with greater warmth and enthusiasm than in Sydney, which made me like Melbourne. It had the feel of a large English provincial city about it. However, nothing of any substance materialised. Nairne introduced me to Merv Tozer, who ran the Chadstone Centre, Australia's biggest mall, who offered me $500 for a week's work in October at their 10th birthday celebrations. By Friday, I had a few calls still to make, the next being an agency called Sellers Phillips Scott. I'd less than $15 in my pocket and used my last 5-cent coin to phone them. I managed to speak to Geoff Scott. 'Can you come and see me next week?' he asked. 'No,' I replied, 'I'll be back in Sydney.' He hesitated, then: 'I have to see a client soon but you can come over now if you like. I can't give you much time, but what you've told me is interesting.' I dashed down St Kilda Road to Albert Road and crashed through the door of No. 66 ten minutes later. Geoff Scott, a compulsive smoker, listened to what I had to say, picked up his briefcase and said: 'Look, I'm interested in this for one of my clients, a paint manufacturer. I've started drawing up a campaign but I can revamp it to include you. I'm off to see them now. Can you come along and help me sell the idea?'

Driving along, he filled me in on the company's background. Integrity Paints was run by a larger-than-life American in his thirties, Jack Bitting, who had started the company seven years before with pundits predicting its early failure. Integrity Paints survived and grew, but had gone through a bad financial patch a few months back. Geoff Scott introduced them to another of his clients, Swan Insurance, a major company in Australia, who invested much-needed capital, giving them a controlling interest in the business. Geoff was highly regarded, and this soon became obvious. 'Hi'ya, Scottie,' yelled Mr Bitting, his conversation splattered with expletives. 'How the hell are you?' We sat down. 'This young man is Richard King,' Geoff began. 'I think he may have the answer to our problems.' He said we'd worked long hours devising what was probably the most important publicity campaign ever mounted for the paint company. 'But Richard can explain the details of it to you.' He gave me a conspiratorial wink and I launched into a presentation I'd rehearsed at dozens of meetings over the past two months. We would appear in all their TV, radio, press and poster advertising, and make 'point-of-sale' appearances in all their major outlets – shopping centres, big department stores and hardware stores – with Roselands in Sydney and the Chadstone Centre in Melbourne already interested in us. I was confident of getting major editorial coverage in the press, and on TV and radio, for The Philanderers' world tour in a bus would also be news. The bus would display large banner advertisements for Integrity Paints and carry special sales literature with offers tied to the stores we would be visiting. My enthusiasm brimmed over; we would also give concerts at schools, clubs and hotels, appear on TV and radio shows and would be Integrity Paints' ambassadors. The main paint brand in Australia, British Paints, was running a campaign using Rolf Harris, but you could only see life-size cardboard cut-outs of him in their stores. With Integrity Paints' Philanderers you would be seeing the real thing – live! 'Holy Shit, Geoff!' cried Jack, leaping out of his chair. 'This is going to be even bigger than "Buy One – Get One Free!"'

I drove back to Melbourne with Geoff in a euphoric daze and a fug of tobacco smoke. His client had bought the whole idea. We would be contracted for six months. They would settle our debt with BOAC, give us an immediate advance and start the campaign in six or eight weeks' time, paying us $500 for three days' work each week. We could also take on a second sponsor at the same rate, if we could find one, and make extra money from giving concerts and performing on TV and radio. We agreed to meet the next week in his

Sydney office and tie up the small print. I phoned Clive from Geoff's office with the good news, said goodbye and rattled back on the tram to Toorak, where Nairne, his mother and I toasted our success with a glass of sherry before settling down to supper. I still couldn't believe it. I caught the daylight express back to Sydney, getting my first glimpse of the countryside of this vast continent: fields, farmsteads, groves of eucalyptus trees, wind pumps, cattle, thousands of sheep, rocky outcrops, undulating hills and small country towns. This wasn't the Outback, it was rural Victoria and New South Wales, and it looked green and inviting.

The following day, we enthusiastically discussed our good fortune. Almost to a man, everyone looked forward to giving up their jobs as soon as the bus arrived and getting it ready for our tour. While I had been away, there had been a major crisis. Clive had visited the BOAC office to be told quite casually that London had rejected our arrangement to pay off our debt at $200 a week, and that the whole of the balance would fall due the next day. He quickly called Tony, now working at the Grace Brothers department store at Bondi Junction, and Tony immediately phoned his grandfather in England – getting him out of bed at 3 a.m. – who promised to look into the matter as soon as he got to his office. The crisis atmosphere in the flat was quickly dispelled the following morning when, to everyone's great relief, Tony received a telegram that read: 'BOAC HAS AGREED TO EXTEND CREDIT TO SEPTEMBER THIRTIETH – TELL THE BOYS TO GET CRACKING. GRANDAD.'

I spent the following Wednesday with Geoff Scott and Integrity Paints' Jack Bitting and Peter Mulhall, the promotions manager, at the head office of Grace Brothers, who also owned Roselands, discussing them stocking Integrity Paint. My credibility was enhanced when the Grace Brothers directors said they already knew about

The Philanderers' involvement in the planned two-week promotion at Roselands. The afternoon was spent in detailed negotiations at the agency, with both agency and client as keen as ever, and we agreed the terms of a contract to be drawn up by their solicitors and ready for signature in ten days, by which time the bus should have arrived. Back at the flat, there was a mixture of amazed delight and relief that, in the teeth of all the odds and in the face of the cynicism of the doubters amongst us, I had managed to bring about a complete change in our fortunes. We decided that everyone should keep working until the contract was actually signed and we'd received the first payment. But the seeds of future dissention were already being sown. As Tim reported: 'Alan had already decided that he would probably be happier working as a fitter than making a fool of himself in Supermarkets; other members of the group with no illusions about themselves were delighted at the prospect.'

During the rest of the week I sorted out insurance and registration for the bus in Australia and, with the help of Mr Phillips, got to grips with how our arrival should be publicised. He suggested we try to get exclusive coverage on ABC TV's peak-hour News Magazine, *This Day Tonight*. Do this, he said, and everything else would follow. I went to the ABC studios, found the *This Day Tonight* office, told them our story and talked them into agreeing to film an eight-minute feature for the programme, starting with the bus being unloaded from the ship and culminating in a studio performance by The Philanderers.

Our social life, which had been pretty non-existent, was improving now that our financial position was looking up. Brinsley Smith was a regular caller. Mick Harris appeared whenever the *Oriana* was in Sydney, and other sundry characters began to populate our lives. Barton Furze-Roberts, another YC from Petersfield, had also met up with us. Saturday lunchtimes still found us at the pub up the road doing our 'stout and cider' routine, but the barman now had a bottle of cider and glasses ready on the counter when he saw us coming. Another watering hole was 'The Bunch of Grapes', a wine bar above the beach in Coogee, where cider was 80 cents a bottle – twice what I paid at our more basic local. Saturday food shopping had also become a ritual, and it took several of us to struggle home with the weekly shop following our lunchtime sessions at the pub. Brinsley's wife Natalie had tipped us off that it was much cheaper to buy a side of lamb and get the butcher to joint it rather than buying various cuts individually, but this meant that we existed off a diet consisting almost exclusively of lamb. On Sundays we would have a roast, and we all became proficient cooks – although John was acknowledged as being the best – and gradually the numbers for Sunday lunch increased as more of our new-found friends joined us.

New tenants moved into the adjoining flat – three English law undergraduates, working in Australia for three months on an English Speaking Union exchange before starting college in October. They would sometimes join us at the pub and share our Sunday lunch. One Saturday in mid-July we went to a party at Clovelly, the first we'd been invited to in Australia, in a modern block of flats, and were welcomed by a vivacious girl called Sue. 'I'm sure I've seen you somewhere before,' said a puzzled Clive, always one to remember a pretty face. 'No, I don't think we've met,' said Sue. 'I know! You were in Belgrade!' he said enthusiastically. She was one of the party in the Land Rover and minibus that had parked next to us in the campsite there. We spent the rest of the evening drinking heavily and comparing notes, with Sue becoming very envious of our overland adventures. It was a merry party and, much the worse for wear, we staggered home at 3 a.m. and crawled into bed. Tim discreetly recorded:

'Tony suffered most from over-indulgence and succeeded in making Richard's night decidedly uncomfortable in his drink and sleep-sodden search for the lavatory.' Actually, I thought I was having a terrible dream. It was pouring with rain and I was getting wet. It must have been somewhere hot, I reasoned, as the rain was warm. I woke with a start to discover that a half-awake, half-naked and very drunk Tony was peeing on my bed!

On Friday 17 July, the 'Vishva Vikas' finally docked at Pyrmont docks and, after a few false starts resulting from the casual attitude of the ill-tempered, wild-looking young gang-leader – who even tried to extort money from us by threatening to drop the bus if we didn't slip him something – Hairy Pillock 2 was finally unloaded the following Monday, with an ABC camera crew filming the event. Tony, Tim, John, Clive and I were there to sort things out, deal with the paperwork and reclaim the cine camera from the captain. The bus was towed to a parking space next to the dock gates to await customs clearance, which took a couple of days. The bus needed to be thoroughly steam-cleaned at the Department of Supply's establishment at Rosebery. With the trailer base reassembled, I drove the bus there. It was good to get back behind the wheel. The bus itself was still full of the contents of the trailer and was in quite a mess. 'God, it's filthy,' said the quarantine inspector when he saw it. 'All this lot will have to come out.' We had to rent a large van to take everything back to the flat, where it filled the small back garden and all the space available indoors, making our home look like the yard in *Steptoe and Son*. The next Saturday we were finally allowed to drive the bus to Stanley Street. We parked it across the road from our flat and started work refurbishing and repainting it, repairing all the damage sustained on our overland journey, replacing three cracked windows, stripping out the inside, renovating the fridge and cooker, fitting a transformer which powered the interior lights from a mains supply, thus conserving the batteries, re-carpeting the lower deck, fitting new lino in the kitchen, washing all the curtains, and polishing and repainting the outside. After a week of hard work, Hairy Pillock 2 was in a better condition than when we'd left England. I took the bus to the Government Registration Department, also at Rosebery, where it was tested by some very sympathetic – mainly English – government inspectors, some of whom knew Leyland PD2s. After fixing a few minor problems, such as getting the brakes to work properly, the bus' UK registration was accepted, and we were given a permit to operate in New South Wales as an over-height vehicle.

On 31 July it was Tony's 21st birthday. A few days before, he received a letter from his father which contained a major bombshell. He offered Tony the exciting prospect of setting up an export department at Temple Building Products, the family business near Liphook – a marvellous career opportunity – but he had to take up the post by October. It seemed he had little option but to accept. Tim and I went for a long walk down to the sea at Bondi Beach with the devastated Tony. He really didn't want to go, he told us, and would feel a sense of personal failure if he were to quit now. We had become good friends and looked forward to completing the trip and getting the group back to England together. I told Tony I believed it was unfair of his father to force this choice on him now, and that he had made a big mistake. Then Bob returned to Sydney after six weeks in the Flinders Ranges with the distressing news that he had virtually made up his mind to stay in Australia and quit the trip. He was so well regarded that his foreman had offered him a 25 per cent rise, giving him $100 a week, and he really enjoyed the challenges of his new career in the Outback. Bob's other more laudable reason was that he wanted to send money to his estranged wife Pat and their two children in England. In doing so he would be facing up to responsibilities he'd left behind by coming with us. During our long talk I told him there was absolutely no reason why he should not leave the trip if he felt it was the best thing for him to do, but that we would miss him enormously. When Bob returned to South Australia a couple of days later, none of us were sure when, or if, we would see him again. With the prospect of losing both Tony and Bob, we ran through a few numbers without them. It sounded dire. Added to this, Integrity Paints' solicitors were slow in drawing up our contract, which we were told was 'in the post'. The sceptics thought the deal was secretly falling apart and were beginning to wonder if, with so many things seemingly stacked against us, the whole trip were about to collapse and we should just give up. If we were down to six in number and the Integrity Paints deal fell through, Alan thought, it would be pig-headed to attempt to go on. It would take forever working to earn the money in Australia to complete the trip. I was inclined to agree. Only Clive, Dick and Tim were determined to keep the thing going, John declaring that he would go bumming around the Americas on his own. After all we'd been through together, was this really how it was all going to end?

The next day, the elusive contract arrived, signed and sealed by Integrity Paints, immediately lifting our spirits. With our income now secure, everyone handed in their notice. We swiftly signed our copy and sent it to England to have it formally engrossed with our company seal. Then Tony's birthday arrived. He had been agonising about the decision his father had asked him to make and, with the paint contract secured, his view had hardened, believing that he would be letting himself, and the rest of us, down if he didn't complete the trip. He phoned his parents so that they could wish him 'Happy Birthday' and to say as much, only to discover, to his immense relief, that his mother and grandfather very much wanted him to finish what he'd started. His father had written without discussing the implications with Tony's mother. It seemed that it never occurred to him that his offer might cause an upset with either Tony or the trip itself, and the job could wait until he returned. We all heaved a great sigh of relief.

Over the past ten days, John had been baking a magnificent iced birthday cake for Tony. Two girls, Chris and Elaine, whom we had met at the party in Coogee and who then visited us for Sunday lunch, invited us to celebrate Tony's birthday in their apartment with a wonderful harbour view in Neutral Bay, which they shared with two other girls, both called Mary. We sat down to a splendid candlelit three-course dinner. Tony was genuinely amazed and delighted when the surprise cake, with twenty-one candles on it, was placed before him. The girls presented him with a silver key mounted on a varnished wooden plaque with an engraved plate reading 'From four friends in Australia – Chris, Mary, Elaine and Mary', and embellished with two kangaroos. He was deeply touched by all the efforts we had made and was sad when we had to return to our squalid little flat.

There were thirteen to roast lunch the next Sunday, which Tim prepared with a high degree of élan, and the following day we started work filming for *This Day Tonight*. We collected reporter Peter Ross, recently back from a spell with the BBC presenting *The Money Programme*, and crew, who filmed the bus crossing the Harbour Bridge and The Philanderers playing on a jetty at the Botanical Gardens. This was followed by an afternoon drinking beer, courtesy of ABC TV, in a pub near the studios. Those still in employment were now quitting their jobs. Alan regretted leaving Marvelcraft. 'It was nice doing an honest day's work,' he told us sadly on his last day. 'I don't really like advertising – it's all trying to con people,' he said morbidly, 'and suits and bowler hats just don't suit our kind of music.' But he agreed to carry on for the sake of the group and the opportunity of seeing Australia.

The paint contract allowed for other sponsors, and various agencies came up with ideas, none of which came to anything. I was intending to return to Melbourne by train to finalise our itinerary when Masius Wynne Williams, another big Melbourne agency, asked if I could be at their office at 9 a.m. the following morning to discuss a promotion for a client, Acrilan, which would involve visiting trade fairs in all the eastern state capitals in the company of eight female models, once our paint contract was over. I eagerly took the early morning flight with Ansett, met account manager Peter Seal, and worked out the details. Then it was on to Sellers Phillips Scott. Geoff Scott was away, and I was greeted by David Miller, the agency's art director, and Robin Lovell, the creative director, who was married to Geoff's daughter, also called Robyn. They were my age and we had much in common, and soon became firm friends. David invited me to stay at his home, out in the country in a village called Wonga Park. There I met his delightful wife Sylvia, a 'Pommie' immigrant who had arrived in Australia as a child, and their two young children, Serafina and Ben, and enjoyed a happy weekend in their company, working on a detailed itinerary for the first weeks of our paint contract. We lunched with Claire and Tony Hofmann, Sylvia's sister and brother-in-law, who was a bassist with the Melbourne Symphony Orchestra. On Monday, after another day at the agency, I flew back to Sydney with the agreed itinerary, which would commence the week of 17 August.

The final day's filming for *This Day Tonight* took place in the bush at the Ku-ring-gai Chase National Park, where Peter Ross spoke to camera while driving the bus, with the cameraman sitting on the bonnet and pinned in position by me hanging onto the headlamp and a handle on the cab bodywork. Publicity photographs were taken for the Integrity Paints posters. We had already had a big photo session for a proposed feature in *Woman's Day* magazine. With our circle of friends growing, most weekends were now turning into parties; Dick manfully catered for twenty-three at lunch one Sunday, and while I was in Melbourne the others had attended a party where Tony famously asked in his loudest booming voice: 'What's that smell?' when he picked up a whiff of the marijuana being smoked illegally by other partygoers. Here they met a freelance sound recordist, Peter Margrave, who became another friend, came to our Sunday lunches and invited us to a party at his house in Mosman, which was mainly used as a store by a private hospital and was full of mattresses.

With the trailer moved to Brinsley and Natalie's bungalow at Toongabbie, our flat at 2/23 Stanley Street, Bondi Junction was finally vacated, the landlord retaining our deposit in exchange for disposing of all the rubbish we'd left behind in the back garden. Daniel Pearce-Higgins, one of the English students from next door, was invited to join us on our tour. Dan would be returning to Bristol University in a few weeks and we were happy to have him along, especially as he played the banjo and claimed to be able to sing. Peter Mulhall gave us a celebratory dinner at a hotel in Manley, and the next day we set off to our first engagement with Peter leading the way in his Chrysler Valiant, and a new chapter in our adventures began.

20

On the Road Again

Hairy Pillock 2 swung into the car park at Wollongong's big shopping mall, the Worrowong Centre, and, as the bus came to a halt, an enthusiastic TV cameraman filmed us leaping out and rushing past fountains and startled shoppers into the complex along a red carpet that had just been rolled out to celebrate our arrival. This was our first appearance for Integrity Paints. We ran through the Big W store, charged down an 'up' escalator – to the great amusement of Peter Mulhall and Integrity's cheery area manager, Ebby Peppler – mounted a small stage that had been erected in front of the paint store and lurched into a rendition of 'This Land is Your Land', followed by a long spiel from me about the virtues of Integrity Paints, all this being recorded on film by John. It was the start of something we would be doing, in one form or another, for the next six months. 'Between appearances,' wrote Tim, 'a gentleman boarded the bus and said in a delightful North Country accent, "Noumber tan! I used to drive this bouss!" ... He signed the visitors book "Mr Gordon Dutton, ex-driver of this beautiful bus."' At the end of the afternoon, a delighted Bill Macallum, the centre's enthusiastic manager, gave us $50 in appreciation of our efforts publicising his shopping mall. During the afternoon though, disaster struck. Heading for the stage, Dick and I were running along with my 120-year-old, three-string double bass – already held together with sticking plaster – when it slipped from Dick's grasp, dislocating the neck. During the following performance it kept going flat and, as I tightened the strings, the inevitable happened, and the neck slowly folded over and came away from the rest of the instrument, much to the amusement of the audience. I was distraught. We returned to the campsite and decided, after our appearance in Nowra, a few miles down the coast, to return to Sydney on Saturday afternoon to buy another bass and get my broken one repaired. The campground, next to a lake, was full of families with young children whom we'd entertained whilst practising the evening before. It was the first we'd stayed in since Teheran. After many months living in Bondi Junction, it was strange sleeping and cooking on the bus once more, and it felt odd being without Adrian and Bob, although Dan – whose background, character and temperament were similar to Adrian's – was soon accepted by us as a suitable substitute. The reporter from Wollongong's newspaper, the *Illawara Mercury*, in an article headed: 'Boys String Along via Vocal Visits', got right up Dan's nose by misquoting his name, calling him Daniel Piggins, which John quickly took up.

We received our first payment of $2,000 from Sellers Phillips Scott and banked it in the account Pillock Ltd had opened with the agency's bankers in George Street. From this we paid off half the remaining BOAC debt, with the final instalment being covered by our next monthly payment in September. In total, we would earn $13,000 for three days' work each week – but I would be nervous about our finances until we'd cleared our debt with BOAC and had a significant sum in the bank. With Bob away, I was the only experienced driver, and stubbornly refused to let anyone else take the wheel until all our debts were cleared. An accident, I argued, could de-rail our tour and scupper our arrangement with the paint company. Some of the others felt I didn't trust them and wasn't prepared to delegate enough. On stage I was also the frontman for the group. In Wollongong, Clive and I were interviewed by the local radio station. 'You haven't said much, Clive,' said the disc-jockey. 'When Richard's around, no one else can get a word in edgeways,' he replied. In the joke calendar we had sent to The Deers Hut from Teheran, Adrian had me down as 'Dick "The Mouth" King'. It was a name that stuck.

Having given up the Stanley Street flat, we no longer had a base in Sydney, so Tony phoned Peter Margrave, who was happy to have us park outside his house in Mosman and use the facilities there. We headed to 11 Erith Street and another party, where I met and became friends with a delightful, slightly Scottish, girl, Marion Tweedie, and she became a regular visitor whenever we were in the Sydney area. By Tuesday morning we had found a second-hand bass for $120, and renewed our gas cylinders. Next stop was Canberra, staying the night at Goulburn on the Hume Highway, the main Sydney to Melbourne road, our route taking us through country districts like those I'd seen from the train. Canberra is Australia's capital city and home of the Commonwealth Parliament. It sits in its own 926-square mile territory in southern New South Wales, a site chosen in 1908 but, although construction started in 1913, it wasn't until after the Second World War that the city really began to grow. It was designed by an American architect, Walter Burley Griffin, following an international competition, and the lake in front of the Parliament buildings bears his name. A garden city, it contains thousands of native and European trees and many green, open spaces. We were impressed by the layout and some fine buildings as we drove along avenues pink with cherry blossom in the Australian spring. Our arrival was filmed by the local TV station and we did a press call for the *Canberra Times*. 2CA, the local radio station, interviewed us, and eventually we arrived outside Rogers Department Store, Canberra's Integrity Paints stockist who, despite the adverts they had placed in the press, showed little interest in our appearance for them. Clive had contacted some old family friends, Wing Commander and Mrs Nicholls, who invited us to supper and, with the bus parked in the rain outside, we stayed the night, moving to Canberra's Motor Village the next day.

We were in Canberra for six nights, singing in a remote corner of Rogers Store for three days and appearing at a rather low-key fashion show there. The advertisement in the *Canberra Times* referred to us as 'delightful gentlemen' and 'comical characters'. We attracted some teenage girl fans, and spent some time sightseeing with them, including a visit to the huge War Memorial, a combination of museum and shrine to Australia's war dead, designed after the First World War and emphasising the sacrifices of the ANZAC troops who died in that conflict. The broad ANZAC Parade sweeps imposingly down from the War Memorial to the lake – with its recently installed 450ft-high Captain James Cook Anniversary Water Jet and the National Carillon, a gift from the British which was unveiled by the Queen during her visit that April – and a view across to Australia's gleaming white Parliament building. We all liked Canberra, comparing it favourably with New Delhi and Islamabad, but all too soon we were on our way.

Arriving in Albury at dusk, we found our chosen campsite closed due to heavy flooding on the Murray River, but were intercepted by Integrity representative, Tom Smith, who guided us to an alternative campground. Next morning we taped an interview for the local TV station, and at a press photocall for the *Border Mail* their cameraman took some

The directors of Pillock Ltd, March 1970. From left to right: Bob Hall, Clive Hughes, John Wilson, Dick Hayes, Richard King, Tony Hough, Adrian Bird, Alan Hughes, Tim Palmer.

The Philanderers performing at the Oberoi Intercontinental Hotel, New Delhi, March 1970.

Hairy Pillock 2
being unloaded
from SS Vishva
Vikas, Sydney,
August 1970.

Attracting a
large crowd at
an Adelaide
shopping mall,
April 1971.

Performing 'live'
on Channel 9's
Woman's World,
Perth, May 1971.

The Philanderers on TV in Perth, May 1971.

Stars of the popular *Spotlight* show, Perth, May 1971.

The Philanderers welcomed in Mobile, Alabama, February 1972.

With Miss New York at the International Auto Show at the Coliseum, New York, April 1971.

Appearing on *To Tell the Truth* in New York, December 1971.

At Avis headquarters, New York, with Sir Colin Marshall, December 1971.

Appearing on television in Phoenix, Arizona, January 1972.

Clive lies about his age on television in Phoenix, Arizona, January 1972.

Modelling Austin Reed suits in San Francisco, January 1972.

A publicity photo taken in San Francisco, January 1972.

Playing at Town East Mall, Dallas, February 1972.

Performing 'Toe-a-Tapper', Houston, February 1972.

Posing with a Triumph Spitfire at British Auto Services, Rockville, Maryland, February 1972.

Left: At the Capitol Building, Washington, February 1972.

Above: Pillock Ltd's logo.

Below: Returning home to meet Prime Minister Edward Heath at 10 Downing Street, July 1972.

In Graz with Miss World and James Bond actress, Eva Rueber-Staier, October 1969.

Playing outside one of Hornig's Cafés in Graz, Austria, October 1969.

Hairy Pillock 2 beneath the Acropolis, Athens, November 1969.

Replacing the water pump bearings at Camping Attikon in Athens, November 1969.

Driving through the Kabul Gorge, February 1970.

The perilous Turkish mountains. Note Tony using binoculars from the upper-deck emergency exit, December 1969.

The bus crossing a river in Pakistan. Bridge in the background is out of action, February 1970.

The bazaar in Kabul. Me buying a pottery drum, February 1970.

Clive, Tony and me hitching a ride on an elephant in Khajuraho, India, March 1970.

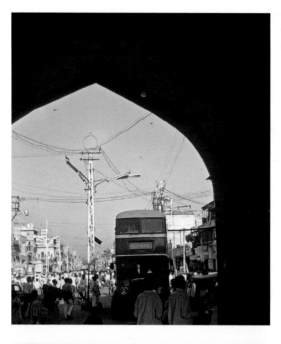

The bus as seen through an archway in Delhi, March 1970.

Me at the Taj Mahal, Agra, March 1970.

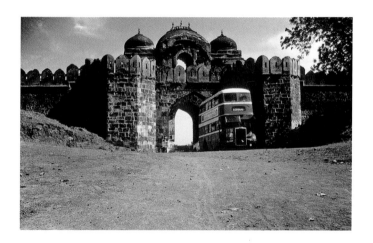

Hairy Pillock 2 at the main gate at Khuldabad, central India, April 1970.

Sydney photoshoot, August 1970.

The Philanderers playing in the Warrawong Centre, Wollongong, Australia, September 1970.

The Philanderers at Albury 'Folk Pot', November 1970.

Hairy Pillock 2 in the shadow of Sydney Harbour Bridge,
September 1971. Note the Australian number plate.

Photocall outside the Los Angeles Press Club, January 1972.

In Alaskan waters on board the *Oronsay*, July 1972.

The triumphant homecoming at The Deers Hut, Liphook, July 1972.

The bet is won! In front of The Deers Hut with landlord, Bert Oram, on the far right, July 1972.

splendid photographs and gave us large prints of them. The article read:

> If you want to travel around the world with several friends and remain friends, take a double-decker bus. The Philanderers spokesman, Richard 'The Mouth' King, explained that they averaged one good row a day. But in a double-decker bus there was room to get away from the rowing partner, and cool off. Consequently these brash, adventurous young businessmen-cum-folk singers have made it halfway around the world with no major catastrophes.

We appeared at the Integrity Paints stockists in Albury, Wodonga and Wangaratta, under the watchful eye of Integrity's Tom Smith, Geoff Sullivan and Peter Mulhall, who provided us with a small public address system to amplify our sales messages. At Gogoll's Hardware in North Albury, an earnest young Methodist minister, introducing himself as George, invited us to play at Albury's folk club – the unfortunately named 'Folk Pot' – offering us the door take, and so on Saturday evening we made our first appearance in Australia before a paying audience, for which we received $82.69. The venue was an old print shop and the compere, a laid-back English folk singer called Ted Jenkins, who lived on the premises with his wife and family and an odd assortment of hangers-on, fed us before our performance. The evening was a sell-out and a great success, our blend of comedy, chat, and a mix of funny and serious folk songs going down so well with the young audience that we were invited back whenever we were in town. Back in Wangaratta on Monday – where on Saturday we had met a rather creepy local entrepreneur called 'Mouse', who had invited us to drinks at the local Returned Servicemen's League Club and unsuccessfully attempted to organise auditions for us at various local hotels – we visited Brown Bros vineyard and were presented with some good wine, including a large bottle labelled 'Champers'. This we decided to drink at the end of the month on the first anniversary of our departure from The Deers Hut.

Driving to Shepparton, we passed through Glenrowan, where bandit and folk hero Ned Kelly had made his last stand, commemorated by a very primitive home-made statue showing him dressed in his bullet-proof outfit and helmet, looking like a Saracen warrior and menacingly clutching a revolver which, on closer inspection, turned out to be a 'Lone Star' toy cap gun! In Shepparton, we were filmed for the local TV station. It rained so hard that the presenter ended his report with: 'Welcome as they are in Shepparton, the boys do seem to have brought with them their own British weather conditions!' After an interview at 3SR, the local radio station, we all went off with the interviewer, Rohan Glenn, for a drink at Bob Dowdell's Overlander Motel, an impressive modern complex, and were invited to supper in the restaurant. Somehow, we became involved in a talent contest, which Rohan and I ended up judging. We appeared at Vibert's – Shepparton's Integrity Paints stockist – and then we were off to Kyabram, even further off the beaten track, where we were to play at Knights Big Store, a full page advert in the local paper promoting our appearance. We were also dinner guests of the local Rotaract Club, when I gave a short speech about our travels. The highlight of our short stay in Kyabram, though, was an early morning visit to two local primary schools. One of the classes at the Haslem Street School made us a book – thirty children in class 2H had drawn pictures of the bus and written messages to us. 'I like you all because you are kind. I have never seen those kind of hats. Have you got a long way to go? I like the old double-decker bus. I wish I can come with you – Roslyn' was a typical comment. We were

so touched by this book, presented to us at lunchtime at the
store by the school's young female teachers, that we returned
to give the school a free concert later in the day in the school
quadrangle. The children sat on chairs and benches, cheeirng
and applauding each number, and when Dick sang 'Puff, the
Magic Dragon' the entire school sang along with him.

Next, we visited the legendary gold-rush town of Bendigo,
where our performance at Fitzpatrick's was recorded by
3BO, the local radio station. We then drove 75 miles back to
Shepparton, where store owner David Vibert had offered us
$100 to play at a big Saturday night family party celebrating
the homecoming of his younger sister, Liz, who had travelled
overland to India and married her boyfriend in New Delhi. The
evening was a triumph, and we made a lot of new friends,
one of whom, Nola Cox, a local girl then living in Melbourne,
agreed to give Tony and Clive a lift to Melbourne the next
day, where they would try to organise bookings and publicity
for us. She was also persuaded to put them, and also me, up
for a few nights at her flat in Manningham Street, Parkville,
not far from the Melbourne suburb of Moonee Ponds, home
of Barry Humphries' fictional Edna Everage. It was also about
this time that John gained a new nickname. A couple of girls
told him they thought he looked like a wizened gnome. John
being the smallest of us, with an unkempt hairy beard from
which protruded a red nose and two beady eyes, it was a tag
that suited him. From then on, when we wanted to tease him,
we called him 'Gnome'. On Sunday, I drove the bus back to
Bendigo, where local freelance cameraman Bob Auslebrook
filmed us in our suits and bowler hats greeting the arrival
of two magnificent steam engines pulling a trainload of rail
enthusiasts from Melbourne, and then travelling around
Bendigo on the town's crowded antique trams. No sooner
had we parked at Bendigo's campsite at the end of the
afternoon than my lift to Melbourne turned up and I headed

off to join Tony and Clive at Nola's flat. While Alan, Tim, John, Dick and Dan enjoyed sightseeing in Bendigo, Tony, Clive and I did our best to launch The Philanderers on the Melbourne entertainment scene.

Tony and I spent a restless night sharing Nola's double bed, desperately trying not to bump into each other, while Clive slumbered uncomfortably on the bedroom floor and Nola snuggled down on her sofa. The next day at Integrity Paints' office, I discovered just how poor a financial state the company was in. They had sacked many of their field staff and were withdrawing from the Queensland and South Australian markets to concentrate their sales efforts in Victoria and New South Wales. This dashed our hopes of seeing a large part of eastern and southern Australia. 'Where are we going next?' I asked Peter Mulhall, reminding him that in five weeks' time we were committed to work for Grace Brothers in Sydney for a couple of weeks. 'Well, Richard, I'm not quite sure. We've got it in hand and we're working on an itinerary. No, we haven't actually got in touch with any of the stores yet ...' Peter lent me a company car and I drove to meet Clive and Tony at Geoff Scott's office. They had spent the morning arranging radio, TV and press coverage, and attempting to get bookings for us, discovering that no big venues were prepared to book acts except through an agent. As a result, Geoff had arranged for Tony and Clive to see an agent friend, Jeff Joseph, who immediately got us a booking on Australia's Saturday morning teenage pop show, *Happening 70*, and said he would try to get editorial coverage of us in *TV Week*.

Meanwhile, I'd visited Masius Wynne Williams, who were still floating ideas about us to Acrilan and having them all knocked back. The three of us then called on the legendary Frank Traynor, who ran Melbourne's biggest folk club, famous throughout Australia. A pleasant Aussie in his mid-

forties, Frank said he would mention us in his newspaper
column and agreed that we should play at his venue. This
was an old candlelit house where different performers played
simultaneously – one upstairs, one downstairs – but we
would only receive a cut of the door take. The next day, Geoff
Scott confirmed what I'd suspected about the short-term
cash difficulties of his client, and told us that they would be
happy to release us from our contract should we find another
sponsor. Then we discovered that we couldn't drive the bus
anywhere in Melbourne without obtaining permits for each
journey from the Country Roads Board. This was a real bind
but, by the time we were driven back to Bendigo by Geoff
Sullivan, I'd obtained a permit and oversize vehicle route map
which would at least enable us to reach a campsite near the
Integrity Paints factory the following Saturday.

Our journey from Bendigo to Melbourne took us to
hardware stores in several towns. In Castlemaine, we also
played to the residents of an old folks' home, much to the
delight of the nursing staff. In Maryborough, we visited the
local primary schools and broadcast on local radio and, in
Kyneton, the *Kyneton Guardian* reported:

> ... crowds packed into Turners' for a closer view of the group.
> During the morning The Philanderers made a popular visit
> to the local primary schools ... They were enthusiastically
> received by the children, who oggled at the red double-
> decker bus ... Those who saw the musicians in action at
> Turners' Store voted the group first-class musicians. For
> many people, it was their first and last opportunity to see a
> genuine English double-decker bus.

The chilly, dull and showery spring weather, large numbers
of mature deciduous European – and currently leafless –
trees, and the solid Victorian and Edwardian buildings in

these towns all suggested that we were in a kind of strange alternative England, and we spent quiet evenings on the bus indulging in nostalgic games of Liphookopoly and organising chess tournaments. Arriving in Melbourne on a damp Saturday afternoon, we pulled into the Five Ways Caravan Park near Moorabbin and settled ourselves in for a month's stay in Australia's second-largest city. Helpfully, Integrity Paints had loaned us a car, which some of us used that evening to go to Frank Traynor's.

'Sunday brought an agonising reappraisal of the position of Pillock Ltd,' wrote Tim. 'It was becoming obvious that the high hopes with which the founders had set out had turned sour ...' We were facing the fact that we had failed as a trade mission and as export representatives. 'I said it would never work,' said Alan smugly, reflecting the views of several of the others. We just didn't have the time, energy or commitment to promote the products we were supposed to be representing. After a lot of soul-searching, we decided to write to them explaining the position and regretting our lack of success on their behalf. Discussion then turned to what form our American tour might take. The only thing most of us could agree on was that we should try to make as much money as possible. But it was difficult to see beyond this. Views differed. It was the start of a long and sometimes acrimonious debate about the ethics underpinning what we were doing, with Alan arguing that we were prostituting ourselves and sacrificing our integrity as musicians on the altar of promoting Integrity Paints, and that we were wasting our time and their money talking to illiterate journalists and idiot disc-jockeys just to secure pointless publicity. This didn't seem to bother the rest of us too much – it was all a means to an end – but I was forced into having to justify signing us up to months of purgatory in hardware stores performing to audiences of paint brushes and lawnmowers.

As the weeks passed, so the fruitless debate continued, but at least we had now finally repaid our debt to BOAC and were better off financially than we had ever been. But it was slowly becoming apparent that we would never earn enough in Australia to pay for the rest of our trip and get the bus and ourselves back to England, and that without sponsorship for an American tour our trip would founder here in Australia, and we would have failed.

21

Making it in Melbourne

Melbourne was Integrity Paints' heartland and manufacturing base. They sold a limited range of primary gloss paints and over 1,500 different pastel shades of emulsion, which were all mixed in store from a selection of dyes which were squirted into cans of white base and then shaken vigorously by a machine. In the month we were in Melbourne, we appeared at ten Integrity Paints stockists, and to reach each of them we had to obtain individual permits and travel on approved routes. Integrity Paints lent us an enormous ten-seater American Ford Galaxy estate car – the only one in Australia – big enough to carry eight of us together with our instruments, including my double bass. This enabled us to reach TV and radio stations and other places where turning up in the bus was not essential, and get out and about both socially and on business.

Our first Monday in Melbourne saw us arranging press coverage and visits to TV and radio stations. Clive, Tony, Dan and I went to see Ron Tudor, a friendly chap in his forties with a light-coloured curly beard, who had recently established the Fable Label and was currently one of the biggest record producers in Australia. By recording local cover versions of UK hits, he'd taken advantage of a dispute between commercial radio stations and the major international record companies, who were now seeking copyright payments for the use of their records. Ron agreed to record an audition tape of us later in the week.

We'd arranged a photocall with *The Herald*, Melbourne's popular evening paper, resulting in an article with a large picture of us alongside the bus – kicking up our legs like a lot of bowler-hatted chorus girls with our umbrellas held aloft to keep off the rain – which filled page three of the paper and heralded our arrival in the city. This triggered visits from a number of the Australians we had met on our travels, including John Potter, whom we'd met at the Vienna campsite, and who invited us all to dinner.

Thursday that week was a memorable day for us. We cruised from one radio station to another in our gigantic American estate car, recording a song and an interview at 3KZ, then a forty-minute live interview with Lois Lathlean at 3AW, the city's top talk-radio station, where we also sang a couple of songs. Back in the car, we heard ourselves on 3KZ as we sped towards the row of terraced houses in Albert Road, South Melbourne, where Fable Label's recording studios were located. Until now we had only been recorded 'live' at radio or TV studios, and this was our first venture into the world of record production. We were ushered into a tiny, cramped, sound-proofed room full of cables, mike stands and other clutter. After various soundchecks, Alan, Clive, Tony and I were told to record the music backing to our first choice of song, 'Courtin' in the Kitchen'. This was then played back for us to sing the words without the instruments. We had recorded the accompaniment far too fast, and had to hurry our way through the first of our two tracks. The second, produced in the same way, had me singing 'Twice Daily', an Adge Cutler song, also at breakneck speed. Ron Tudor was sufficiently unimpressed not to offer us a recording contract. Back at the Fiveways Caravan Park, we settled down for the evening listening to the LP *Bridge over Troubled Water*, our current favourite, and wondered if we would ever make our own record, when some more Aussies from the Vienna campsite came to call and brought with them some very welcome cans of beer.

Our work for Integrity Paints that week started inauspiciously on a cold and damp Wednesday in a quiet but pleasant enough store in Ringwood called Stoney's. The report in the following week's *Ringwood and Croydon Mail* had a big jokey photograph of us posing in front of the bus with Dan standing in a small dustbin. In the text he was referred to as Daniel Piggins again – the reporter must have got his name from John. Things picked up on Friday, when we played for Neil Howard to an enthusiastic crowd outside his hardware store at the Parkmore Shopping Centre near Dandenong. We'd played at a secondary school earlier that day, and a bevy of pretty teenage schoolgirls, including Neil's daughter, skipped lessons to hear us again and spent most of the rest of their day tidying up the bus for us. Keith Ford, Integrity's general manager, bought us all fish and chips, including the girls, who became members of the burgeoning Philanderers' fan club and had christened themselves 'The Bus Cleaners'. Our week ended at the Old Orchard Shopping Centre at North Blackburn, where our friends David and Robin from Sellers Phillips Scott were on hand to help John film our performance. They loaded John onto a shopping trolley to take some tracking shots, pushing him slowly towards us through crowds of children and their parents, much to everyone's amusement. Ex-Liphook immigrants Ray and Audrey Cutting and their family emerged from the crowd to tell us how much they loved life in Australia. This was the last time Dan would perform with us. That evening we took him to the airport for the first leg of his journey back to England, taking with him films, tapes and personal knick-knacks for us. Within a few days he would be in Liphook with our parents and friends, as my mother had arranged an evening to show some of the film we had taken and mark the first anniversary of our departure. Both Adrian and Dan would be there to provide their own personal testimony. We had grown fond of Dan and enjoyed his wry amusement at what we were doing, and were sad to see him go. He couldn't be persuaded to stay, though, being committed to return to Bristol University.

The next week, we auditioned for the popular *Mike Walsh Show*, and the rather precious producer, Joe Latrona, was so impressed that he immediately offered us a slot the following week – with a billing in *TV Week* – for a fee of $100. That evening we celebrated the anniversary of our departure. We had stuck together for a year through thick and thin and, after travelling halfway round the world and overcoming all the difficulties and obstacles in our path, we were still friends. We wondered what Bob was doing, thought about Adrian and Dan at my mother's anniversary get-together 10,000 miles away and toasted ourselves with the Brown Bros 'Champers'. Tim cooked a celebratory meal of mushroom soup, roast beef with roast potatoes, cauliflower, peas and sprouts, followed by fruit salad and cream, which was washed down with a couple more bottles of wine. With the meal cleared away, we sat quietly thinking about what we had managed to achieve so far and what life could possibly have in store for us all in the year ahead.

For the rest of that week, we helped to celebrate the 20th anniversary of Integrity Paints stockists Courtney and Brear, starting with a cabaret spot, to great acclaim, at the surprise party at the Springvale Golf Club for the two founders, who still managed the store. Performances in the store, and a splendid lunch at one of Melbourne's pleasant, recently built large family pubs, hosted by Mr Courtney and Mr Brear to thank us for entertaining them at their party, rounded off the week. Integrity's managing director, Jack Bitting, was also around to hear reports about what a fantastic success his promotion had been. But the high point was our appearance at Frank Traynor's famous folk club. With audiences accustomed to mumbled introductions from solo artists who failed to connect with them on a personal level and then sang sad dirges with no humour, about protest, failure, death and the sorrows of the world, the Philanderers came as something of a surprise. I had always enjoyed introducing the songs we sang, and relied on spontaneous wit and humour to win over an audience. We also genuinely liked what we did, and in particular playing to people who warmed to our strange mixture of folk and comedy songs, and it showed. After years of doing this together, we worked well as a team on stage and were obviously happy in each other's company. At Frank Traynor's it all paid off. With our friends David, Sylvia, Robin and Robyn in the audience cheering us on, and my not being afraid to take the mickey out of the dismal end of the folk scene between songs, we gradually won the audience over. By the end of the evening we had convinced almost everyone present that The Philanderers were something special, that folk music could be enjoyable and fun and had the audience following us wherever we played in the house. Our reward wasn't just our £20 share of the door take, but also the knowledge that our act had been a great success at Australia's top folk song venue. David and Sylvia invited me home for the rest of the weekend, and I was grateful for the opportunity to get away and unwind. They lived in a new, open-plan, single-storey house that David had designed and built on plot 23 in Toppings Road, an unmade track, surrounded by undeveloped bush. It sat tucked into the hillside to protect it from bushfires. David introduced me to Edna Everage and enjoyed giving highly entertaining recitations from a book entitled *Let Stalk Strine*, a supposed lexicon of modern Australian usage. 'Stwence, Vistas, New Strines – Learn the Strine language!' it said on the cover, asking, 'Do you have a Gloria Soame? What is an egg nishner?' The introduction explained its genesis. English author Monica Dickens was in a Sydney store signing copies of her latest book. A woman handed her a copy and said, 'Emma Chisitt', thinking that this was the woman's name, she wrote 'To Emma Chisitt' above her signature on the flyleaf. 'Nair, Emma Chisitt' said the customer. She was actually asking the price. I successfully used Strine myself. Catching the bus into downtown Sydney from Mosman, I would say 'Weird!' and the driver would sell me a ticket to Wynyard, a 'trine' or 'rye-wye' station and bus terminus in the city! After a relaxing day and wonderful meal on Sunday, we sat on their porch in the sunset, drinking wine and listening to the crickets in the native woodland that surrounded the house, and I felt at peace with the world and wondered if I would be happy living in Australia.

Our tour of Melbourne's suburbs continued with performances at Bizz Buzz stores at Essenden and Northcote, a Mitre 10 store at Burleigh, and Gippsland Hardware in Dandenong, but the work was emotionally unrewarding. At Essenden we were accosted by an Irishman who asked us to sing 'Whisky in the Jar'. When we said we didn't know it, he volunteered to write down the words for us. We offered him a beer. 'I don't drink,' he told us. We learned the words he'd written for us and sang them for years afterwards, and even made a record of the song, not realising that they were a garbled version of the real thing with two verses missing, which goes to show that you can't trust a teetotal Irishman.

We purchased a set of flared, black, pin-stripe trousers to wear with our Afghan jackets on stage and TV shows. Back at the caravan park, we'd become firm favourites with all the children there. A resident Dutch couple, the Van Zanens, had three delightful but noisy children, Jan, Dennis and Cynthia, aged 9, who was madly in love with Clive, as was 12-year-old Debbie Spears from another nearby caravan. They specialised in waking us up early every morning and treating the bus as a second home. Although we had occasional run-ins with the site management – who described me to the others as 'the smart alec one' – our month's stay at Fiveways was pleasant enough. Most Friday evenings found some of us at Craig Forster's, a teacher who held open-house every Friday and, having read about us, invited us along. One evening there, Tony had fallen foul of a tall and powerfully built Welsh girl called Bronwyn, and spent the rest of our time in Melbourne trying to avoid her at all costs, renaming her Blodwyn, and was put completely off his stride at Frank Traynor's by finding her in the front row of the audience. Meanwhile, I was spending most weekends as the guest of the Millers, who were beginning to treat me as one of the family, and was thankful to get away from the claustrophobic and, to me, increasingly stressful atmosphere on the bus. John joined me one weekend to go canoeing with David and his family on the River Yarra. Robin and Robyn turned up, as did other relatives, and we spent a pleasant Sunday picnicking on its bank. Back on the bus, Alan was preparing the Sunday meal when Nola Cox turned up and stayed for supper. They started to form what was to become a deep mutual attraction, which was to have a lasting impact on the rest of us.

On Monday evening, on our last week in Melbourne, we arrived at the studios of Channel O to record the four-hour Saturday morning pop show, *Happening 70*, which was networked throughout Australia. It was recorded 'as live' – the tape kept running and the show carried on, whatever happened. Tim, our knowledgeable popular music specialist, became a juror on the *Juke Box Jury* segment and passed judgement on a number of mediocre new records by locally famous pop stars totally unknown outside Australia. The whole proceedings were hosted by teen idol Ross D. Wylie, and we rubbed shoulders with John Williamson, who mimed to his hit record 'Old Man Emu', and a host of other 'stars'. The performances were all uniformly greeted by the same screams and applause, which was unsurprising as the audience existed only on tape. 'We're just not the kind of group people scream at,' I protested to the producer, but was sternly told: 'You are on the only nationally networked teenage pop show and that means you get screams whether you like it or not!' Our time came and, dressed in our new group trousers and our Afghan waistcoats, we launched into 'This Land is Your Land'. We finished to screams and applause from the pre-recorded audience. In the course of my cheery televised chat with Ross, I managed to plug Integrity Paints an incredible number of times, to the amusement of everyone in the studio. They all seemed to like us, and we were invited to appear on the show again whenever we were in Melbourne. Climbing into the big Ford at the end of the show, to our surprise we were mobbed by teeny-boppers, all of whom seemed to know about The Philanderers, calling for Clive by name.

Three days later, we appeared on the *Mike Walsh Show*, transmitted live at 9.30 p.m. before a large audience from the Channel Seven Theatre, an old converted music hall. The Galaxy had transmission problems, so at the last minute we were ferried to the studios in two cars by Peter Mulhall and his family, who joined the studio audience. At 7.30 p.m. there was a soundcheck and camera run-through, but a major local disaster – the collapse of part of the new Westgate Bridge over the Yarra River that was under construction and had already killed thirty-two workmen – disrupted the programming to allow for live coverage of the rescue of those still trapped, and no one knew exactly what was going on. Mike Walsh, a typical thirtyish TV personality, stuck his head round the door of our dressing room. 'Sorry lads, with this bridge thing we're having to cut down the show, so no chat, just a couple of songs.' The start time of the show was delayed by twenty minutes. Amazingly, in view of the great disaster unfolding at the Westgate Bridge site, the show started with a female singer gustily belting out 'On a Wonderful Day Like Today'. The running order kept changing. The other acts came and went and, at the end of each turn, large green 'Applause' signs flashed rapidly telling the audience what to do. Now near the top of the bill, we were told that the programme would run for its full ninety minutes. During a commercial break, Mike Walsh dashed over and said he would chat with me on-air after all, then suddenly we were on. We opened with 'This Land is Your Land', with John making his TV debut as a banjo player. Mike Walsh came over to me. 'I had a letter from some of your fans,' he said. 'They say, "Thank you for having that great group The Philanderers on your show." They sign themselves The Bus Cleaners.' In the audience some girls holding up a large placard saying, 'We love The Philanderers' screamed. I was now chatting to the audience as much as to Mike Walsh – and making them laugh. Our last number, 'The Wild Rover', finished with wild and spontaneous applause, and as we left the stage we got the biggest hand of the whole show. Our first appearance as guests on a live TV entertainment show in front of a big audience had been a great success.

Our last assignment for Integrity Paints in Melbourne was at Moores in Prahran, a big department store and local landmark resembling a mini Harrods. It was an important new account for the company. Our last appearance there was on Saturday 17 October. We attracted a large crowd that morning. They had come to see these new TV personalities in the flesh and greeting us from the crowd were a couple who remembered meeting us in Spain two years, before when we had travelled there in the original Hairy Pillock. So far our promotional tour for Integrity Paints was working out in just the way I had described to them three months before. With our obligations in Melbourne finally discharged, we were off to Sydney to work at 'Roselands', Sydney's biggest and most prestigious shopping centre, and have the bus fitted with a new set of springs. I was still pig-headedly insisting that only I should drive the bus, and so drove the 200 miles to Albury, where our cheery friend, the Rev. George Davis, fixed a date in November for another concert at the Folk Pot. At six o'clock the next morning, we headed for Sydney, 370 miles away. When I climbed out of the cab outside 11 Erith Street at seven o'clock that evening, I'd spent more than eighteen hours behind the wheel, driving over 570 miles. I was completely exhausted, but I'd now worked out exactly what we would have to do if we were to successfully complete our world trip. All I had to do was to convince the others.

22

Swanning Around in Sydney

Apart from trips to Albury and Wyong, we would be in Sydney for seven weeks and began to think of the city, and 11 Erith Street, Mosman, as our home again, and Alan arranged the ridiculously low rent of $13 a week with the owner. Mosman Bay Wharf was not far away, and Circular Quay and downtown Sydney only a short ride on the harbour's antique, wooden yellow and green ferries, from which we enjoyed spectacular views of the half-built Opera House and the massive Harbour Bridge as we travelled to and from the city. We'd negotiated a month's break from the paint contract, and were paid $1,000 for the first couple of weeks working as entertainers for Grace Brothers, Sydney's premiere department store chain. Our first engagement was at Roselands – 'the largest shopping centre in the southern hemisphere' – where we were the star attraction in their 'Ports o' Call' promotion, with the publicity photo of us and our bus filling their full-page press advertisements. Roselands seemed to float like a giant aircraft carrier on a sea of bungalows that stretched for miles in every direction. Sometimes we sang to audiences of 200 or more from a huge stage several times each day, and between sessions were fed by the centre's management. John shot umpteen reels of film of us playing, and we made the acquaintance of the beautiful, blonde Shelley Young, recently crowned Miss New South Wales, whom we occasionally met on our travels around the state. Performing at Grace Brothers' department store at Paramatta – a splendid late 1930s art deco building – the staff told us that they had greatly enjoyed our visit, and presented us with a toy koala which became my constant companion in the bus cab. We also played in Ryde, Bondi Junction (where Tony had worked briefly in June), Chatswood and Brookvale, as well as at their original store in Sydney's Broadway. I was having a great time doing the introductions. 'Richard again found a responsive audience,' wrote Tim, 'and flew off into such flights of ingeniously idiotic fancy that it seemed that the songs were mere interruptions to the outpourings of his wit.' By the time we'd finished, we knew our way around most of Sydney's featureless outer suburbs pretty well.

Over supper in Erith Street, we argued about the future. I now believed that the only way we would pay for our visit to America was if I went ahead of the group to find a sponsor there. Some thought this very sensible, while one or two others, Alan in particular, thought it fanciful in the extreme and, perhaps with good reason, rubbished the idea of me going to New York and caused others to question whether it really was a good idea – but then, Alan always enjoyed 'debate'. We had never taken a vote on our decisions, and didn't take one now, but it was slowly becoming apparent that we would never earn enough money in Australia to fund a trip to Central America and the US, and the majority thought that my suggestion was probably the only way we would ever complete our journey and arrive home with some money in our pockets. A bit of research showed that New York was where the headquarters of most major advertising agencies were located, and I began to look into the logistics of getting there. We finally agreed that, once we had saved a thousand pounds, we would use it to fund the quest for a sponsor for our tour of the US, and that I should undertake this. The rest of the group began to practise playing without me and I started to take a back seat, giving the others the opportunity to try their hand at introducing the songs and doing the commercials. Tim made the best job of it and, once I had left, would take my place as the frontman for the group. Tony had been keeping the accounts and running our finances for several months now, and it seemed that between them they would happily manage without me. Living next door to us in Erith Street was Honey Clarke, a cheery, attractive and very determined 17-year-old who had recently moved in with her grandmother and become a great friend to all of us. She and her friend Glenda joined us on the bus for a Sunday excursion and picnic with Brinsley, Natalie and their two daughters in the Blue Mountains, an area famous for its dramatic scenery, with steep cliffs, waterfalls, bushwalking trails and eucalyptus forests which give rise to the bluish haze which give the distant mountains their name. It was a nice break and a genuine piece of sightseeing – our first real experience of the native bush, with its tinder-dry eucalyptus trees, Australia's dominant tree with over 700 different species across the continent. The next day, I took the bus to Leyland's main depot, where it would remain for a week to be fitted with its new springs.

Alan returned to Melbourne to be with the jolly Nola Cox. Tony wrote in a letter home:

Alan Hughes, our accordion player, has gone down to Melbourne for a couple of weeks and is staying with a girlfriend which is a holiday for him. Actually Alan is our main problem at the moment because he is full of doom and gloom which is infectious. Since he has been away everybody has been quite cheerful.

Alan was growing noticeably more uncomfortable about earning a living as part of what he saw as a promotional gimmick. The rest were enjoying it, didn't mind our brief moments of fame at all and hoped I would pull off something similar in America. With Alan away, the arguments within the group lessened and harmony briefly reigned. We appeared without Alan's accordion on a number of TV shows, including *For Ladies Only*, Channel 10's lunchtime talk and entertainment show hosted by TV glamour boy John Mahon. With the bus now at Leyland's, we relied on taxis and Peter Margrave, with his ageing Ford Zephyr estate, to get us to the TV studios, and Peter filmed us performing before the cameras. At dawn the next morning we were off to Epping and Channel 7, which was marketing itself as 'The 7 Revolution', where we were to appear live on *Sydney Today* between the breakfast weather report and the traffic news. Dick had recently started playing a recorder to accompany and introduce a few of our numbers, and got the introduction to 'Leaving of Liverpool' hopelessly muddled, but the rest of us carried on regardless. No one else seemed to notice, though, and the entire studio crew burst into a round of spontaneous applause at the end, which was most gratifying. There were more TV appearances, and Tim and I were guests on *Ray Taylor Today*, a televised discussion show on Channel 10.

We were still trying to find markets for our UK sponsors' products, even though we had written to them all saying that this was now very difficult for us. Tim and I visited Alec Boyd, the commercial counsellor at the British High Commission high up in Gold Fields House, overlooking the harbour at Circular Quay, who confirmed our view that we wouldn't have much success in Australia. I also went to see an accountant about our tax position. I walked to his office at Milson's Point through sunny residential back streets, a cool wind relieving the hot sun, wondering why they had such deep gutters and yawning storm drains on the hilly streets here. I had grown fond of Sydney and its beautiful harbour. My destination was at the north end of the Harbour Bridge, and I sat for a while on the grass next to the massive steel gantries that carried the road and railway to the familiar steel arch that curves over the harbour with the carriageway suspended beneath. The wind had dropped and the atmosphere was sticky as I entered the accountant's building. When I came out it was raining steadily, huge droplets splashing on the pavement and, as I made my way to the bus stop on the bridge approach road, a blinding flash of lightning and a great clap of thunder immediately overhead heralded the worst downpour I had ever seen. Black clouds swept across the tops of the low skyscrapers in North Sydney, which loomed eerily through the sheets of cascading rain. Water poured from everywhere and the cars, all with headlights blazing, seemed to be driving along deep rivers. I stood watching from the shelter of the elevated railway which curves westwards to North Sydney after leaving the bridge, waiting for my bus. Thunder and lightning crashed and rolled around the bays and inlets of the harbour, and great curtains of rain blurred and obscured everything. As I saw torrents of water push boxes and great piles of rubbish onto the expressway lower down the hill, I at last understood why all the streets had such wide storm drains. I had never seen rainwater run with such force and, as the storm grew, so the floods in the gutters increased. My salvation came when a bus pulled up and I was able to hop on board, getting soaked in the few feet between the concrete canopy I was sheltering under and the open doorway of the bus. I arrived back in Erith Street wet through.

At the Leyland depot, John had been carrying out repairs and maintenance on the bus, touching up paintwork, rehanging cupboard doors and putting things in order for the next tour. Honey and Glenda had taken the bus curtains to a laundromat and came back with three large, green plastic garbage sacks full of clean, dry curtains. These were then stowed in the house porch. The dustmen, known in Australia as 'garbos', do their work at night and, a couple of days later, Dick and Peter heard them outside in the early hours of the morning. 'We're not really meant to take these, you know,' said one of them to Dick as he handed them the three green garbage sacks he'd found in the porch, and Dick watched gratefully as the garbage truck disappeared into the night. It was Friday the 13th, and later that morning Dick and Peter spent several hours at the local rubbish tip unsuccessfully attempting to retrieve the missing bus curtains they'd thrown away! Honey, her grandmother, and other charitable neighbours spent the next week running up a new set of curtains for us. We were very grateful.

One evening in mid-November, a battered Holden pulled up outside the house and out stepped Bob. He had finished his contract with the Outback survey team and was considering re-joining us for our remaining time in Australia. We welcomed him home like the prodigal son and set off for the Strata Motor Inn on Military Road to celebrate his return. It was as if he'd never been away. Tanned, fit and raring to go, he was like a breath of fresh air, and it was good to have his positive energy back with us again. He quickly decided to return to the fold, and we were all delighted.

We had been inveigled by Channel 10 into helping to promote an Aussie vs Poms celebrity charity cricket match to raise money for the Royal Far West Children's Hospital in Manley. With the bus and its new springs back from Leyland's, we visited the hospital, which catered for children, mainly from the far west of New South Wales, suffering from malnutrition and other long-term physical and psychological problems. It was full of the most delightful young tots –

aboriginal, mixed race and white – many with one leg in a plaster cast to help heal a degenerative condition brought on by poor diet. In the wards, we sang to the kids, who were all over us, which stiffened our resolve to raise as much money as we could for them. We returned and sang to them again the following week, posing with the bus and some of the children for a photo for the *Manly Daily*. We then passed out leaflets in Manly's main street for the next day's charity match at the Manley Oval. The Australian celebrity team was captained by popular Australian actor John Mellion and featured several well-known show-business personalities. The Pommie team (Pommie being a term of affectionate abuse used to describe the English generally and recent British immigrants in particular – derived, we were told, from 'Prisoners of Mother England', or 'Prisoners of Her Majesty'), captained by British-born TV personality Tony Barber, was so short of members that Tony, Dick, Clive and John were all pressed into service. The umpires were the famous Australian film star Chips Rafferty and a much-loved, jolly, rotund singer/comedienne, Beryl Cheers. Tony wore a grey top hat and tails and, after a day of everyone joking around on the pitch, gave up an easy catch which ended the match in a diplomatic draw. A large picture of Dick and Tony, described as members of The Philanderers Touring Folk Group, featured prominently in the best-selling *Woman's Day* magazine, landing us firmly in the show-biz fraternity. The night before the cricket match, Peter Margrave threw a big party to celebrate his 21st, but his actual birthday was the following week. Peter's open, cheerful character inspired love, affection and the need for mothering from his neighbours, and we all prepared a surprise candlelit birthday dinner for him. Speeches were made and Peter was overcome by being presented with two candle-bedecked cakes, one baked by John. Eighteen of us sat down to dinner on what was a highly civilised occasion.

Two days later, we drove to Merrylands for the first of three Integrity Paints appearances in Sydney. Here, for the first time, The Philanderers, now including Bob, appeared without an accordion or a bass, and without me out front doing the introductions. Tony and Tim took this on, and it all seemed to work well. Watching them perform, I was now sure that I could leave for America while the rest of them completed the Integrity Paints contract. We then set out for Albury, where we were booked to appear at the Folk Pot, this time with Honey and her friend Sue on board. We stayed overnight in Goulburn again and, having driven the bus everywhere for the previous four months, for the first time in Australia I was once again sharing the driving with Bob. We set out early the next morning with Bob at the wheel (or so I thought), and I decided to stay in bed until we stopped for breakfast. We were bowling along quite merrily when Bob woke me up. If he was here, I wondered, then who the hell was driving the bus? It was Clive. Bob had given him a quick tutorial and off he went. I then realised how stupid and foolish I'd been in insisting on doing all the driving myself. This was another example of my lack of trust and inability to delegate. We parked in Albury's Noreuil Caravan Park next to the Murray River, now transformed by the warm, early summer sunshine from the flooded mess it was in when we'd previously visited. Alan and Nola arrived from Melbourne in Nola's Cortina and, for the first and only time in Australia, all eight of us performed together. It was a joyous event. The audience of over 200 gave us a rousing welcome, and the stereo recording of part of our performance captured the happy atmosphere which, for me, was tinged with regret that I would soon be leaving my friends and the easy life we were now living in Australia. It was my last appearance on stage there. With only two store appearances in Sydney for the paint company to come, plus a couple of TV appearances that Tim had been able to book, Alan decided that he would prefer to return to Melbourne with Nola, and I cadged a lift with them to say goodbye to Nairne Butchart and his mother, Geoff Scott, who had saved our bacon four months earlier, the people at Integrity Paints, the Lovells and the Millers, who had become firm and lasting friends. Meanwhile, the bus returned to Sydney, driving through the rolling Snowy Mountains, and visiting Canberra to meet Honey's married sister Penny. On the way Honey celebrated her 18th birthday.

It was now early December. Back in Sydney, six Philanderers performed quite creditably without either Alan or me – proving that none of us were indispensable – appearing on John Mahon's radio show on 2CH, returning to *Sydney Today* – where Dick repeated messing up his introduction, this time to 'Whisky in the Jar' – and as star guests on the peak-time *Joe Martin Show*, hosted by a popular Australian club comic and TV comedian, where they managed to get the bus right inside the studio. There were two more jobs for Integrity Paints, a Mitre 10 store at Richmond and the Timber and Hardware store at Wyong, 50 miles north of Sydney, where Tony had arranged free beer, accommodation and dinner at the Beachcomber Motel in exchange for performing in the motel's big club bar during the evening. I flew back to Sydney from Melbourne to finalise the details of my trip to America. By using a charter flight, the cost of travelling to New York via England was no more expensive than flying across the Pacific. It would also be cheaper and easier for me to prepare sales brochures, edit and copy films and tapes and organise photograph albums and press cutting books there. There were two other underlying reasons for returning home for Christmas. My father was to undergo serious heart surgery which had only an average success rate, and I wanted to see him again before the operation. Also, I missed my girlfriend, Gale, and wanted to ask her to marry me once our bus trip was over. On Saturday 5 December, Bob drove me to Sydney Airport in his old Holden and I took off on the first leg of my trip home. The bus then headed south again to continue the Integrity Paints tour in Victoria.

Alan wrote to Adrian Bird, now back in Cambridge:

Wotcher A, I have just had a great holiday for five weeks with a rather nice bird who has a flat in Melb. whilst the others were playing around in Sydney. Australia is being pretty good to us nowadays and we are having a great time here ... As you know RK has left us for the States via home. I suppose it is what he wants. I think his father is pretty sick, isn't he? Actually we don't miss him as much as we thought we would. Tim makes a very good job of introducing the songs etc. His jokes are as good as Richard's. e.g. 'Clive, our blue-eyed boy of English folk, will now have a pull at "Grandfather's cock"'. We've learned a few new songs at last and wild Willie now plays (at) the banjo. Tony is a bit upset at the moment because Clive wondered rather loudly where he obtained his hobnailed plectrum. Yes, even Tony has long hair now. Dick has a moustache. John is almost invisible. I think Tim is the only one who is getting less hairy and that's only because he is going bald rather rapidly. Bob is back with us again, much to our relief – he is a pretty good singer and a lovely lad ... Everyone (except Tim and I) is driving the bus now – it's a real chuckle to hear them criticising one-another all the time. They all play some very interesting tunes on the gearbox. Australia isn't a bad place really except for the pubs – it's like drinking ice cold lager in the pisshouse – bloody tiles everywhere ... We still argue as much but we seem to be a bit more good natured about it now ... It will be funny to have Xmas on the beach with sand in the turkey and a crowd of Aussie surfers around ... Give my love to everyone (especially the ladies), tell Bert he's a bald-headed old fool and ask him where our Christmas present is. Have a great Christmas, don't drink too much and leave me a couple of cigars. Love, Alan.

23

Home for Christmas

As we had already discovered, Australia shut down at lunchtime on Saturdays, and when I arrived in Adelaide it was closed for the weekend. I checked into a hotel and went for a walk downtown. Nothing was open. If this was Saturday, what would Sunday be like? Back at the hotel, I enquired whether there was anything for a tourist to do in Adelaide on a Sunday and was told there wasn't. 'You could take a coach tour. They visit either the Barossa Valley or Victor Harbor – it's very scenic there.' I booked for the Victor Harbor trip, had supper and went to bed. Next morning it was overcast. The coach left early and was half empty. When we eventually arrived, Victor Harbor, once a whaling station and pretty by Australian standards, was closed, too. There was a long and rather rickety wooden pier that led to a place called Granite Island, a few fishing boats, and hardly anywhere to eat. Looking eastwards down the coast, I could just make out the mouth of the great Murray River through the distant spray of the great breakers of the Southern Ocean. To the south there was nothing between us and Antarctica. We returned to Adelaide and the next morning I flew to Perth.

Perth was a buzzing, attractive city. I stayed with Liz Benham, an old friend from England who had recently emigrated with her boyfriend, Bob, and spent a happy ten days exploring Perth and Freemantle and the beaches up and down the coast with her. We spent an evening at 'the trots' at the Gloucester Park stadium – gambling at trotting races was a favourite pastime in Perth. They showed me the plot of land in the bush where they planned to build their house. Time passed quickly and I was soon boarding a Quantas jet to Singapore, where I was to collect my ticket for the charter flight to Stansted. I had with me $2,200 US in traveller's cheques. In Australia there was over $2,750 in our account – a far cry from the £185 we had twelve months before. This time I had no trouble getting into Singapore and a two-week Visit Pass was stamped in my passport. The Sydney Travel Agents, Patrick Travel, had booked me into the Bencoolen Hotel in Hong Kong Street, in the heart of the city, where the agent with my onward ticket would contact me. Apart from a receipt from the travel agents, I had no paperwork at all. Eventually, Robin Nederkoorn, a suave young Dutchman who spoke perfect English, found me and said he would collect me at 7.30 a.m. the following morning and take me to the airport. The next morning, we drove to the airport in his MGB. He handed me my ticket and took me to a line of passengers queuing for the 10.30 a.m. flight in the collection of huts that formed the terminal buildings. To qualify for a seat on this charter flight, I had to have been resident in Singapore for six months. 'Don't worry about that,' said the smooth Dutchman, 'it's only a formality – they never check,' and cheerily said goodbye. The line shuffled slowly forward and when I was two passengers away from the check-in counter he rushed up and dragged me away, apologising profusely. 'I'm so sorry. The authorities are checking everything today. You won't be allowed to board. Come with me to my office and we can arrange another flight.' Once in his pokey little room in the city, he made a few frantic phone calls. 'There's a flight on Wednesday we can get you on,' he said. 'Meanwhile, you can stay on at the hotel at our expense – I'll run you back there now.'

I spent the next couple of days sightseeing, exploring the colourful old quarter teeming with rickshaws and dilapidated buildings, with the adjoining waterways full of aged sampans and rowing boats, and treating myself to an up-market afternoon tea at Raffles, Singapore's famous colonial hotel. Back at the airport on Wednesday, Monday's saga repeated itself. 'I really am most sorry about this.' My Dutch friend's voice oozed insincerity. 'They're still checking every passenger. There's a major crackdown. Too many people are abusing the charter flight rules. You won't be able to fly to England from here. I'll get you on a flight to Stansted from Kuala Lumpur tomorrow.' I spent the rest of the day in the Botanic Gardens. The next morning, as the sun rose, I was taken in the MGB to the airport to catch the early Malaysia–Singapore Airlines flight to Kuala Lumpur. 'What about the ticket to London?' I enquired. 'Our agent will hand it to you when you get to KL,' I was told. 'Where will I find him?' I was instructed to report to the information desk there and he would find me. The flight in the new Boeing 737 took less than an hour and, once inside Kuala Lumpur's brand-new international airport, I found myself standing around with about 180 other Brits all heading home for Christmas and looking for the man who had their tickets. A small, balding Indian gentleman appeared, sat down, opened his briefcase and looked about him. He was immediately mobbed by everyone and we finally got our tickets home, only to discover that the plane, a second-hand Boeing 707 parked at the end of the runway with 'Lloyd International' on it, had only just flown in and the crew had gone to a hotel to sleep for eight hours. We boarded the plane, squeezed into the 189 seats fitted into a cabin originally designed for 110 passengers, and discovered from the logo on the seatbelts that it had originally belonged to Pan-Am. Hours later, having refuelled at Karachi and Athens, we touched down at Stansted at

4 a.m. in the morning. I eventually arrived at Liphook station on the milk train. 'Morning, Richard,' said Arnie Bennett, the porter there, 'thought you were in Australia' – I was home.

I spent the next five weeks preparing to sell The Philanderers and their bus to the Americans. I produced an eight-page brochure entitled 'Introducing the Philanderers' and had hundreds printed. 'Universal in their appeal, unique in their experiences,' it read. 'Are you looking for a new approach to an advertising problem? A new and exciting way to present a product? A campaign that is news? Take a look at The Philanderers, and what they have to offer.' It told our story and was full of photographs and ideas about how we could be used. Photographs were copied and enlarged and put into albums, press cuttings reorganised, film edited and tapes duplicated. I bought two smart new suits and some second-hand bowlers, which I sent to Australia to replace the ones we were rapidly wearing out. The companies we represented were understanding about the difficulties we had had in securing orders and agencies for them and, much to my relief, accepted that we were unlikely to produce much business for them. The families and parents of the other boys were reassured to hear that their sons were in good health and high spirits and that our trip should be concluded within a year. Adrian was down from Cambridge for Christmas and we caught up on the detail of what had happened in Bombay, and the traumas we had been through in Australia. When I delivered our home-made Christmas card to Bert and Queenie at the Deers Hut, Bert greeted me as if I'd never been away. 'Welcome home, Sir Richard,' he said, 'half of cider?' The locals really enjoyed the insulting letters and ingenious cards, jokes and presents that we had sent to the pub since we left, but it seemed to be quieter than usual, until it dawned on me that most of my noisy drinking companions were 10,000 miles away. Standing in the bar with Adrian, we both realised that our experiences had created a strange bond between us all which no one else could ever share. The doubters who thought we would all be back by the previous Christmas slapped me on the back and told me they always knew we would make it to Australia. Nobody really cared after that and, after feigning a brief interest, they carried on discussing their own affairs. It was a strange homecoming.

Underneath it all, though, I was guilt-ridden about being home again. Although my father's heart condition required a serious operation early in the New Year and I felt that it was right to come home to see him, I found it hard to come to terms with enjoying Christmas with my family while the others were stuck on a beach in Australia eating sand with their turkey. Had I subconsciously – knowingly, even – thought up the idea of going to New York simply because I was homesick and could use it as an excuse to see my family and girlfriend again? I genuinely didn't know. Did the others think that? I wasn't sure. In the early days we had talked idealistically about the 'spirit of the trip', a shared adventure in which we 'happy few' would stick together through thick and thin – a 'band of brothers'. But we had split up before. In Kabul, Tim had gone on ahead to Rawalpindi to find work and get publicity for us. Tony and Adrian had stayed behind in Bombay to ship the bus, and we always knew that Adrian would part company with us. In Australia, I had gone off to Melbourne to find a sponsor, Bob had been away working in the Flinders Ranges, and Alan had taken five weeks off to stay with Nola. Maybe I shouldn't feel too bad. At the turn of the year, Gale and I got engaged, to the delight of our parents. We talked about her coming to North America, and she decided that the only way to achieve this would be to emigrate to Canada, where she could work as a French-speaking English secretary in Montreal.

There was a lengthy postal strike in the UK and it was impossible to send or receive any mail. As a result, I had no idea if letters sent to their contacts in New York by Tony's parents had arrived. Any replies would not have been delivered either. When I set off for America I had absolutely no idea if anyone there was expecting me, or even knew of my existence. On Tuesday 26 January 1971, Gale and my family drove me to the airport. Between us we lugged heavy cases full of brochures, photographs, press cuttings, films and tapes to the check-in desk. I had to pay an extra £15 – almost a week's wages – for excess baggage on top of £104 for my return ticket. A single ticket was not an option because to enter the US I had to demonstrate that I was able to leave again. After fond goodbyes and with $1,240 in my pocket, I boarded BOAC's flight 501 to New York. In eight hours' time the biggest test of my life would begin.

24

New York, New York!

'So that's why I'm here, Joe,' I said. Over supper I'd been telling my host about our world trip and explaining why I was visiting New York. Joseph L. Smith, a family friend of the Houghs, had generously invited me to stay at his apartment on East 64th Street. Joe was slightly built, dapper and meticulous – a business consultant who had become friends with Tony's mother and her family when he was stationed in England with the American army during the Second World War. He was an officer in the medical corps, as I found out when he instructed me in great detail about folding the sheet corners on my bed! He was divorced, with a son of about Tony's age, and divided his time between his New York apartment, which he used for business, and an eighteenth-century cider mill near Westport, Connecticut. 'I'm driving up to the cider mill tomorrow and YOU are coming with me,' he announced at breakfast the day after I arrived. The next day we collected Joe's metallic gold Rolls-Royce 'Silver Cloud' with its personalised plate, JLS 81, from the multi-storey parking lot across the icy street and glided effortlessly into the traffic. At the turnpike toll booth he asked for a receipt. 'My accountant needs them to prove that I spend more time in Connecticut than in New York,' he said. 'The taxes are cheaper there!' Leaving the city, we found ourselves in a frozen landscape of rocky outcrops, woodland, small farms with open fields, and pretty settlements with white-painted clapboard houses and broad, grassy lawns all deep in snow.

The cider mill was a stylish conversion, beautifully furnished with antiques. Joe opened a highly polished old chest in the hallway and pulled out two flags; one the original thirteen-star Stars and Stripes, the other the eighteenth-century Union Jack, both of which he ran up the flagpole in the centre of the snow-covered lawn. 'Now they know we've arrived and I've a guest from England,' he said. Joe was an ardent anglophile. That Saturday night we were dinner and overnight guests of the charming Robert Fulton, his wife and two sons, Robert and Rawn, who lived in grand style in a huge house with a living-room like a barn and acres of grounds which included an airstrip. A successful architect, inventor – an ancestor is widely credited with developing America's first commercially successful steamboat – pilot and businessman, who travelled between Connecticut and his factory in Texas using his Second World War Mustang fighter, Bob Fulton was no stranger to overland travel. In the early 1930s he had ridden a Douglas twin motorbike overland from London to India, China and Japan and then across the USA – visiting twenty-two countries on three continents in eighteen months. We spent the evening talking about his extraordinary adventure and what it had taught him, and the places we'd both visited. A gentle, self-effacing man, he had filmed and had written a book, *One Man Caravan*, about his adventures. Bob only had one copy, and I spent most of that night reading it, feeling that our achievements were rather tame by comparison, but he thought our trip, and travelling in a double-decker bus, was wonderful.

Joe and I returned to New York the following morning and spent the rest of the day cleaning his apartment – I couldn't understand why he didn't have any domestic help – and on Monday I started searching for a sponsor. Tony's grandfather had given me an introduction to Bob Buchanan, a vice president of Ford's advertising agency, J. Walter Thompson, who offered the agency's help. JWT were the world's largest advertising agency and in my first weeks in New York I used the facilities at their Lexington Avenue headquarters to produce a sound film of us performing in Australia. I'd hoped that they would use us for one of their clients, but they never did. I spent days in New York's magnificent Public Library, an imposing Beaux-Arts building and National Historic Landmark. Each morning I passed between two haughty-looking marble lions that stood guard over the entrance, climbed the impressive marble steps that rise from Fifth Avenue to the library's splendid classical portico, and left the freezing streets for the impressive, and warm, Main Reading Room to make endless lists of contact details for the major advertising agencies, their clients, and the top 100 companies (by advertising spend) based in New York. Joe cast a critical eye over the brochure I'd written and helped produce a harder-hitting, two-page document headed 'Who Can Capitalise on THE PHILANDERERS?' I spent hours on the phone making dozens of appointments. At the end of the first week I had contacted the top twenty-five agencies and visited ten of them. Starting on the West Coast in June, I estimated that in six months we could make three major shopping centre presentations in seventy or eighty big population centres – totalling some 250 appearances. At $1,000 each, it would cost a sponsor $250,000 – the equivalent of sponsoring a peak-time half-hour TV special. I would have to cook up some figures to show that we would

reach as many – or more – people than a TV special. I wrote
to the boys in Australia to report on my progress. I ended:

> The weather is bitterly cold here. I'm already sick of being
> penniless and without friends ... Bob, I miss your cups of
> tea in bed in the mornings ... when I see the films of us in
> Australia I wish I'd never left. Funny, but looking back on it,
> we didn't get on too badly together, did we?

The week after I arrived, I celebrated my 28th birthday,
and Joe and his friend Marie Bernolfo gave me cards and
presents. At the weekends, Joe took me through streets
still heaped with snow to art galleries and museums, and
we returned to the cider mill. In the evenings, we would eat
supper on the sofa while watching reruns of *Star Trek* and
The Avengers. He also introduced me to some of his business
friends, including the copywriter from Foote, Cone & Belding,
who made his name by thinking up Contac capsules' slogan
about '600 tiny time pills'. Another friend, Dick Mascot, a vice
president at Reader's Digest who also played double bass,
took me to lunch at New York's historic Players Club and told
me that he got his job selling advertising at Reader's Digest
by producing a large painting of a big cob of corn at his
interview, telling them: 'THAT is what we're marketing!'

Piles of frozen snow filled the gutters and steam rose
through manhole covers in the uneven, poorly surfaced and
icy side streets. I needed a warmer overcoat and better shoes.
I discovered that a good way of escaping the icy winds was
to walk to different parts of mid-town Manhattan through
stores like Bloomingdale's, hotels such as the Waldorf Astoria,
and the lobbies of big buildings including the Rockefeller
Center and Grand Central Station. I found it easy, with my
English accent, to get appointments. 'Gee, don't stop talking
– I love your accent,' was a regular response, even if I was

just asking someone the way. By the middle of March I'd had over a hundred meetings with agencies and potential sponsors, the majority of whom were encouraging, but I couldn't tell whether I was wasting my time. I worked on the principle that at the next meeting someone would say yes, but all I usually got was, 'We like the idea and will put it to our clients.' When I followed anything up, it was always, 'We're still thinking about it.' Whenever someone said, 'Why don't you go and talk to so and so?' I would do it immediately. I was getting dispirited and downhearted and, then to add to it all, the inevitable happened.

'In New York, Richard, when people are invited to stay, it's understood that they are welcome for four or five days,' Joe said one day. 'Charming and delightful as you are, you've been here for over a month and you really should think about moving on. You don't expect me to put up with you forever, do you?' He wasn't exactly throwing me out, but Joe did have other friends who wished to visit, but couldn't while I was there. Also, Gale was due to arrive soon on her way to Montreal and I needed to find somewhere for us both to stay. I really enjoyed Joe's company; he was cultured, refined, amusing and quite different to most of the Americans I'd met. He would pull my leg mercilessly, but was also a sympathetic listener. I would miss staying with him, and was embarrassed that I had no way of repaying his kindness and hospitality. 'You could check in to The Pickwick Arms – it's on East 51st between Second and Third,' he suggested later. 'People stay there between apartments – it's not expensive.' He was beginning to sound desperate.

I started scanning the papers for somewhere to rent, following up an advert about a room in a large apartment at 50 East 86th Street, close to Central Park. It was still occupied by someone who was supposedly just leaving, and I arranged to move in the next day, a couple of days before

Gale arrived. I said goodbye to Joe, put my heavy suitcases in a locker at Grand Central Station, and early that evening took just an overnight bag to my new accommodation. It was a disaster. Apart from Brenda, the woman who was subletting the room, there had been no one else in the apartment when I'd first looked at it. Now, it was full of the most unpleasant and unhelpful people I'd met so far in New York. The room was still occupied and I was offered a small broom cupboard with a mattress on the floor instead. It was late, I had nowhere else to go, so I dossed down in the cupboard but left early the next morning to check into The Pickwick Arms. Outside, the rain was turning to sleet, but the hotel was hotter than a steam bath. I had a shower and lay on the bed. At just over $10 a night, I couldn't afford to stay there long. Thumbing through the *New York Times*, I came across an advert for a studio apartment on East 78th Street and First Avenue, picked up the bedside phone and dialled the number. A woman with a German accent answered. It was still available. I was there within half an hour. The door was opened by an attractive blonde, a young German artist and fashion model called Karina Jakobi. She was returning home for five weeks and wanted to sublet while she was away. Her friend, Miyo Endo, a Japanese-American lady who seemed well connected in the New York arts scene, would look after things for her while she was away. The tiny studio was on the first floor – in America it's the second floor – above a Chinese laundry. It was warm – the ancient iron radiators and pipes were so hot you couldn't touch them – clean, brightly painted and furnished, full of artist's materials and personal touches which made it feel homely, and was available the next day. There was a phone, radio and TV. The advert described it as having a 'Pullman Kitchen', which turned out to be a sink and a cooker in a fitted cupboard off the living room. I paid $250 plus a $50 deposit against the phone bill and moved in the next afternoon. As I arrived, Karina was off to the airport in a taxi so I cadged a lift, helped her with her bags and waved her goodbye at the departure gate before rushing round to the arrivals hall just in time to meet Gale off Icelandic Airways flight 203 from Reykjavik. I was so pleased that she was there, and amazed her by cooking her a delicious dinner.

By early April, I had contacted every one of the top 100 advertising agencies in New York and dozens of major companies and smaller agencies. Eighty of these had copies of the brochure. I'd shown films of us to over twenty organisations and made almost a hundred presentations to account executives and vice presidents. Every second person I met seemed to be a vice president of something or other! To save money, I'd traipsed up and down Madison Avenue, where over a quarter of the agencies were based, and walked to appointments all over mid-town Manhattan. I had endless lists of possible leads, and potential sponsors were 'seriously considering' using us, but the truth was that nobody had actually committed themselves and my money was quickly running out. Early in February, I'd contacted Clyne Maxon Inc., the thirty-fourth largest agency in the States. There I'd talked to Leonard Garbin, who dealt with the Cutty Sark Scotch Whisky account, and he'd suggested that I also speak to Jack Morris at Rubenstein, Wolfson & Co., a public relations company. They in turn introduced me to Ron Greenberg, who produced television game shows through his own company, Ron Greenberg Productions. Ron was keen to represent us and produce a TV 'special' about us. I'd screened our films for him, including the ABC TV feature on *This Day Tonight*. The company had a tiny studio at 112 E 40th Street where they made game show pilots, and he videotaped an interview with me there which they used to interest the TV networks. Larry, Ron's brother and business partner, and I met regularly. Ron's ideas for us included records, TV, radio, tours, product endorsement, 'Philanderers' comic strips, and card games – a whole range of things which would only work if we caught the public's imagination and became an overnight novelty sensation. I got the impression that they saw us as The Monkees on wheels. Knowing I needed money, Larry offered me $600 for a six-week exclusive option. I said I'd think about it.

While Gale was with me in New York, winter turned to spring and the snow slowly melted. Most evenings we ate in, and were invited to drinks and supper by Joe Smith and Miyo Endo. A visit to the cinema was a real treat. At weekends and when I had no appointments we were tourists and marvelled at the fabulous view from the top of the Empire State Building, at 1,450ft the tallest building in the world when it was built in 1932, but now recently surpassed by the twin towers of the World Trade Centre, which was still under construction. We watched the St Patrick's Day parade and people skating on the rink in front of the Rockefeller Center, walked down Wall Street and toured the Stock Exchange. We took a trip on the Staten Island Ferry – cheap at 5 cents each – visited the Frick Collection, the Metropolitan Museum of Art and the Cloisters, the latter reconstructed from derelict medieval French monasteries and abbeys, funded by John D. Rockefeller, and an oasis of calm at Washington Heights overlooking the Hudson River. We strolled around Greenwich Village and Central Park, where over 100,000 people were spending a balmy Easter Sunday. The Rockefeller Center was now adorned by thousands of Easter lilies. We toured the UN Building on the East River, with its beautiful murals, tapestries and gifts from member countries and, on Gale's birthday, took the Circle Line boat trip around the island of Manhattan.

As the weeks went by, though, there were more disappointments on the sponsor front. Herman Vandenberg of The Marschalk Company, No. 62 on my agency list, was keen to use The Philanderers and their bus. They tried to sell our six-month, $250,000 tour to Heublein, an alcohol and food company and distributor of many famous liquor brands, and when that fell through turned to CorningWare, the cookware company, but without success. My letters to the boys in Australia were full of potential sponsors, and requests for the bus to be ready for shipping at a moment's notice, but each letter had a new set of names, the previous ones silently disappearing. On 21 April I wrote:

> You'll be sad to hear that Gale left for Montreal on Saturday after a five-week stay during which she washed my socks, ironed my shirts, got my meals and generally made my miniature living unit a home, so now I'm all on my own (boo, hoo etc.)...

My time at Karina's little pad was up, and I'd now been offered bed and board with friends of friends of the Houghs, Basil and Lorene Candela and their teenage family, in their beautiful home at 454 Westchester Avenue, Yonkers, forty-five minutes from Grand Central Station in Westchester County. This was Norman Rockwell country and Crestwood, their local station, had even appeared on one of his covers for the *Saturday Evening Post*. Basil had a high-powered job in a government 'think tank' at Yale, and every night when he arrived home helped himself to a large Scotch, a routine in which I was immediately invited to join. The Candelas were straight out of one of those amiable American sitcoms about perfect upper middle-class American families, with a nice big detached house with wide lawns and three cars in the driveway. I was soon adopted as one of the family and given my own, very pleasant, room. All the kids loved me; there were two sons at college, a teenage daughter, a boy of 13 and a girl of 12. Sadly, they lived in the wrong place, as I could ill afford the daily $2.10 return fare to New York and really needed to be based in Manhattan. By the end of April, with less than $500 left, someone suggested I might 'caretake' furnished apartments while permanent tenants were being sought, and someone in the real-estate business said he would help. After a couple of weeks as a guest of the Candelas, I moved into a nice apartment back in Manhattan in the next street to Joe Smith. However, there was no linen, cutlery, pots, pans or crockery, so I had to borrow them. There was no telephone, so one of the Candela boys, Steve, who was a Bell Telephone 'boy scout', produced an old telephone and somehow wired it up to the network – but we'd no idea what the number was. I had been using this for a few days when I picked it up to find two other people talking and discovered that he'd hooked me into next door's phone. They were unaware of this, thankfully, but would be billed for my calls, including some to Montreal. After a couple of weeks I had to move out.

Miyo Endo had invited me to a fondue party she was giving as a farewell to Professor Marcus Cunliffe, a British historian, currently a visiting professor at the City College of New York and now returning to England. It was a smart, academic affair, and I was near the door of Miyo's mid-town apartment when the bell rang. I opened it to find a slim, short, attractive girl with a quizzical look on her face. 'Is this Miyo Endo's place?' she asked, in a beautiful, cut-glass English accent. 'Yes, it is,' I answered. 'You're English?' she said. 'So are you,' I replied. Her name was Susan Tobin, and we spent the rest of the evening comparing notes about America and Americans. She worked for Professor Cunliffe, lived on W 17th Street near 7th Avenue and had been in America since the middle of the Sixties. I told her that I was looking for somewhere to live. 'Well, you could stay in my place in June while I'm in Mexico if you like. It's a bit tiny. Come and have supper and see what you think.' I soon appeared at 3A, 222 West 17th Street, a rent-controlled apartment building, and was introduced to Norma Harrop and Liz Esterly, who occupied two of the three other apartments on Susan's floor. Her apartment was very small but I was thankful to have found somewhere to stay for a few weeks.

I finally decided to accept Ron Greenberg's offer and signed an agreement produced by his solicitors. I opened an account at the Chase Manhattan Bank's Madison Avenue Branch, the Greenberg's bankers, and paid in their $600 advance. My hands were now tied for the next six weeks. I was also downhearted and depressed. I had been in New York for three-and-a-half months and had achieved little. I badly needed a rest and, with nothing to do and nowhere to live until June, I headed off to the 8th Avenue Port Authority Bus Terminal, paid the $32 round trip fare to Montreal and on 14 May boarded the Greyhound bus at gate 24 to visit Gale. My big ideas about us earning a quarter of a million dollars had come to nothing and I had to accept that I should aim for something less ambitious. I wrote to the others:

> Suddenly he realised that the forces of doom were drawing even closer, making him feel that further effort was useless … The whole enormity of the thing that he was trying to do dawned upon him … this vast, self-imposed task, upon the outcome of which hung the fate of himself and his friends, seemed more impossible … King not only had to fight the battle of finding the sponsor so badly needed for the trip to continue but also the battle for survival and the unending mental struggle against the forces of doubt and … More next week.

Was all this driving me out of my mind?

25

Abroad in Australia

Back in Australia, my companions continued to fulfil our obligations to Integrity Paints, spending months driving between Melbourne and dozens of small hardware stores in unknown country and Outback towns, mainly in Victoria, some so far from the tourist trail that they were rarely visited by people from overseas, let alone a bowler-hatted English singing group in a double-decker bus. Many of these places had familiar-sounding names such as Croydon, Richmond, Ryde, Eltham, Hampton, St Albans, Horsham and Albury – their original counterparts all being within 60 miles of the Deers Hut. Other towns with names from the rest of the British Isles included Torquay, Cheltenham, Portland, Liverpool and Hamilton. Some places conjured up more exotic locations – Heidelberg, Sorrento and Ararat – and many more boasted creatively Australian tongue-twisters: Echuca, Geelong, Kerang, Naracoorte, Tooronga, Warracknabeal, Warragul, Warrnambool, Wodonga, Wollongong and Wurruk.

In December, Integrity Paints had scheduled a visit to the Gippsland Lakes, 120 miles south-east of Melbourne, where it always seemed to rain. This was followed by a trip to Geelong and then Ballarat, to the north-west, where the boys visited newly opened Sovereign Hill, an open-air museum and historical park recreating the time of the 1850s gold rush, where they drove the bus into the main street and

John filmed the group performing. Back in Melbourne, our friend Neil Howard asked for another Philanderers visit. Here the Philanderers were reunited with 'The Bus Cleaners', our earliest and most ardent fans. Neil was a generous host, and his home became a favourite haunt of the group, and John became friendly with Neil's daughter, Marilyn, who would lend him her car. Another home from home in Melbourne was the Kew flat of Alison Read, who regularly ferried everyone around in her little VW. The seven left in Australia, particularly Bob and Clive, seemed to attract a great number of girls, who would turn up at the most unlikely times and locations. A week rarely went by without an invitation to a party. Whenever in Melbourne, the bus parked at the attractive Crystal Brook Caravan Park at Warrandyte, on the city's rural outskirts. It seemed to have been carved out from the bush. Tim wrote:

> The tall, mottled eucalyptus trees were alive with bellbirds which filled the morning with their crystal note, like a little gong being struck. Flights of kookaburras drop in for frequent visits, making the air delightfully hideous with their maniacal laugh ...

Christmas in Australia was spent on the beach at Torquay, near Geelong. Tim roasted what seemed a nice piece of beef which, once tasted, turned out to be salted boiling beef. Nevertheless, the seven enjoyed their Christmas meal on the bus. On Boxing Day with the 37°C heat, softened by a sea breeze, they built an enormous sand castle in which everyone sunbathed while Bob, wearing bow tie, tails and a bowler hat, served them with afternoon tea, much to the amazement of a crowd of gawping onlookers. A couple of days later, John filmed a Surf Carnival at Torquay. Teams of lifesavers paraded like Roman legions landing in Britain and undertook feats of manly endurance, while crowds of spectators cracked open tubes of ice-cold beer. On their days off from the paint contract, The Philanderers earned $100 promoting Joseph Saba's Stag Shoppes, a local chain selling trendy menswear, before setting off for Fidler & Webb's department store in Mount Gambier, their first visit to South Australia.

Mount Gambier sits on what is considered to be a dormant volcano and is famous for the Blue Lake at the bottom of one of the craters, which, for six months of the year, is a magnificent deep blue colour. It was the town's water supply and, while thousands of gallons were drawn from it every day, the water level remained constant throughout the year. Here above the lake, in the middle of a 37°C heatwave, the group made a comical three-minute film for the local TV station, and the copy they were given was occasionally shown by other TV stations they visited. The Commodore Motel chain became a regular venue for the group, and they received $75 for playing at the Mount Gambier Motel on Saturday night before starting on a 300-mile trek north to the Murray River and Mildura, Kerang and Echuca. In bright sun and blistering heat in Mildura, on the way to singing at the Howey Brothers store, a top-of-the-range Holden Brougham reversed out of a parking bay in Deakin Avenue straight in front of the bus. Tony stood on the brakes, but it was too late and with a loud, sickening crunch he smashed into the back of the Holden, spinning it through 45 degrees and completely wrecking the rear of the car. There was little damage to the bus. 'All my fault. I really should have seen that coming!' said the driver cheerfully. 'Oh, the car was worn out, anyway,' he said as they parted, but it was Holden's most expensive model and less than 3 years old. In Echuca, the manager of the tourist bureau invited them to take a veteran paddle steamer cruise up the Murray River on the small and delightful *Canberra* and listen to Australian folk songs from the on-board folk group. Back in Melbourne, they played at various down-at-heel suburbs, before a return visit to the Gippsland area. Tim continually called John 'Gnome' when introducing him to the audience, and Clive was always referred to as the star – 'our blue-eyed boy'. Then it was back to Neil Howard's house to celebrate Australia Day, the public holiday commemorating the landing of the first fleet of convict ships from England at what is now Sydney Cove on 26 January 1788.

The group spent early February in southern Victoria and Melbourne. Integrity Paints' lack of initiative and enthusiasm for using us to promote their product was now compounded by the attitude of the parent company, Swan Insurance, who had put in a general manager to sort out Integrity's dire financial situation and who considered us to be a total waste of money. Luckily, Geoff Scott was on our side and despaired of the paint company ever doing anything right. In our support, Integrity's Keith Ford produced evidence that their sales had risen in relation to the previous year's figures, at a time when every other paint manufacturer was in decline. Neil Howard told them that we were 'the best promotion I have ever seen in the hardware business', but volatile managing director Jack Bitting, forgetting his early enthusiasm for us, still seemed unimpressed and continued to undersell The Philanderers.

Tim had finally succeeded in interesting a record company in The Philanderers. Australian country singer Gavan Arden, who hosted a popular weekly country music show on 3UL on which we'd appeared a couple of times, had spoken to Murray Sampson, the proprietor of Valley Records, a small Melbourne outfit, who was prepared to release a single for us. One evening in mid-February 1971, at Melbourne's Crest Record Studios, supervised by Gavan Arden, The Philanderers, plus an electric bass player, recorded 'Whisky in the Jar' and 'Grandfather's Clock'. It was the only record we ever made, and it never hit the charts.

Two more weeks in the Melbourne area, making store appearances that were generally sparsely attended, mainly due to lack of both publicity and interest by the store owners, brought our work for Integrity Paints around Melbourne to a close, the final assignment there being, appropriately, at Neil Howard's store. Peter Mulhall, Keith Ford, Tom Smith and Ebby Peppler all arrived to say farewell. Keith invited the group back to his house for lunch, prepared by his wife, Bernice – known by everyone as Mrs Keith – and the evening was spent at Neil's once more, where an appreciative audience watched the film John had recently shot in Australia. Supper the following evening was with Mrs Coghlan, a kind, bustling Australian housewife, who had regularly fed us on earlier visits to Melbourne and this time had invited every relative she could find to say farewell to 'her boys'.

Then it was north to Sydney and our final appearances for Integrity Paints. The last stop in Victoria was at Benalla, where Evans Grain Store had sensibly arranged for The Philanderers to visit the local convent school, the Senior Citizens Club, and the local hospital. Here the boys said goodbye to Integrity's helpful Geoff Sullivan and presented him with an engraved tankard. An overnight stop in Albury allowed Tim and Clive to finalise arrangements with Ted Jenkins for concerts there at the end of March. Then the bus headed up the Hume Highway to Sydney, with just three more weeks of store appearances at Buckingham's department stores at Ryde, Liverpool and Oxford Square, Darlinghurst, before the paint contract ended. Everyone believed that Peter Margrave had left Erith Street to work in Western Australia, and so, for the first time in Sydney, the group was forced to stay in a campsite. However, after a night on a garage forecourt in Ryde, having unsuccessfully attempted to find one, Peter miraculously appeared and invited the bus back to Erith Street, which he now shared with a couple of girls, and thereafter it became home whenever the bus was in Sydney. The Ryde store appearances were dismal except for Saturday, when a good crowd gathered. Buckingham's management made little effort to gain any value from the group, and the next week in Liverpool was just as bad. The final three days at Buckingham's Oxford Square branch were, as Tim wrote:

> a sadly fitting epilogue to the Integrity Paints adventure: but a handful of people wandering about the store all day; the Integrity rep., after dropping the group off absent all morning. A disappointing end to a disappointing campaign, which, while very successful in patches, nevertheless realised a fraction of its potential.

It all ended not with a bang, but with a whimper. The paint contract had been completely discharged to our considerable credit. We had appeared at the advertised times at all our venues and had fulfilled all that was required of us to the letter. In the process we had garnered publicity for the paint company in the press and on radio and television wherever we went. The same commitment could not be said of Integrity Paints and, as the bus drove away from the final venue, Integrity Paints still owed us $3,000.

By March 1971, when the paint contract ended, the bus had travelled over 10,000 miles around Australia and we had earned over £9,000, initially from working at various jobs individually, and then promoting Integrity Paints, giving concerts and appearing on radio and television. The Philanderers and their bus were now well known in Australia and had a great many supporters and 'fans'. Sadly, Tim, Tony and the others were unable to capitalise on this because every letter I sent asked them to be ready to ship the bus to America immediately. They were unable to make any serious forward plans, but the boys were eager to move on, see the rest of the world and make their fortunes in America. But they were also keen to see Queensland and the real Outback before finally leaving Australia.

Free of the Integrity Paints contract, the group was now able to undertake cabaret performances and shopping centre promotions anywhere in Australia. But finding work was difficult, and the agents we approached usually said that there was no real market for our style of folk singing, which they believed was virtually unsaleable, even though our experience showed them to be wrong. While in Sydney, several other things were also dealt with. Brin and Nat had invited them to Sunday lunch at Toongabbie – and to remove the trailer and all the rubbish we had stored under their house! Luckily, two dragon-like English girls who were opening a bric-a-brac shop in Mosman appeared in Erith Street one day, marvelled at the bus and were persuaded to take and sell for us our trailer, the old generator and some of the junk. The rest eventually ended up at the tip. Tony investigated getting the bus to America and found a new roll-on roll-off shipping service to the US' West Coast which could take the bus. He also negotiated a 20 per cent discount with UTA, a subsidiary of Air France, on air fares to Los Angeles, in exchange for a small advert on the back of the bus. It was also decided that the bus should be repainted. They bought two gallons of matching red paint and Dick and Clive set to rubbing down the paintwork and applying the new coat. Tim arranged another appearance on *Sydney Today*, which included use of the Mt Gambier film, and also arranged for them to drive up to Newcastle to spend a week working for his uncle, John Palmer, who managed the big Co-operative Society there. A new phase in the world trip was about to begin.

✕

Newcastle, at the mouth of the Hunter River, was the second-largest city in New South Wales, and one of Australia's earliest settlements. The discovery of coal made it a major industrial centre and home of the mighty BHP steelworks, which dominated the city and was a major source of local employment and bad air pollution. Tim's uncle, his wife Min and Tim's grandmother, Cicely, insisted that the bus be parked outside their house in Fairview Avenue, and the group spent a week making personal appearances around the city for 'The Store', as the local Co-Op was known. Adverts were placed on the sides of the bus. The Philanderers appeared as guest stars on NBN3's *Here Tonight*, with Neville Roberts, the only TV entertainment programme produced in Newcastle, in company with old acquaintance Tony Barber, who had captained the Pommie cricket team at the Manly charity match in which four of the group had played. Even better was discovering that the surprise guest was the highly desirable Miss New South Wales, our friend Shelley Young, who seemed pleased to see everyone again and who joined them the following morning in 'The Store' at Hunter Street, where they were playing. Tim's uncle arranged a conducted tour of the great steelworks. This was an awe-inspiring complex covering 700 acres, with its own wharves employing over 11,000 staff and producing 2.3 million tons of iron and steel each year. The plant used 1,260 million gallons of water every week, much of which disappeared into the atmosphere as steam, known locally as BHP rain. At the end of the week, a final lunchtime barbecue with Tim's relatives preceded a tearful farewell and a four-hour drive south through tall eucalyptus forests to Sydney. Their next commitment was the Albury concert being set up by Ted Jenkins, followed by a two-week shopping centre promotion in Adelaide for Bill McCallum, the centre manager we had met in Wollongong at our very first appearance for Integrity Paints. Bill had moved to Adelaide as general manager of the city's major shopping centre complex and, after Tim had contacted him, was keen to use the group there.

In Albury, Ted Jenkins proved less able to do the business than everyone had thought. In spite of a radio interview by Clive early in the week, and the bus parading around promoting The Philanderers' presence, as well as a series of personal appearances locally, the Thursday night concert booked at Wodonga's venerable Melba Theatre found the group playing to rows of empty seats, with just eighteen people in the audience. Alison Reid had driven up from Melbourne to join the boys for the weekend and had brought with her a hundred copies of the group's new single, four of which were immediately bought by people at the concert. Earlier in the day, the group visited the Kalliana sheltered workshop for the mentally handicapped, where their half an hour of songs delighted everyone, with the exception of one little girl who suddenly became terrified and had a fit during one song. 'Don't worry, love,' said Tim, 'our music takes a lot of people that way!' Next day the boys visited the Albury Base Hospital and sang in a couple of the wards, where Tim reported that they were rapturously received. One old lady was reduced to tears by the unaccompanied rendition of 'Wild Mountain Thyme'. 'Don't worry, love,' said Tim again, 'our music takes a lot of people that way!' Another dozen records were sold there. Only 200 of the 800 seats in Albury's brand new Civic Centre were filled for the Albury Arts Council-sponsored concert that evening, but it was enough to provide a good audience. The Philanderers – ably supported by Ted's Mamas and Papas-style group, 'The Four Tunes' – gave a highly professional performance, assisted by high-quality amplification, excellent acoustics, and an audience keen to be entertained. A good-quality stereo recording of the whole event was marred only by Charlie, a bass player hidden behind the curtains, who, despite Clive's tutoring, consistently played the wrong notes. The Albury visit was not the success they had hoped for, but they did sell seventy-five records. 'Heaven knows why people buy them,' said Dick, cynically.

In January, Alan had written to me in New York saying he wished to leave the trip if it lasted beyond September. He wanted to sign on at college back in England and also to be with his Australian girlfriend, Nola, who was already there. The others had agreed, and said that his $500 fare home should be paid by the company. Another letter from him in February confirmed that this was what he intended to do. He wrote:

> I feel I ought to try and do something about becoming a teacher, and unless I get home before September I will have to wait for another year. I really think a lot of Nola and we haven't had much time together ... I don't think a year's separation will help much.

I had worried – unnecessarily, he reassured me – that he might be leaving because he and I argued all the time and had never really seen eye to eye about the way the trip was organised and financed. He continued:

> It won't be easy to leave the group. The bus means a lot to me really, even if I don't admit it, and it will be hard to leave the emotional security provided by the bus, but I think that if anything goes wrong between Nola and I, I will kick myself for not having the courage to leave ... I love you too in my own way. Alan

Albury was the last time that Alan played the accordion with The Philanderers on our world tour; he then returned to Melbourne with Alison to spend a couple of months working to get some money behind him before returning to England, where he would marry Nola and sign on at college. Tim wrote:

> His decision to leave was obviously a wise one. He had not been at all happy working as a musician and became increasingly disgruntled with making appearances at stores. Recording and TV studios held no fascination for him, and the trip made him realise that what he really wanted to do was to settle down and qualify as a teacher of engineering.

Ten thousand miles away, I had mixed feelings. I was happy for Alan that he now knew the path that he wished to take – something that, I thought, had yet to be revealed to the rest of us – yet sad that we had lost one of our number, however sound the reasons. The effect that Alan's departure was likely to have on all of us was concisely put in an unusually perceptive letter from Dick. 'Good luck to him,' he wrote to me shortly afterwards, 'I think possibly it will make your life a lot easier and generally speaking I feel a lot more will be achieved.' The Philanderers in Australia had become a six-man group.

Returning to in Sydney for three weeks, the anniversary of our arrival in Australia came round, and everyone, except for Tony, who only reached Sydney in June, applied for, and were granted, residential status. The group's record was pedalled around Sydney's radio stations and Tony was interviewed at length on 2GB by the Reverend Roger Bush. Maintenance and repairs to the bus engine and brakes were undertaken and the repainting continued. With the work in Adelaide now confirmed, the group drove to Canberra and through the Snowy Mountains to Jindabyne, where they were Saturday night cabaret artists at the Commodore Motel for a fee of $80, before continuing to Adelaide. Their route took them over one of the highest roads in Australia, the Alpine Way, around Mount Kosciuszko which, at 7,310ft, is the highest point in Australia. Unimpressive, merely a bump little higher than the other bumps, thought Tim. Tony drove on through forests of eucalyptus made mysterious by the misty autumn rain, the giant gum trees rising tall from the steep slopes that dropped away on either side of the narrow, unsurfaced road. After a while, a steep descent began under leaden skies and through driving rain, with pale blue-green gum trees contrasting with the glistening reddish-brown rock exposed where the unsealed road had been hacked out of the hillside – the bus engine screaming in low gear, acting as a brake and the exhaust producing great clouds of vapour in the damp air. The next day, they passed through the flat, dull countryside of southern New South Wales and northern Victoria, farmland slowly giving way to dry scrub where the kangaroos seemed quite at home. Crossing into South Australia the following morning, the road took them through seemingly endless green pastures. To avoid the low bridge at Murray Bridge, they crossed the wide, sluggish and brown Murray River on the old chain ferry at Tailem Bend before driving through the delightful Mount Lofty Ranges. The bus finally arrived at Adelaide's Marion Shopping Centre to meet Bill McCallum, after a 700-mile, four-day journey.

Adelaide, with a population of three quarters of a million people, has no convict legacy and is a city of wide streets and large public squares lined with many pleasant buildings that were old by Australian standards, all surrounded by parkland. During the next two weeks, The Philanderers and their bus took Adelaide by storm. They appeared at the Marion Centre and Tea Tree Plaza – the city's two main urban shopping malls – on alternate days, sponsored by Coca-Cola and Top Brand, a local fertiliser manufacturer. Adverts were stuck on the bus, a car was provided for the group by a local Ford dealership and the Marion Centre's promotions manager, Peter Schrader, organised interviews and features on local radio and every one of Adelaide's four TV channels. Bob and Clive became friendly with Rhonda, who worked for Channel 9, and her flatmate, Rosie, who had them all round for supper one evening. The weather was dull and most days it rained intermittently. Quite a number of the Adelaide population were originally from the south of England, and they came across several ex-Liphook residents who had emigrated to Australia. Clive discovered some old friends of his parents. 'I can remember you when you were so high,' they said. One of the occupants of the Land Rover with 'Trans World Expedition' on it that we'd met in Athens appeared one day and took the boys to Adelaide's folk club. By the end of two weeks, The Philanderers had been guests on Channel 9's popular *National Country Music Hour*, which was networked around Australia and which, a year before, we had fantasised about appearing on when we were penniless in our squalid Sydney flat. They performed for Channel 10's *Saturday Tonight Show*, and also on Channel 7's local version of 'I've Got a Secret', where Clive's secret was that he had 'mooed for milk in Athens', recalling the time when he had unsuccessfully tried to buy milk. Having run out of all the foreign words he knew for milk, he resorted to crouching down and miming milking a cow, to the blank amazement of all who watched him. He was away for hours. When he returned empty-handed, I upset him by going out with an empty milk bottle and coming back with several full ones in less than five minutes. The panellists failed to guess his secret, with one suggesting afterwards that Clive could have failed because, maybe, Greek cows didn't moo. The Philanderers then mimed to 'Whisky in the Jar' and the programme presenter, Bob Francis, interviewed Tim before closing the show. During their second week in Adelaide,

Tim confirmed the group's booking with Merv Tozer at Melbourne's Chadstone Centre in mid-June. This left them free for the next five weeks. They realised that it was far easier to have a major impact on a community the size of Adelaide, compared with Melbourne or Sydney, and that it would be worthwhile seeking work in either Brisbane or in Perth, which were of similar size. As this was the nearest they would ever get to Perth, 1,700 miles to the west, they decided to pay the city a visit, although Clive and John were keen to drive north to Alice Springs. A couple of phone calls got them tentative promises of work there, but it would be a challenge crossing the Nullarbor Plain, a journey which would involve hundreds of miles of dirt road. On Monday 17 May 1971 they set off to drive across the Australian desert. Not since northern Iran had the bus faced such a challenge.

26

'We'll Take Good Care of You'

The Greyhound bus roared up the ramp of the New York Port Authority's bus terminal and out into the spring sunshine. I was on my way to see Gale. The 370-mile journey, broken only by a three-quarters of an hour stop at Howard Johnson's restaurant at Saratoga Springs and half an hour's border check, lasted eight hours and took me through forests of budding beech, birch and aspen, with great rocky outcrops and mountains that faded blue towards the western horizon. Strings of lakes and the rushing torrent of a mountain river were all viewed from a landscaped four-lane highway that wound gracefully through the vast Adirondack National Park. Once in Canada, the road signs in Quebec were in both French and English, and it was a shock to discover that the native tongue of 80 per cent of people here was French.

The next two weeks relaxing and sightseeing with Gale included a trip to see the amazing display of spring tulips in Ottawa, Canada's capital city. Princess Juliana of the Netherlands and her daughters had been guests of the Canadian Government there during the Nazi occupation of Holland in the Second World War, and in 1945 the Dutch royal family sent 100,000 tulip bulbs to Ottawa in gratitude and to acknowledge the role played by Canadian soldiers in liberating their country. Now, a million tulips bloom in Ottawa each May, attracting hundreds of thousands of visitors.

Gale was living in a room in a shabby terrace, 'The Commonwealth Apartments', at 1117 Greene Avenue, Westmount, which was full of people from far-flung outposts of Britain's former empire. Montreal was a cosmopolitan, vibrant place, full of young people, with bars, underground shopping plazas and a superb new 'metro' system built for Canada's Expo '67. This had become a permanent exhibition – 'Man and his World' – which we visited with Gale's childhood friend Julia Phillips, who was also living in Montreal. That evening, the three of us treated ourselves to Irish coffees in the rooftop bar of the Queen Elizabeth Hotel with its wonderful view of the St Lawrence River and the city's sparkling lights. We climbed Mount Royal, with its splendid view over the city, and visited St Joseph's Oratory, somewhat reminiscent of Lourdes and underlining the Catholic faith of the people of Quebec. At Montreal's modern theatre complex, the Place des Arts, we attended the packed first-night performance by the Georgian State Dancers and Singers, who were victims of anti-Soviet protesters who, after throwing pamphlets from the balcony where we were sitting and letting off stink bombs, caused a disturbance by releasing mice into the auditorium. The perpetrators were sitting right next to me, and during the interval I helped the police identify them. Others let off smoke bombs which totally obscured the stage. Panic ensued but, as the dark smoke slowly cleared, the Georgians were still dancing and were greeted by a great cheer and applause from the now highly sympathetic audience.

Refreshed, and with my batteries recharged, I returned to New York on an overnight bus, arriving on the morning of 1 June. With nowhere to stay, that night I visited Miyo Endo, where I'd left my belongings, and she offered me her couch. I then phoned Susan Tobin and arranged to move into her apartment the next day, when she left on her Mexican trip. The Greenbergs told me that they were trying hard to sell The Philanderers, but so far without success. 'We have two script men putting together a scenario/proposal for the networks for a TV special, Richard,' Larry told me. They only had four weeks to go before their option expired but, as I now had over $900 in the bank, including their option payment, I couldn't grumble. Miyo had tickets that night to a new musical that had just opened to rave reviews at the intimate Cherry Lane Theatre and invited me to go along. The audience was full of celebrities and the theatre was so small that the interval refreshments were served from stalls on the sidewalk outside. I wrote to the boys: 'Went to theatre here in Greenwich Village, saw super thing called "Godspell". Could be a big hit! Also nearly met Leonard Bernstein, who stood next to me during the interval but didn't introduce himself (obviously didn't recognise me?).' The next day I settled into Susan's tiny 222 West 17th Street pad.

I had completely revised my ideas about our American trip and had concluded that to attract sponsorship I needed to downscale everything. A July start was out of the question. My new idea was that we would launch our tour at the San Francisco British Week in late September and end up three months later in New York. We would need at least $50,000, plus some additional expenses, which I thought could most easily be achieved by finding five sponsors who would pay $10,000 each. I'd calculated that we should still return home with some money in our pockets. This was really important, as some of us had no assets and we would need a financial cushion to help us get back on our feet at the end of the trip. In a week or two, Ron Greenberg's option would end. It was becoming obvious that their original optimism was misplaced, so the next thing for me to do was to find a 'host' sponsor, and I had a pretty good idea whom I should approach first.

I had contacted BOAC in March, when I met Tony Fussell, their US advertising manager, who promoted the airline with the slogan 'We'll Take Good Care of You'. He was interested in The Philanderers' US tour, and offered free air travel for a part of the action, but there was no way they could look at the big figures I was then talking about. I had kept in touch, though, and just before my trip to Montreal he had introduced me to the person who was to become the saviour of our North American venture – BOAC's formidable US promotions manager, Ouida Huxley. In her early fifties, Ouida was American, large both in character and stature – 'During the war,' she told me, 'I was known as the Allied "yes – yes" girl, as "Oui" is "yes" in French and "da" is "yes" in Russian.' She was raised by an aunt, the wife of Basil Rathbone, the Hollywood-based British film star, and married David Huxley, Aldous Huxley's half-brother, who had been Attorney-General of Bermuda and was now a New York City financier. Ouida ruled BOAC's PR function with an iron hand. The week after returning from Montreal, I walked into the American Brands building at 245 Park Avenue, took the lift to BOAC's offices on the 29th floor and sat down with Mrs Huxley to talk through my revised ideas. We arranged to meet again the following Tuesday. This time she was like a galleon in full sail, introducing me to her colleagues John Meredith, BOAC's deputy US marketing manager, who became a helpful friend, and the cheery and rotund Barry Barratt, their special promotions manager. I pulled out all the stops, suggesting that The Philanderers would appeal to college campus audiences and could sell BOAC's low young persons' fares, while at shopping centres we would concentrate on marketing the airline's package holidays. Talking about press, TV and radio coverage, I demonstrated how much we'd already achieved in Australia. For what I was offering, $10,000 was nothing. I was sure that once the ball was rolling we would have no difficulty in getting others on board. Everyone agreed. Now it was up to their boss, Jim Harris, head of BOAC's North American sales operation. This was the final hurdle – if Jim agreed, then the deal was in the bag. We saw Jim on 15 June. He was enthusiastic and was immediately sold on the proposal. 'Yes, Richard,' he said:

> It's a great idea. I'll authorise BOAC to put up $10,000 at once and we'll throw in air travel for you and your group to the USA and back to England when it's all over. We'll also help you find the rest of the money. You can have a desk here if you like, and use our resources to find other sponsors. You and Ouida can work out the details. Now – when can you get started?

'Next Monday,' I replied, shaking his hand. Monday was the day the Greenberg option expired.

This was the pivotal moment. I had been in New York for almost six months. I had done so much research, eliminated so many different options and ideas, overcome so many objections and obstacles, made so many contacts and got so deep under the skin of the American advertising business that my time here could hardly be called wasted. Without those months of demoralising and unrewarding effort I might never have closed this particular deal. I met Ouida a couple of days later to get things moving and wrote a lengthy letter to the boys in Australia telling them to prepare to come with the bus to San Francisco for September. There was a lot to do, but at last I felt things were now under way. All I needed were more sponsors.

Domestically, I'd settled into West 17th Street and become pally with Norma Harrop and Liz Esterly, the occupants of the other small apartments on Susan's floor. Norma was in her forties. A journalist and copywriter, she swanned around her tiny apartment, the only one with an air-conditioning unit, in kaftans and dressing gowns, her hair dyed jet black and her face heavily made up. She loved her cats and a glass of wine, and mysteriously entertained her married 'swain', Robert, every Thursday evening. Liz was about my age, an occupational therapist with close-cropped hair who dressed as if she were off to scout camp, never wore make-up, and was illegally subletting from Diana, who was in Israel. Liz was shortly to move to San Jose, California. Norma and Liz regularly invited me to eat supper. Liz introduced me to David Cox, a dark-haired, virile-looking – but totally penniless – out-of-work actor in his early thirties who lived on the floor above. 'I was in a Hitchcock film once,' he told me, 'I played a mounted policeman outside the Plaza Hotel in "North by Northwest", but you couldn't see my face – all that ended up on the screen was the rear of the horse!' When Susan returned from Mexico, I moved in with him – my upfront payment enabling him to clear his overdue back rent. The single room we lived and slept in was tiny, and our bed sheets covered pieces of foam laid out on the deep pile-carpeted floor. Placed against the wall, they doubled as a sofa when we weren't sleeping on them. There was no air-conditioning. During the hot, humid mid-summer weeks I gradually fell into a routine of the girls inviting me to supper in turn during the week, and on Fridays I would cook Susan, Norma and Liz supper in David's flat. Joe Smith, now on an extended visit to England, had introduced me to Miss Dolan, who ran a message service. If Joe didn't answer his phone after a number of rings, Miss Dolan intercepted the call at her ground floor apartment at 240 East 55th Street with 'Mr Smith's Office' and took messages for him. I gave people Miss Dolan's address for my mail, and her phone number, where she took messages as if she were my secretary, for which she charged $26.50 a month.

The hunt was now on for the other sponsors. Jim Harris had arranged for me to see John Manton of Avis, the car rental firm, who, after a bit of persuasion by BOAC, agreed to join in and put up $10,000. John Meredith introduced me to John Watson of British Rail, who immediately offered to take a $5,000 share to promote BR's 'youth' rail passes. I was very keen to get the British Tourist Authority on board. With their involvement we would then be promoting travel to Britain for Britain's government-funded tourist organisation, which would really legitimise the whole thing. Back in March I'd met Ed Antrobus, BTA's diminutive and perpetually harassed number two man in the States, who was interested but had nowhere near the money I was then seeking. I did discover, though, that he and his boss, BTA's American chief, Jim Turbayne, had organised a goodwill tour of America by three London Transport double-deckers in 1952, inviting Americans to 'Come to Britain'. Ouida fixed another meeting with him to discuss their participation in our new scheme. 'BTA are a load of sour gits,' I wrote to the boys afterwards. 'There's no money there unless I can get BR to influence them. There's odd talk about us going back to Sydney for a week in November for the BTA, who are at a convention there.' I finally met Jim Turbayne, a balding, big cheery Scotsman and, three weeks later over lunch, we finally reached a deal, but it would involve a dramatic change of plan. In early November, the American Society of Travel Agents – known in the trade as ASTA – held an annual convention. This year it would be in Sydney, and BTA's participation in our American tour depended on our agreeing to appear with the bus as the star attraction at their hospitality suite there. Sydney would be host to thousands of influential American travel agents, and we could 'launch' our tour at the convention and start our journey from San Francisco in January 1972. I had little option but to accept, and it was agreed that I would fly back to join the others in Australia and we would ship the bus to the States as soon as our work at the convention was over. During July, I wrote reams to the others about the arrangements for our US tour. The breakthrough moment came when we finally got BTA to commit to paying $10,000 if we appeared at travel trade presentations for them across the States during the tour, which meant that I only had to find another $15,000 and we were home and dry.

The approaches that BOAC, the BTA and I made were a list of British and UK-associated companies who promoted their goods and services in North America. We talked to Trusthouse Forte, the UK hotel chain, Cunard, the shipping line, various Scotch and gin distillers, British European Airways, Whitbread, Raleigh bicycles, Barclays Bank, Blades, the trendy Savile Row tailors, Wedgewood, Schweppes, Cadbury's, Lea & Perrins and dozens of others. After an exhausting couple of months, the remaining funding eventually came from British Leyland, who chipped in $10,000 for us to promote Triumph sports cars, and P&O, the cruise line, from whom I got the final $5,000. Lipton tea said they would provide us with an endless supply of tea bags, Hart Schaffner & Marx offered us clothing, including several suits and jackets each from Austin Reed, in which they had a financial interest, and Pringle gave us some Union Jack sweaters. Guy Norman, BOAC's holiday projects manager, arranged for us to use a Commer Highwayman campervan, sign-written to promote 'Landcruise', Wilson UK's BOAC-promoted camper holidays and currently in Toronto, as a back-up vehicle for most of the tour.

Back in West 17th Street, life with David Cox had become easier as he'd taken a night-time job looking after a computer complex. This meant that he slept during the day when I was out, and at night I had the place to myself. It was now July, and the temperature soared, sometimes touching 37°C, with high humidity making it unbearably sticky, made worse by the still air. It was impossible to see the horizon down New York's long avenues as exhaust fumes produced a hazy smog, the pollution being officially rated as 'unacceptable'. The subways were like a furnace. Every so often there would be a terrific thunderstorm and a great downpour, which always came as a wonderful relief. Everyone went into the street to stand looking up into the rain as it cooled the air and freshened everything. Unfortunately, this would only last a couple of days. The children along the block turned on the fire hydrants when it was really hot and splashed around under the high-pressure jets. The Fire Department then fitted them with sprinklers, which produced a fine spray and kept the pressure in the system high, but the kids found more fun in the blast of water which almost knocked them over.

Over the Independence Day weekend, I returned to Montreal for a few days. Gale had now moved into a spacious apartment at 4216 Boulevard de Maisonneuve Ouest, a beautiful, tree-lined avenue, sharing with two other girls, a nurse and a teacher, both of whom smoked pot. This was kept in the toilet where they could quickly push it through the window into the inner courtyard below if there was a police raid! The apartment was bright, airy and tastefully furnished, a far cry from the rooming-house in Green Avenue. We visited Upper Canada Village, where old buildings had been relocated from areas flooded by the St Lawrence Seaway project, recreating an early nineteenth-century Canadian settlement. People dressed in period costume talked to visitors about life in Canada's early days, worked water-powered saw and textile mills and farmed the land using traditional methods.

Back in New York, I got a call from an old girlfriend, Jane Harbury, who had emigrated to Toronto from Liphook in the mid-Sixties and was now 'girl Friday' to the singer/songwriter Tim Hardin, who lived with his entourage in a twenty-two-room mansion at Woodstock. 'Are you into the sweeter things of life?' she asked me. I wasn't exactly sure what she meant, but said I didn't think I was. 'We're coming to New York next week. Tim has a $2,400 a week habit,' she said casually. He was a heroin addict and was making his regular visit to a classy Upper East Side clinic for his methadone treatment. We met for coffee at a pavement café opposite the hospital, and the composer of 'If I Were a Carpenter' sat sullenly in the hot afternoon sun until it was time for him to go for his regular 'fix'. Jane and I then had a long and animated chat, but as soon as he returned they swiftly disappeared back to Woodstock. Drugs were a major concern in the US, and I regularly met people who told me how 'great' they were, but I kept as far from them as possible. I sensed that some potential sponsors feared that we had been floating around the world on a sea of dope and, so to allay this, Geoff Scott provided me with a written testimonial which concluded:

> Everyone concerned – Client, Agency, Retailers and Buying Public – found The Philanderers to be a very welcome change to the currently accepted concept of a Musical Group. Clean-living, humorous, energetic, enthusiastic, responsible, fun-loving young gentlemen who smoke nothing but cigarettes. And with a knowledge of what they are paid for – to promote product.

I began working on a detailed itinerary, and took the Greyhound bus down to Washington to visit the Federal Highway Administration, from whom I learnt that the new Interstate Highway System had bridge clearances of at least 16ft to enable missile-carrying military vehicles to pass under them. We would, however, have to get transit permits for our 'illegal' overheight vehicle from every state we intended to cross. Having worked out and agreed an itinerary, I then wrote to all the relevant States and soon had a large file bulging with details of routes and permits which I eventually passed to Clive. Our sponsors drew up legal agreements which a solicitor friend of Joe Smith checked for me. Early in

August, I opened Pillock Ltd's new account at Barclays Bank in Park Avenue and paid in the BTA's initial retainer. Our cheques even had our logo on them. I looked into whether we needed to join the Musicians' Union, and eventually concluded that, as we were only being employed to promote travel to Britain, it would be better if we steered clear of that particular complication. Our sponsors agreed.

Socially, Susan Tobin and I had dinner at the Huxleys' luxurious penthouse apartment on Washington Square one evening, and I went with Liz and Susan to open-air concerts in Central Park and barbecues with Liz's friend, Ian Bubb, a Londoner who had travelled extensively on cheap local buses in South America, and his heavily pregnant American wife, Susan, at their apartment on Staten Island. I continued to be a regular visitor at Joe Smith's, usually at the end of the day around cocktail time. Daniel Pearce-Higgins came to supper on his way to a summer job in Pennsylvania, where I visited him one weekend at a great mausoleum of a resort hotel at Buck Hill Falls, deep in the wooded Pocono Mountains, where he was a cocktail waiter. He'd got his degree and was off to the Inns of Court in the autumn. Liz eventually took off in her little VW Beetle to California, leaving an empty flat and a lot of displaced cockroaches, many of whom sought refuge in my apartment, and often the steps I'd take in the night across the kitchen could be traced the next morning by the trail of squashed roaches on the floor. The City Council employed operatives to get rid of these pests; they would regularly bang on our door, shouting 'Sturminator!' and come in to spray 'cockroach doom' everywhere. I typed interminably long and rambling letters to the others in Australia, mainly about the arrangements for the tour, which included little details about how I was living. On 18 August I wrote:

Hell, folks, I've been trying to write this all night and it's now twelve-twenty. I started at seven, but decided to have a gin with Susan Tobin, and ended up getting dinner for us both. Then, after a while (at about eleven) just as I'd started David appeared at the door and said he'd bought us a great pizza, which I should come down and help eat, so David, Susan and I all traipsed into Norma's (air-conditioned) apartment and waded into this bloody great pizza which must have been 18in across, swilling it down with a bottle or two of red wine … so now I'm full up, hung up and only capable of a good kip …

Early in September, Gale came down for a long weekend and met many of my new friends, including the Huxleys. I'd been working flat out for months and really needed a break, so we decided to take a couple of weeks off to explore eastern Canada, and the following week I took the Greyhound bus to Montreal. BOAC's Guy Norman was developing a Montreal-based fly-drive camper holiday package and, at short notice, arranged for us to use one of the VW campervans. We spent two idyllic weeks driving first to Quebec City, one of the North America's odlest and most magnificent settlements, with its stone buildings and narrow streets and undoubted French influence, then up the south side of the St Lawrence River to the scenic, but rather foggy, Gaspé Peninsula, through the forests of New Brunswick to the Bay of Fundy, and onto the ferry to sunny, pastoral Prince Edward Island. We drove through the rugged beauty of the Cape Breton National Park to the tip of Nova Scotia following the 'Cabot Trail' and returned through the mountains of Maine, New Hampshire and Vermont to Montreal, covering 3,500 miles in under two weeks. It was a refreshing change, and after a few more days I reluctantly caught the bus back to New York.

'It's no use, you'll have to find somewhere else to live,' announced David when I arrived back at the flat and, seeing the place strewn with female clothing, I understood why. So I was back on the street again, but the Bubbs took pity on me and I moved into their spare room at 19 St Mark's Place, Staten Island, where I stayed until leaving for Australia three weeks later. The trees along their street were now turning gold and yellow, and I spent the early fall shuttling across New York Harbor past the Statue of Liberty on the Staten Island Ferry, before catching the subway to Grand Central Station and BOAC's office. The journey on the ferries, with their distinctive black and mustard yellow paintwork, cost a nickel, 5 cents, and was considered to be the biggest bargain in New York City. I wrote the copy for the colourful leaflet that would accompany our tour – 'The Philanderers invite you to Visit Britain' – scripted the commentary that would accompany two short films for American TV stations, recorded promotional tapes for local radio, finalised the details of our route and generally tied up loose ends, but I had yet to resolve getting the bus properly insured. Following the travel agents' convention in Sydney, we would fly to New York to familiarise ourselves with our sponsors' products. I had supper with Dan, on his way home to pursue his career as a lawyer, and on 30 September celebrated the second anniversary of our departure from the Deers Hut by calling on Joe Smith, when we raised our glasses of kir to the success of The Philanderers' North American adventure. Eventually, on 21 October, after a quick trip to Montreal to bid farewell to Gale, I boarded a Sydney-bound BOAC VC10 at New York's JFK Airport, wondering how I would get on with the others in Australia. It was almost eleven months since I'd started on my lone quest for North American sponsors, and I'd managed to survive in New York from January to November on less than £1,000.

Earlier in October, Tim sent me what he admitted were his highly subjective views of the group. He described Clive as glowing with self-righteousness over the way he believed that, musically, he had carried the group single-handedly on his broad musical shoulders since Alan had left, which he used as an excuse to avoid doing his share of the usual menial duties if he could get away with it. In Tim's view, Bob, although erratic and unpredictable, was more useful musically than Clive thought he was. Bob hated confrontation and disagreement and had become the conciliator when it came to disagreements within the group. Tim said nothing about Bob's key role in keeping the bus on the road, though – something I considered important. Tim thought John conscientious but still capable of going off into 'blidges', and believed John's banjo playing was a considerable asset to the group. John also looked after the food very well, with none of the sullenness that Tim felt Dick used to bring to it. Dick he dismissed as playing the recorder, painting the exterior of the bus and normally siding with Clive. Tim's main praise was reserved for Tony. He was still the faithful lieutenant, more self-assured than a year ago, conscientious and dependable, looking after things like shipping, taxation and finance magnificently. He was my man through and through, Tim assured me. Writing about himself, Tim felt he had gained something by being de facto in charge in my absence, was still capable of being bloody-minded, but still had no confidence in his ability to achieve anything – considering everything, I believed he had been amazingly successful during my absence. He believed himself to be the outsider of the group – but I suspected that we all felt that about ourselves from time to time – and he was surprised that the others held him in high regard. All this left me thinking about what they really thought of me, and wondering what I would actually find when I got back to Australia.

27

Five Thousand Miles in Five and a Half Weeks

In mid-May as I was speeding up to Montreal at 70mph on the Greyhound bus, my friends in Australia were leaving Adelaide in Hairy Pillock 2 at a sedate 38mph on their way to Perth, having made many friends in Adelaide and becoming well known there. John stocked up with food for the journey in Port Augusta, the last big town towards Perth along Australia's Highway 1, and by nightfall on the first day they had travelled over 350 miles. The surfaced highway took them as far as Ceduna, 500 miles from Adelaide and the last significant settlement before the vast expanse of the Nullarbor Plain. Here the dirt road began, continuing to the border with Western Australia, 320 miles away. It was being upgraded and surfaced, and a lengthy detour to avoid the roadworks took the bus along dusty, unmade tracks, smothering everything on board in a fine, silvery dust which penetrated everywhere. The flat, uninspiring scrub, relieved by a few eucalyptus trees, none much higher than the bus, merged into poor grazing country dotted with sheep. Bob had worked in this area the previous year, and the bus called at a sheep station he'd visited, before stopping overnight at a local motel which Bob knew. The next day, the trees became fewer until there was nothing but 6in-high salt scrub in a vast, greyish-white, sandy, treeless emptiness which stretched to flat horizons in every direction; the only features on the wide, graded track were the mileposts. To the north, a great unexplored nothingness extended for over a thousand miles. Nullarbor is not aboriginal in origin, but comes from the Latin, meaning 'no tree', and this was certainly true. Crossing the border into Western Australia, the track suddenly became a new blacktop highway and the bus was able to cruise at top speed for hour after monotonous hour through thick bush country. In order to reach Perth by Thursday evening, which, Tim thought, might enable them to get some publicity on Friday's TV news magazine programmes, they decided to drive on through the night. Kangaroos were spotted here and there along the road, with the bleached bones of those hit by passing vehicles littering the edge of the highway. Tall gum trees became plentiful, and the earth a reddish orange colour, and a shiny steel water pipe followed the road for hundreds of miles. By mid-afternoon, the bus was driving through farmland and by 8 p.m. they finally reached Perth's Orange Grove Caravan Park, which had been advertised by large red-and-white signs all along the highway.

With a rapidly growing population, then still under 700,000, Perth was the fifth-largest city in Australia and is one of the remotest cities in the world. Set on rising ground above the banks of the Swan River, where this widened into a large, attractive lake, Perth was like a mini-Sydney, with its solid, traditional Victorian and early twentieth-century buildings being replaced by modern glass and concrete towers housing the headquarters of big companies involved in Western Australia's mining boom. Unlike Adelaide, where publicity for the group had been organised by the shopping centres, Tim and the others had to arrange everything themselves. It was to Tim's credit that, within hours of their arrival, they had broadcast live on Channel 9's lunchtime *Woman's World* and appeared on the news programmes of all three of Perth's television stations. They were booked as guest performers on Channel 7's *New Faces* the following week, were to be featured in *TV Times* and *TV Week*, and had photos and articles about them in both Perth Sunday papers. 'Did you ever come across that Foden steam lorry that's doing a world tour on your travels?' asked one of the journalists. They were quickly discovered by Liz Benham and Bob Baker – with whom I'd stayed the previous December – who, having seen them on TV, had been out searching for the bus. On their first evening in town, they sang three trial numbers at 'Pinocchio's', a Perth nightclub, whose manager quickly decided that they weren't right for his club, but offered help with other introductions. Having made phone calls to them from Adelaide, Tim had hoped to find at least two weeks' work with Boans, Perth's big store and shopping centre group, but in the end had to settle for a few days, worth $70 a day. The group spent a lazy weekend around the campsite and met up with Lewis Williams, who had been at our Teheran Christmas dinner and was now working in Perth. Bob went looking for his brother, Gerry, his wife, Alexandra, and their two toddlers, who had recently emigrated to Western Australia, Gerry joining the RAAF. Bob eventually tracked them down and the bus became a fixture outside Gerry's house in the northern suburb of Balga for the rest of their stay. Gerry let the group use his clapped-out 1950s Wolsley, which had an air of faded gentility about it and continually broke down.

A highlight of their time in Perth was when The Philanderers featured as special guests on the popular *Spotlight* show,

Channel 9's equivalent of *New Faces*. Nationally famous presenter, Graham Webb – known in England as the voice at the Australian end of *Two-Way Family Favourites* – flew to Perth from Sydney each month to record several editions of the show, and the group were given star treatment. This was the nearest we came to having our own show on Australian television. Other than passing judgement on one or two amateur performers, the whole programme was devoted to The Philanderers' songs and adventures, and was presided over by the laid-back Webb. Everyone was introduced individually and the group's professionalism, easy confidence and relaxed approach contrasted strongly with the uptight nervousness and wooden performances of the amateur participants. The Philanderers were turning into experienced professionals. They very nearly missed the phone call to Gerry's asking them to appear on the show. 'Can I speak to Phil Andrews, please?' the rather dozy secretary at Channel 9 asked. 'There's no Phil Andrews here,' was the reply. 'He's a singer, I think,' said the secretary. 'You mean The Philanderers, don't you?' It was quickly sorted.

During the group's appearance as guests on *New Faces*, Tony had spoken briefly to Frank Baden-Powell, one of the judges, who ran a number of entertainment venues in Perth and Freemantle. A couple of days later, Tony called in to see him. Frank was in his early forties, with thinning hair, dancing eyes and a mischievous smile. An earthy raconteur with a quick wit and a robust sense of humour, he told Tony: 'I've no vacancies for entertainers but I really do want to use you and your bus. How about driving around with adverts for the Old Time Music Hall on the side and a couple of the girls to help you dish out leaflets for us?' 'Great!' replied Tony enthusiastically. 'Now then, what do you want for it?' Frank asked. 'I'm hopeless when it comes to money,' stalled Tony, and so Baden-Powell offered him $150 plus meals at both the Music Hall and 'Dirty Dick's', his Elizabethan banqueting place in Freemantle. As this was far more than Tony expected, he swiftly accepted. This almost doubled their income in Perth and they were soon spending chilly lunchtimes in the city centre with a couple of shivering, scantily clad showgirls, handing out leaflets to crowds of curious passers-by, which gave John something interesting to film. Later, in Freemantle, they parked outside the Music Hall before it opened, advertising 'Take Tea with The Philanderers', with three girls in Victorian costume making tea on the bus for a stream of customers while Flanagan and Allen sang on the record player. While the bus was in Perth, engineers at the Lucas depot overhauled the fuel pump, fitted a new lift pump, cleaned the injectors and reset the governor, giving the bus an impressive amount of extra power. Post was forwarded to the group from Sydney to Perth's Central Post Office, including my letter explaining my arrangement with Ron Greenberg. This would delay them leaving Australia for at least six weeks, they thought, planning to use the time to visit Queensland and the Barrier Reef once they had finished the shopping centre work already lined up in Melbourne.

After a couple more shopping centre appearances for Boans and two evenings organised by Tony playing at the 'Galaxy' nightclub in Charles Street, they said goodbye to the friends they had made in Perth and retraced their steps back across the dusty, arid and featureless Outback towards Adelaide. They went sightseeing in the old goldmining town of Kalgoorlie, which Tim described as:

a riot of colonial and border town architecture. The main feature of the almost flat landscape, apart from a number of gaunt wooden pitheads ... is the slime dumps, huge low flat-topped rectangles of slowly settling fine earth, almost washed clean of its gold, but nevertheless still holding several fortunes in gold dust if anyone could find an economic way of getting it. The whole area little more than a clearing several miles wide in the seemingly endless Western Australian bush, and bears an incredible sense of isolation.

Across the South Australian border a couple of days later, they stopped on the Nullarbor Plain for a late breakfast and to film the bus on the dirt road when a car sped up and screeched to a halt in a cloud of dust. 'We've seen you on television – can we have your autographs?' demanded the occupants. They spent that night in Penong, the only place they'd come across with a dirt road for its main street. Scattered around the outskirts of this tiny settlement were dozens of windmills that pump water from the Anjutabie Water Basin to provide the local water supply. The only bit of the street with a decent surface was in front of the local garage, which, they discovered, was because that was where the mechanics threw all the old sump oil.

Back in Adelaide on Friday, the boys parked at the home of Joan Shaw and her family. A big, jolly woman from the North of England, she had provided two enormous meals for them on their previous visit, and had insisted they stay with her on their return. They renewed acquaintance with other friends they'd made there and joined Joan and her family for Australia's firework night, the second Saturday in June – mid-winter in Australia – which was the Queen's official birthday. They left on Sunday before dawn, driving through mist and drizzle beyond the Mount Lofty Ranges to pasture and arable land where huge concrete grain silos sat at the roadside at each of the settlements they passed. They reached the Ballarat campground in pouring rain at dusk, and by lunchtime the next day were back at the Crystal Brook

Caravan Park at Warrandyte in time to clean up and prepare for their appearance the following morning at the Chadstone Centre, which also claimed to be the biggest shopping centre in the Southern Hemisphere. The promotion was a great success, and four days working for centre manager Merv Tozer earned the group $400 and clocked up the sale of fifty records. A visit to Jack Bitting at the Integrity Paints offices resulted in a cheque for half of the $3,000 outstanding from our contract – immediately banked by Tony – and a promise of the balance by mid-July. The cheque, however, wasn't cleared until 26 July and their final payment reached our bank on 5 October! Meals at Alison Read's Kew flat and a quick call on our old friend Neil Howard by John, Clive, Dick and Tim, concluded the group's activities in Melbourne and, five days after they arrived, the bus headed north to Albury and an unscheduled Saturday evening appearance at the Folk Pot. This was followed by an impromptu party at Wodonga the same night, and the bus finally came to rest once more outside 11 Erith Street, Mosman, at 7 p.m. on Sunday evening, where Elaine Groves was now in residence.

In the post was an unexpectedly optimistic letter from me telling the boys about BOAC's acceptance of my proposal for a three-month tour of the US starting in September. They decided to put on 'hold' the proposed trip to Brisbane, just in case the bus needed to be shipped to America quickly, and Tim, who in my absence had become the business manager of the group, set about trying to find work in Sydney until they heard from me again, and arranged three days' work at Westfield shopping centre in the North Shore suburb of Hornsby the following week. Since our arrival in Australia, the bus had been driving around using its British registration, but its UK tax couldn't be renewed without a British MOT certificate. It now had to be properly registered in Australia and was taken back to the testers at Rosebury who, as before, were very sympathetic. Bob was worried about the brakes, which had never been very efficient, but all that was required by the inspectors was that a few easily remedied defects be put right, such as replacing a faulty tyre, renewing a rubber mounting at the back and fitting some additional rear lights. The bus was then issued with bright yellow New South Wales registration plates bearing the number BQH 472, which Clive screwed onto the bus over our British ones. The girls with the bric-a-brac shop had unsuccessfully tried to sell Bob's old Holden, so Bob reclaimed it for a while, after which he finally found a buyer. Clive and Tim visited the tiny music shop at the bottom of Pitt Street and the little old man who had sold me my double bass and made such a good job of repairing my old one bought Alan's accordion, which we had acquired for just $40 when we first arrived in Australia. After several more encouraging letters from me suggesting the bus needn't be shipped for a few weeks, they decided to head off to Brisbane as soon as they could and visit Queensland and the Barrier Reef.

One significant complication in everyone's lives in Australia, particularly for Bob and Clive, were girls. Tony wrote home:

> We have just said goodnight to five girls who suddenly descended on us. Actually all five are separate girlfriends of Bob and really the whole evening was very funny as they just sat and virtually spat at each other. The rest of us gave Bob one hell of a time and most of them left in a huff, but they will all come slinking back in 2 or 3 days' time.

The easiest way for them to escape was to move on somewhere else and, as soon as the three days at the Hornsby Mall were over, Tim went to Newcastle for the weekend to see his relations, while the rest of the crew, after a Saturday night party, went off with various girlfriends before driving to Newcastle on Monday to collect Tim and stay the night at Tim's uncle's house before setting off for Queensland.

North of Newcastle, the highway passed through more forests of gum trees as it wound its way up the coast, and the following morning the bus arrived at the resort of Surfers Paradise on Queensland's Gold Coast. After unsuccessful attempts to organise advance bookings as cabaret artists at the beachside hotels on the way back to Sydney, they carried on to Brisbane, where the suburban railway system gave them a few problems with low bridges on the way to their campsite. Tim phoned the Brisbane studios of ABC television, and his contact, Tony Joyce, was very enthusiastic and arranged for a reporter and camera crew to visit the caravan park early the next morning, which they did while everybody was still in bed. This resulted in a four-minute slot on the Brisbane edition of that evening's *This Day Tonight*, the country's top news magazine programme. Promotional work was arranged at Indooroopilly Shoppingtown, another new Westfield development, where the manager, Rob Richards, was keen to have them perform in a couple of weeks' time. With work lined up for their return, there was nothing to keep the boys in Brisbane, and so they drove north to Cairns and the Great Barrier Reef. Tim reported:

Bob was up early and seemed anxious to get into the city and the post office before the bus left, and when he returned he had with him a couple the group had met the previous week at various Mosman parties: Richard, a 21-year-old American radiographer on the first leg of a world tour, and his girlfriend Leonie, a feature writer on the *Sydney Telegraph* who was on a week's holiday –

and as they moved their stuff onto the bus, everybody else assumed that the others knew all about it, and were anyway much too polite to enquire.

The bus pulled onto Highway 1 once more and, with its augmented crew, set course for Cairns, over 1,000 miles to the north, and a two-week holiday.

28

Keeping Afloat

Five days later, they arrived in Cairns. Much of the way the poorly surfaced road was lined with what appeared to be the same type of eucalyptus trees as those they had seen everywhere else in Australia, frequently giving way to clearings providing pasture for large bullocks. Tony wrote:

> North from Brisbane along the coast with the Dividing Range on the left one passes through the big river country, which is the prime beef area. The rivers are huge and fascinating with cargo ships sailing many miles upstream to collect cargoes of beef, sugar cane, bananas and other tropical fruits.

There were fields of sugar cane, tall, thin and thickly planted, interlaced with networks of narrow-gauge tramways used to move the harvested crop, and at Rockhampton – described by Tim as a decaying town with a few half-dead palms and badly in need of a coat of paint – they crossed the Tropic of Capricorn. Stopping in Cairns just long enough for John to stock up with provisions, the bus carried on north to Clifton Beach, 12 miles up the coast, where they found an idyllic campsite on a long, quiet and secluded beach. The temperature was in the high 20s and everyone sunbathed and swam in the warm seas under a benign sun. One evening,

Leonie made an interesting soup from the mussels she had found on the beach. They then moved back to Cairns, leaving Leonie at the Pioneer Coach Terminal, her holiday over, to get the long-distance coach back to Sydney. Tony booked a trip for everyone else to visit the Great Barrier Reef at Green Island the next day. This small coral cay, covered with rainforest and a few palms and surrounded by white, sandy beaches and sapphire-blue waters, lies 17 miles off the coast and sits right on the reef, which is viewed from glass-bottomed boats and an underwater observatory. Brightly coloured fish darted about through the colourful coral, some of which, though, had been attacked and killed by the dreaded 'Crown of Thorns' starfish. It was another idyllic day.

The boys teamed up with an attractive young blonde English actress, Briony Behets – in Australia working on a BBC TV series starring Hugh Lloyd – her friend Sharon, four nurses holidaying in a hostel in Cairns, and a young Frenchman, Didier, and his kelpie dog, Danny. The following day at Tony's insistence, they all made the long, winding climb to the dusty little town of Mareeba, high in the Atherton Tablelands, to visit a rodeo there. They quickly tired of watching riders falling off bucking horses, however, returning to the beach at Clifton, this time to the Moon River campsite, the only one prepared to take Didier's kelpie, and settled there for the week with Leonie's friend Richard, Briony, Sharon and Didier and his dog. They camped on a spit of land which became an island at high tide, and most of them slept there. Didier was a fine cook and produced some tasty and inventive meals. But the idyll was soon over. Richard set off to hitch a lift back to Sydney, Sharon headed towards Darwin, and Briony plus Didier and his dog stayed on board as the bus trundled steadily southwards towards Brisbane.

It was in Rockhampton that the boys received my letter containing the news that they would not be leaving Australia

until November, after the American Travel Agents' Convention
in Sydney, with our US tour now starting in January. At first, this
seemed like a shattering blow but, as with all the setbacks we'd
encountered on our world travels, everyone soon adjusted
to the new circumstances. Once in Brisbane, Didier and the
kelpie said goodbye and Briony flew down to Sydney and her
part in the TV series that was to establish her as a well-known
film and television actress in Australia. My letters updating
them on my progress came in thick and fast. One, saying that
we would have to sing things like 'Down at the Old Bull and
Bush' for the British Tourist Authority, stimulated a heated
debate between those who thought that The Philanderers, as
professional folk singers, should not debase themselves with
this sort of rubbish, and the rest, who really didn't give a damn
if we sang corny old music hall songs or not.

The work at Indooroopilly and Toombul Shoppingtowns
was spread over two weeks and was to have been partly
paid for by Leich Motors, Brisbane's big Holden dealer, for
whom a TV commercial featuring The Philanderers was also
in prospect, but Leich pulled out at the last minute, leaving
an unfilled hole in the budget. Through Tim's heroic efforts,
The Philanderers appeared not only on all the local TV news
magazine programmes, but also on every 'live' television
entertainment show produced in Brisbane – programmes
with exciting names like *Rosemary's Magazine*, *A Crook Affair*,
Breakfast with 9 (broadcast between 7 a.m. and 8 a.m. in the
morning) and *The Channel 'O' Saturday Show*. They appeared
on the Brisbane version of *I've Got a Secret* – with Clive
mooing for milk again. The TV stations were all located on
the summit of Mt Coot-tha and approached via the winding
Sir Samuel Griffith Drive, which was so steep in places that
the bus found difficulty in climbing it. The group's base was
the city caravan park, which was by the river and run by an
English couple, Roger and Dorothy, who took the boys under

their wing. A young English musician, Denis Manning, who once played lead guitar in a Brisbane group, called in one day to get advice about making an overland trip and became a regular visitor. One evening a few days later, he brought along some girls including Jane, who spent the evening totally unrecognised by Clive, even though he had once walked a 4-mile round trip from Bondi Junction to Randwick late one night to visit her after a party. He had completely forgotten her, and was stunned when he was told this after they had left. He was determined to put things right when Denis, Jane and another girl, Irene, accompanied the group to Surfers Paradise a few days later looking for bookings there. I had asked for some up-to-date publicity photos to show potential American sponsors, and an imaginative young photographer produced a set of them complete with instruments, suits and bowlers in rather unusual poses at the Indooroopilly mall, which they sent me. 'What the hell is all that stuff on your face, Tony?' I wrote as soon as I saw them. 'How do you manage to eat with all that stuff in your mouth?' 'I've trimmed my beard,' Tony replied a few days later, 'and I'm told it looks very aristocratic!'

The Broadbeach International Hotel, at the southern end of Surfers Paradise, was second only to the Chevron as the top hotel on the Gold Coast. It was a five-storey concrete and glass slab, built in the mid-1950s, with balconies overlooking a wide, sandy beach. Tim had persuaded the manager, Tony Kinch, to book The Philanderers for at least two weeks at $400 a week. So, in the middle of August, the bus moved down from Brisbane and The Philanderers took up residence on some waste ground just behind the hotel, using the hotel facilities in much the same way as they had done in Pakistan and India. 'I think I ought to say something about Tim Palmer,' Tony wrote to his mother. 'It's due to his efforts that we have continued to make money by folk singing either at shopping centres or at hotels and these next two weeks are due to him, and I hope we don't let him down.' They were contracted to play at lunchtime in the Beer Garden and in the evening from 7 until 10 p.m. in the hotel's 'Kings Road Tavern', six days a week, requiring them to sing for almost five hours each day. Denis joined the group to play the double bass for a while, and friends from Brisbane, including Jane, who was now showing more than a passing interest in Clive, came to visit and to watch their performances. News arrived from England that Nola had accepted Alan's marriage proposal, so the group got Denis to draw a cartoon wedding card with a totally recognisable but wretchedly miserable Alan, captioned: 'This is the happiest day of my life'! The company sent them $150 as a wedding present and I sent them a $10 note from New York – my entire week's allowance!

As The Philanderers' short season continued, some of their supporters from Melbourne who happened to be holidaying in Surfers Paradise discovered them, including the girls they had met at Neil Howard's. Day after day, fans from Victoria, including three female teachers from Melbourne, appeared at their performances to cheer the group on, Tim winning their approval by continually rubbishing Melbourne. Denis returned to Brisbane and another temporary bass player, John Cooksey, took his place. Attempts by Tim and Bob to find other work on the Gold Coast were inconclusive but, on the morning of their final day, Tony Kinch unexpectedly offered to extend their contract for a further week, but at $200 and reducing the number on stage to three or four. All but Dick were reluctantly in favour of this, mainly because it would buy Tim and Bob more time to follow up the leads they had established, and they also needed the money. Tony told Tony Kinch that they accepted his offer and would start the new arrangement that evening but, during a long debate about how a four-man group would work, Dick, who came in late on the discussion and had inflated ideas about the group's worth and strongly resented being offered less money, argued that it would never be successful and that they should move on. He persuaded Clive to change his mind, John soon followed and an impasse was reached until Tony expressed a few doubts and the turn-around was complete. Tim and, to a lesser extent, Bob were furious. To go back on an undertaking so dramatically reflected badly on the group, Tim reasoned, and Mr Kinch made this very clear when Tony advised him of the group's change of mind. With no other work in prospect, the group immediately left Surfers Paradise and two days later arrived back in Mosman, the main reason being to enable John to say goodbye to his Sydney girlfriend, who was just about to leave to tour Australia, and for Clive to see Jane, who had also returned to the city. Tim wrote to me:

> Actually I'm feeling a bit irked, because we're back in Sydney for exclusively sexual reasons & there's no work here at short notice & we'd have done far better to have stayed in Queensland ... We needed the money and it would have given us another week on the Coast to find more work, which I feel we would have done.

In retrospect, it was, perhaps, one of the more short-sighted decisions taken on the trip.

It was time for them to take stock. There were eight weeks to fill before the Travel Agents' Convention, after which the bus would be shipped to the States, but, as Tim had foreseen, getting engagements at short notice in Sydney was almost impossible. They all agreed that they needed to practise, which they did when not otherwise occupied, and Tim phoned every contact he could think of, desperately attempting to find work. A huge shopping complex near

Botany Bay, Miranda Fair, booked them for a day early in October, but otherwise things looked pretty grim. However, when he called Rhys Walker at the Jindabyne Commodore, the group was immediately booked for the coming Friday and Saturday. Meanwhile, a man from the Mosman Council came to call. 'You don't live in the bus here, do you?' he asked. 'Oh no,' lied Clive, 'we live in the flat,' indicating the bungalow at No. 11. The official said that the bus should be locked up, and not connected to an electricity supply, 'because then you might be living in it.' The boys took this philosophically. They actually had been living in the street there, on and off, for the best part of a year, with the tacit acceptance of the neighbours. Clive called on Mrs Conlon, who owned No. 11, and arranged for them to move into the vacant front room. A couple of days later, Leonie, who had accompanied them up to Cairns, found them. She had been promoted to the *Daily Telegraph*, Sydney's biggest-selling daily paper, a tabloid not unlike the UK's old *Daily Sketch*, and now had her own page each Wednesday – 'That Page, with That Girl, Leonie Walther'. She quizzed Tim for an hour and summoned a photographer for a feature on her page the following week. A couple of days later, the group drove down to Canberra and on to Jindabyne, where they were surprised by the unexpected re-appearance of Denis, down from Brisbane, who had decided to join them for a few weeks. That weekend at the Commodore Motel, they had two of the most successful musical evenings they'd ever experienced – helped by the enthusiasm of a group of former Sydney University men, now mostly teachers, who were on holiday and who cheered them on. It was the end of the winter season and they spent their days in the Snowy Mountains attempting to ski. No bones were broken, although several skis certainly were, and a charity concert was promised for the teachers.

Just as the group arrived back in Sydney, Leonie's story hit the streets. She wrote:

> Imagine travelling 1,000 miles from Brisbane to Cairns in a red English Double-Decker bus. Add to that fact that your travelling companions are six gorgeous English guys and you have the perfect holiday. The guys are The Philanderers, a folk group that specialises in bawdy Irish drinking songs. And the 1,000 miles to Cairns is nothing to them – they've already done nearly 35,000 miles since they left England in October 1969.

Leonie went on to eulogise about the trip and concluded with an idyllic description of life on the bus. Tim rang David Coleman at the BTA to talk about the Travel Agents' Convention arrangements and was told: 'Yes, I read it on the way in this morning.' They drove the bus into town and parked it at Dawes Point, where the Sydney buses rest between trips. 'I was reading about you blokes in the paper this morning,' said the inspector on duty. 'Good splash in the paper this morning,' said Mr Clarke, the manager at the bank, as Tim and Tony renewed our letter of credit. 'This is the bus that was in the paper this morning, isn't it?' said the senior inspector when they retrieved the bus from Dawes Point later in the day. 'You can park it here any time you like,' he told them. Leonie proved a good ally, regularly plugging the boys in her weekly column. That weekend, the group, with Tony's girlfriend, Marianne, Shelley Young, in her last weeks as Miss New South Wales and still being pursued by Clive, and Denis enjoyed a superb barbecue with Leonie at her mother's house in the seaside suburb of Harbord, with its magnificent view across the bay north of Manly.

Towards the end of September, much to Tim's disgust, the boys were reduced to taking on gardening and redecorating work at the Alanbrook Private Hospital for Mrs Conlon, and labouring at various building sites, sourced either through the Commonwealth Employment Service, where they bumped into an unemployed Peter Margrave, or from adverts in the *Sydney Morning Herald*. Advertisements for the ASTA Convention were put on the bus, haircuts were arranged, and uninspiring publicity photos of The Philanderers and the bus with the new adverts taken for the BTA for the Convention's literature. At the beginning of October, Denis said goodbye once more and returned to Brisbane, and The Philanderers made another weekend trip to Canberra and the Snowies to fulfil a short, early Friday evening booking at Canberra's Monaro Mall, which earned them $30, and perform at Jindabyne's Commodore Motel again, making them a further $160. Freddie, Pam and Maggie, the teachers they'd made friends with at the Broadbeach International Hotel, came up from Melbourne for the weekend specially to see them. Returning to Sydney, the boys did a charity appearance for Shelley Young to raise money for the Spastics Centre for New South Wales and earned another $120 from a performance at a big promotion at Miranda Fair, where they were billed as 'a livewire group of 6 guys, entertaining their way across the world in a London Double Deck bus!' This involved dancing girls, a resident band, a compere and – the following evening – the famous British pop-pianist Winifred Atwell instead of The Philanderers. The *Oriana* docked at Circular Quay, and Mick Harris smuggled the boys aboard once more for a couple of free suppers and joined them with his Sydney girlfriend at a Saturday barbecue at Shelley Young's parents' house, with Leonie also putting in an appearance to meet Bob. However, it was mainly manual work that kept the wolf from the door during the Australian spring, and between them they earned just over $600 in the weeks before I returned to Australia. On Saturday 23 October they drove the bus to Sydney's Kingsford Smith Airport, and at 8.50 a.m., an hour-and-a-half late and with my luggage lost in transit, I staggered out of the customs hall. After almost eleven months we were all reunited again, and my New York odyssey was finally at an end.

29

Farewell Australia Fair

Tony wrote to his mother:

> So after 11 months Richard is back. We collected him from the airport at 7 a.m. in the bus and it's good to see him again. He is his usual self and now that he is back it's almost as though he had gone down the road to buy a loaf of bread and was delayed a few hours.

That was also how I felt, too, and suddenly all those months in New York seemed like a dream. While John bought the week's supplies, the rest of us enjoyed a lunchtime drink at the Strata Motor Inn. To the others, with their Queensland tans, I looked pale and fatigued. We carried the shopping back in the warm afternoon sun to Erith Street. I was a bundle of nervous energy, fishing out my old clothes, fixing up somewhere to sleep in the old conservatory at the back of the house, and talking incessantly. All day I was too tired to sleep and eventually crashed out at around midnight, happy to be back in Australia with my old friends and to find them just the same as when I had left.

The next morning, Elaine Groves, the big blonde from Warrington who had taken Peter Margrave's room, moved out, which gave us a lot more space, and we became the sole tenants at the staggeringly low rent of $7 a week. We began to rehearse for our appearance at the BTA's hospitality suite at the travel agents' convention, which began the following Sunday. I hadn't touched a keyboard for almost a year, and was rushed round to Tony's girlfriend's house, where we could rehearse the pub songs using her piano. Marianne was an accomplished pianist and was studying for Grade 8 – I'd not got past Grade 4! Clive struggled with my bass while I got my head around the piano accompaniment. The words of 'Don't Dilly Dally', 'Down at the Old Bull & Bush', 'Tavern in the Town' and five other songs were all printed on napkins to be given to the BTA guests. Those not involved in rehearsals carried on with cleaning and refurbishing the bus, including replacing the carpets and lino on the lower deck, in readiness for our debut for our American tour sponsors.

ASTA held an annual convention at venues around the world, and this year, the 41st, it was Sydney's turn to play host to thousands of American travel agents. Everyone who was anyone in the travel business was there to set out their stalls, and hospitality suites tempted agents to promote their destinations. The UK was a prime destination for Americans, but the BTA faced competition from across the globe. Playing to Britain's strengths, they created a 'typical' British pub in the main hall of the Royal Commonwealth Society's rooms at Norwich House in Bligh Street, just behind the 'Wentworth', Sydney's most prestigious hotel, where most of the top travel agents were staying. We looked in on the preparations and I introduced everyone to Jim Turbayne and Ed Antrobus, both just in from New York, who were overseeing the work. The place was a frenzy of activity. Pub signs, a stag's head, dartboards, a large bar with antique pump handles and some Victorian glass, horse brasses, and bits of armour and instruments of torture from the Tower of London were all being thrown together in a pastiche which would be immediately recognisable as a pub to anyone who had never seen the real thing. Lynne Dickson, an Australian who happened to be the world's Scottish Highland Dance champion, was billed to appear, and The Philanderers were there to act as the 'locals', provide 'atmosphere' by performing, and then get everyone in a jolly mood by encouraging them to sing along around an old piano. Invitations had been sent out by the hundred, and large crowds were expected. We spent Friday and Saturday rehearsing *in situ* while BTA staff continually re-arranged the furniture and props until they felt they had the right effect.

Back in Erith Street, we received an unexpected visit from Maggie, Freddie and Pam, our teacher friends from Melbourne, who had come up for the weekend to help clean up the bus. Clive, John and I took them to Saturday night's Narrabeen Folk Club in company with Bob and Leonie – with whom Bob, inevitably, was becoming heavily involved. The girls brought us early morning tea in bed the next morning and cooked us a decent breakfast before flying back to Melbourne later in the day. That evening we sang to our first all-American audience at ASTA's New York Chapter's pre-conference cocktail party at Oxford Square's Koala Motor Inn. It was late – 11.30 p.m. – when we took the stage following a few speeches, having already put away a lot of free food and drink, as had our audience. This was the first time in almost a year that I had played with the group and introduced the songs, and I was understandably nervous. With our BTA and BOAC bosses in the crowd, this was a make or break performance for us, but we were greeted with applause, cheers and laughter, and carried it off surprisingly well. We boarded our bus and drove back to Mosman in a euphoric, if slightly alcoholic, daze. Things had started on the right note. At 8.45 a.m. the next morning, the bus, clean and polished with 'BTA welcomes ASTA Delegates' on one side and BOAC welcoming them on the other, pulled up outside Sydney Town Hall, the convention's main venue, and delivered Jim Turbayne – who had, just seconds before, climbed aboard out of sight around the corner – to the conference so that he could be photographed getting off the bus. After a visit to show off the bus and its adverts at Dawes Point, from where the 1918 barquentine *New Endeavour* was to sail round the harbour for a lunchtime ASTA press reception, we drove to Bligh Street and got ready for the first of four evenings providing the 'colour' at the BTA's now completed 'pub', to which guests were invited between 5 and 9 p.m.

The evenings started with me doing a cocktail bar tinkle on the piano, which sounded fine in the background as long as no one actually listened to what I was playing. Then The Philanderers would sing a few songs on the stage, followed by some eye-catching Highland flinging from Lynne, accompanied by her accordionist. Lynne's dancing was truly attention-grabbing, but the high spot of the evening seemed to be our pub sing-song around the piano. By our third evening, the word was out among the delegates that the BTA hospitality suite was the place to be. Leonie included a paragraph about it in the 'Where It's At' part of her page in the *Daily Telegraph*. By now the 'pub' was full to overflowing, with some delegates returning for a second or third time to join in the fun. 'I can't tell you when I've enjoyed myself so much!' confessed one middle-aged American matron. On the third evening, there was the annual darts match against a scratch team from the Irish Tourist Board, with John and Clive in the BTA team; this resulted in an invitation for us to visit the Irish hospitality suite when we'd finished the following evening. Thursday was the last night, and by 6.30 p.m. it was packed. This time there were queues out to the street. Ninety minutes later, during our session on stage, I was urgently requested to ask people to leave so that those waiting outside could get in. Only a few obliged, and people were still trying to squeeze in when we linked hands, squashed together like sardines in a tin, for 'Auld Lang Syne' at closing time. The BTA were delighted by the great popularity of their 'pub' and our part in it, and our sponsors returned to the US with a warm feeling that The Philanderers' American tour could well be a great success. I was happy that their confidence in me seemed justified. We rounded off the evening by visiting the Irish hospitality suite where, very much the worse for wear, we were persuaded to take the stage for half an hour to liven the place up a bit. It was here that we first met Lewis Roberts, BTA's manager in Canada, who suggested to Clive that we might do a Canadian tour once our commitments in the US were over.

I flew to Melbourne that weekend to stay with David and Sylvia Miller for the last time, to bid farewell to them and my other friends, including the Lovells, Nairne Butchart and his mother – who had so kindly taken me in on my first visit there, when, penniless, I was seeking an Australian sponsor – and Geoff Scott, whose initiative, quick-thinking and immediate confidence in me had resulted in the Integrity Paints contract. It was in Melbourne that our future in Australia was secured, and I regretted leaving behind some good friends when I returned to Sydney early the following week. Travelling by coach overnight along the Princes Highway, which follows the coast of Victoria and New South Wales, enabled me to see some more of the country. I arrived back in Sydney to find that the *Oriana* and Mick Harris were back in port, and that evening all of us, except Bob, who was out with Leonie, crammed into Mick's cabin for a pre-dinner drink before enjoying another free supper in the *Oriana*'s tourist-class restaurant. The following day, Mick joined us to spend the day with TV director George Bradford and an ABC TV crew to make a three-minute film of us for the British Information Services for use on American television.

The Philanderers' final performance in Australia was, perhaps fittingly, in a small, pretty, country town called Singleton with a population not much bigger than Liphook. It was set amid rolling farming country along the Hunter River about 50 miles inland from Newcastle, and a Rotaract charity concert had been arranged with one of the rowdy ex-Sydney University teachers the boys had met at Jindabyne. It was a low-key, home-town affair in a building reminiscent of Liphook's Church Rooms, an old First World War army hut. This also gave us the opportunity to say goodbye to Tim's relatives in Newcastle and shoot some film of the bus in the countryside before returning to Sydney for the last time. A visit was paid to say goodbye to Brinsley, Natalie and their daughters – and also collect the oscilloscope trolleys and display units that were still under their house and which were eventually shipped home to England on the *Oriana*! BOAC used the bus as a mobile cinema for a couple of days, which earned us another $100 towards the shipping costs, but this was after I'd left with Tony for New York.

On Tuesday 16 November I left Australia for the last time. The BOAC Super VC10 – flight BA 592 to New York – flew low across Sydney Harbour and below us in the sunset we could see the famous bridge, the opera house and the wakes of the busy little ferries, and trace the route of Military Road to Mosman and Erith Street – and maybe even see the bus – and then it was only the sea, darkness and supper until we touched down in Fiji four hours later. Tim, Clive and John would follow the next week, and Bob and Dick a couple of days later, once the bus had boarded the 'Paralla', a roll-on, roll-off cargo ship of the Pacific Australia Direct line, which would take it to America for us at a cost of $3,508.41 US, payable on its arrival in the States. Nobody had bothered to note the mileage on the bus when it left Australia, but I reckoned it to be around 61,000 miles, which meant that it had travelled almost 27,000 miles during its eighteen months there. Although some of us really did feel Australia to be the end of the earth, I was sad to leave and would miss the friends I had made there and the laid-back 'She'll be right, mate' attitude of the Australians, all of whom had made us feel very much at home.

Tony and I were both exhausted, and we used our time in Fiji to rest and relax in the hot sun at a pleasant beachside hotel on a palm-fringed sandy cove before preparing to face the rigours of America. Three days later, we landed in a wet and chilly New York. Tony became the guest of Joe Smith and I flew straight up to Montreal to stay with Gale for the weekend before moving in with the Bubbs on Staten Island again. In contrast, Tim, Clive and John saw as much as they could during their four days in Fiji, renting a car and travelling deep into the attractive countryside, past cane fields and groves of coconut palms, up hills and down dales on gravelled roads, past small mountain peaks topped by fluffy white clouds, and getting a cheerful welcome from local people wherever they went. They were quite taken with the peaceful tranquillity and the infinitely varied and uniformly beautiful countryside through which they travelled. When asked later which country he liked best on his world journey, Clive's answer would be 'Fiji.'

America's Thanksgiving holiday was on 25 November and, while Tony went off to Connecticut with Joe Smith to celebrate it there, Gale came down from Montreal to spend the holiday with me in New York, where we were invited by Susan and Norma to join them for a traditional Thanksgiving supper of roast turkey and pumpkin pie in Norma's tiny flat. Tim, Clive and John arrived in New York on Sunday

28 November. Bob had decided to fly straight to New York and should have been on the same flight as the others, but arrived a few days later as he'd been delayed fixing a burnt-out starter motor and dealing with one or two other mechanical problems before the bus was shipped. Dick also left later than expected, but stopped over in Fiji for four days. The seven of us were finally reunited early in December. I'd booked them all into the Hotel McAlpin on 34th Street, but after a couple of days the chubby Barry Barratt at BOAC arranged for them to have two adjoining self-catering apartments at the Middletowne Hotel at 148 East 48th Street at $500 for the month, which was much cheaper and not far from BOAC's Park Avenue offices.

With the contracts with our American sponsors signed and sealed, and their initial payments safely in our New York bank, the money worries that had dogged us for the past two-and-a-half years were over. The $5 a week pocket money we'd allowed ourselves in Australia became $50 a week in the US, to which was added $5 a day to cover meals. As before, the company was still paying for everything. Our unclaimed allowances accrued week by week and the money we had in our own personal accounts with the company grew. We had closed our Australian bank account when we left, converting everything into US dollar traveller's cheques, which gave us $6,100 US to take to America, including $3,000 from the BTA for our work at their ASTA hospitality suite. But we found it hard to kick our old habits and were still very frugal with our funds.

As 1972 approached, so the whole nature of our world trip changed. The 'spirit of the trip' was still there and the bond between us was stronger. We'd grown more tolerant of each other and worked much more closely as a team. We'd started out in 1969 virtually penniless, with no firm idea about how we would fund our journey and with only a half-hearted belief that we could pay our way by acting as export representatives or as folk singers. As export salesmen we had proved wanting, but we had quickly developed the knack of getting publicity for ourselves. In Australia we had appeared as The Philanderers on more than forty television programmes and had done countless radio broadcasts and interviews, and six months of promoting paint in Australia had taught us a lot about how things could easily go wrong. Now our biggest test was just ahead of us. Could we deliver $50,000 worth of benefit for our sponsors in America, or would we be exposed for what we really were – just a bunch of blokes from a village pub in England on a jaunt around the world in a clapped-out old bus chasing a free pint of beer?

30

Go West Young Man: California Here I Come!

We were in New York to learn about our sponsors' products and sort out the detailed arrangements for our American tour. Our days were spent with sales and marketing people from the BTA, BOAC, P&O, British Leyland, British Rail and Avis. We visited the Avis World Headquarters in Long Island and met Colin Marshall, the company's executive vice-president and chief operating officer, and at the time the only Englishman to be boss of a major American corporation. Later, he became boss of British Airways and received a peerage. We sang in the Avis canteen, much to the surprise of the staff, who enthusiastically followed their company motto – 'We Try Harder'. 'Hi folks, we're The Philanderers and we're here to give you indigestion during your lunch hour,' went my introduction. 'Their appearance at WHQ was a single girl's delight,' wrote an enthusiastic Linda Lash in the Avis house magazine, 'as the charming Englishmen are all bachelors ...' We were then taken to British Leyland's HQ at Leonia, New Jersey, by the delightfully named Lyman Gaylord from their PR company, where we test drove a new

Triumph Stag and were treated to a superb lunch. P&O gave us a meal at the 'Top of the Sixes', the forty-one-storey-high penthouse restaurant at 666 Park Avenue. British Rail's John Watson, a smooth operator who reminded me of the English actor George Sanders, also took us out for a decent lunch, and even offered me a job! BOAC worked us hard. Jim Harris, who ended up as British Airways' Director of Marketing, gave us a good talking-to and sent us out with his sales force. We shadowed their reservations team and learned about their state-of-the-art computerised booking system. Ouida Huxley – described by Tim as 'an aggressive expanse of American womanhood who had somehow acquired executive control of the whole tour' – was adamant that her 'charming English bachelors'' reputation should not be tainted by having any females in tow, and my plans to have Gale join us on the trip, and Bob's idea that Leonie might come along, too, were out of the question. If I insisted, then the trip was off, as far as she was concerned. This was a bitter blow, and Tony and I flew up to Montreal to break the news to Gale, who was dismayed but, to her credit, soon accepted the inevitability of what had happened.

As well as the training, we had other things to do. We were measured for new suits, sports jackets, trousers and even bowler hats at Wallach's menswear store in the Empire State Building. These we would collect on our arrival in San Francisco. Marjorie Bassett at the BTA arranged for us to appear on *To Tell the Truth*, a popular and widely syndicated game show hosted by the personable Gary Moore, where a panel of celebrities decided which of three contestants was telling the truth. They screened the short film of the journey to India I'd edited for the BTA and we then sang 'live' to the panel, with the two imposters in the line-up – both of whom did a passable job of pretending to be the real Richard King. We managed to fool the panel and, as well as The Philanderers' $250 appearance fee and my third of the $500 winnings for beating the team, I came away with a dictionary and a pair of bed sheets. Tim and I were interviewed for fifty minutes by the pleasant, well-informed and highly professional talk show host, Barry Farber, on WOR, one of New York's top radio stations, and also on WNCN-FM – an upmarket station favouring classical music – by the respected radio interviewer, Caspar Citron, who always started his show with, 'This is Casper Citron from the Algonquin Hotel, legendary rendezvous for people in the arts.' After breakfasting with Marjorie in the Algonquin's famous dining room, we recorded the interview in one of the historic hotel's third-floor bedrooms, which had been set up as a radio studio.

We made several appearances at BOAC's Speedbird Club at their 245 Park Lane headquarters, where, on 2 December, our first – quite short – performance in America took place. I felt lost without my double bass and afterwards got in touch with Dick Mascot, who kindly offered me the use of his bass for any subsequent performances. The problem was getting it from Dick's penthouse apartment at 333 East 55th Street to BOAC's offices and, as it wouldn't fit in a taxi, we ended up having to carry it across town. Later, to get it to the NBC studios at the Rockefeller Center, I had to take it on the subway! We bought Dick a cover for his bass as a 'thank you' present, and a second one for mine. At the next Speedbird Club session, we were given the keys of the City of New York by a suave official from Mayor Lindsay's office. The actual key didn't fit anything. It was a replica of the key of the original door to City Hall, dating from 1812. The door, we were told, had gone missing, presumed stolen, years before and had been replaced by more securely fixed iron gates. Dick Mascot, Joe Smith and Susan Tobin were our guests at the presentation and performance. Afterwards, Dick generously treated everyone, including some BOAC people, to a magnificent Chinese meal at 'The Flower Drum' on 2nd Avenue, where we were served the same menu that U Thant, Secretary General of the United Nations, regularly gave official guests when he took them there. By popular demand, we played at the club again the next evening and, not to be outdone, Barry Barratt rewarded us by taking most of us to dinner at 'The Four Seasons', one of New York's genuinely iconic eating places. The following weekend, we were the guests of Susan and Norma at the tiny West 17th Street apartments where I'd once lived, when they laid on a tasty pot roast, and on Sunday evening the Huxleys invited us to their Washington Square penthouse for another splendid supper. The next evening, Joe Smith was our host for cocktails at six, which lasted well into the evening. We began to enjoy being wined and dined at other people's expense.

It was now almost Christmas, which was celebrated with a passion, and highly commercially, in New York. The city was full of Christmas trees and lights, the biggest being at the Rockefeller Center. Bloomingdale's, Macy's, and the windows of all the shops on 5th Avenue were elaborately decorated, and each store boasted their own individual Father Christmas. There was a frosty nip in the air, wisps of steam rose evocatively from manholes in the streets, Bing Crosby was singing 'White Christmas' everywhere and it was so cold that it felt as if he might be proved right, but we were so busy that none of the magic seemed to rub off on us. Bob and Clive took the Greyhound bus to Toronto, where they collected the campervan and Clive firmed up plans with BTA Canada's Lewis Roberts for our projected short Canadian tour after our work in the States was over. On the way back, they physically checked the route the bus would be taking across New York State in March, by the ingenious method of fitting a wooden baton to the back of the camper which stuck up in the air. If it hit a bridge, the hinged section at the top was knocked backwards and pulled on a string in the van. It hit fifteen bridges! We wondered how we would fare in all the other states we would be passing through.

Tony wanted to spend Christmas with his parents, and flew back to England on a new BOAC 747. Through the contacts we had made, he was given an upgrade to the first-class cabin. Dick flew off in the other direction to collect the bus from the ship in Los Angeles and drive it to San Francisco. There had been dock strikes on the West Coast and, as another was looming, we agreed that it would be prudent to get the bus off the *Paralla* at its first port of call in America. Dick and the bus would meet the rest of us in San Francisco at the beginning of January. Gale had come down to New York for Christmas but was not sure if she wanted to come with us to San Francisco. She arrived just as the Bubbs were heading for the airport. We had agreed to 'house sit' for them. Gale and I were invited to a magnificent motor trade lunch in the Grand Ballroom at the Waldorf Astoria, where the first prize in the raffle was a brand new MGB donated by British Leyland. Bob and Clive arrived with the camper, which was driven to Audio Visual Innovations in West 42nd Street to pick up two 200w Fender speaker/amplifiers, six Shure microphones, mixer units and four stands – some $1,200 worth of amplification equipment that we'd purchased – to be stored at the Middletowne, with the camper parked on the lot opposite the hotel.

Christmas Eve started with a fire at 5.30 a.m. in the Tamburlane nightclub underneath the Middletowne. '250 rescued as blaze hits a midtown hotel' were the headlines in the afternoon papers, which credited the night manager with the heroic work which was, in fact, done by John and Bob – waking the residents and getting people out of the building. It took seven fire engines and 120 firemen to deal with the blaze, although by evening it was safe enough for John, Clive, Bob and Tim to continue staying there. However, they smelt of smoke for days afterwards. The day ended with Gale and me attending the Christmas Eve carol service at Saint Thomas' Church on Fifth Avenue. Halfway through the celebration, the big Gothic Revival church was plunged into darkness, leaving a single candle burning on the altar, from which tapers held by the choirboys were lit and taken to light candles placed along the aisles, slowly filling the church with warm candlelight. On Christmas Day, the Christmas spirit finally arrived. Gale and I were picked up on Staten Island by the others in the camper and driven to Jack McCullagh's house in New Jersey. In the suburbs, every house was strung with coloured lights and illuminated icicles hung from the eaves, all totally 'over the top'. Jack, a friendly, easy-going Dubliner, was the administration manager for Avis' International Division. He had been in charge of our indoctrination there and invited us to join him and his family for their traditional Christmas lunch. I had fun playing with the model railway in Jack's loft and it wasn't until 9.30 p.m. that evening, feeling full and contented, that we left. The following day, Gale and I locked the Bubbs' apartment for the last time and drove the camper into Manhattan, where Tim, Bob, Clive and John had packed up their gear and checked out of the Middletowne. At the last minute, Gale had decided to come with us, and so at 2.30 p.m. in the afternoon the six of us set off to drive the 3,000 miles to San Francisco.

The camper was grossly overloaded. As well as the six of us, it carried our personal luggage, all the paperwork I'd accumulated during my time in America, the guitars and banjos we'd taken to New York from Australia, the heavy new amplifiers and other PA equipment we'd purchased, and our sponsors' display stands and boxes of literature, including thousands of 'The Philanderers Invite You to Visit Britain' leaflets. With all this weight, it took a long time for the underpowered little engine to get up speed, and even longer for the somewhat inadequate brakes to slow the camper down again. We travelled in three pairs. Starting out, Gale and I sat in the front with me driving, Bob and Clive were in the seats behind us, and John and Tim squashed into the back, surrounded by boxes and suitcases, trying to make themselves as comfortable as they could on bench seats which doubled as beds. After about six hours, by which time we'd crossed New Jersey and were driving through Pennsylvania, we stopped for an evening meal. Then we all moved up one, with Clive driving, Bob in the passenger seat, John and Tim behind them, and Gale and I trying to sleep in the back as we droned on through the night. This routine continued for the next two days, with a stop every six or seven hours to eat a meal and change position. Our route followed the famous Route 66, but was mainly the new Interstate 40, driving through Ohio, Indiana, Illinois, Missouri, Oklahoma, Texas and New Mexico in a headlong dash to reach California before New Year's Eve. By the evening of the second day, we'd covered over 2,000 miles, crossed the Mississippi River, two time zones and the continental divide, and were in Gallup, New Mexico. The next day, we decided to slow down and do some sightseeing. We checked into a trailer park in what turned out to be a futile attempt to get a good night's sleep. The main street in Gallup was covered in garish neon signs and had as many Mexican eating houses as American ones. We had a massive Mexican meal, all beans and chillies, piled back into the camper and fell asleep, exhausted. It was cold outside and the windows were closed, the condensation quickly freezing. As the night progressed, so did our supper, and by dawn we had almost gassed ourselves and the windows were open, despite the heavy frost outside!

After breakfast in a diner, we drove to the Painted Desert and the Petrified Forest National Park, an arid desert landscape famous for its brilliant and varied colours, the hills made up of layers of rock of different shades, from rust red and ochre to steel-blue, grey and white – except that when we arrived the whole area was covered in a dusting of snow which hid most of this from us. Glowering black clouds threatened more snow. Laid down over 200 million years ago by ancient rivers, the rocks were sculpted by erosion to form flat-topped, steep-sided mesas and buttes, and the area is rich in fossils. The ground was strewn with large petrified tree trunks, the remains of logs washed down and buried in sediment and subsequently exposed by erosion, their rainbow colours being due to different minerals. By mid-afternoon, we had reached the South Rim of the 270-mile-long Grand Canyon, formed over millions of years by the Colorado River cutting through the layers of sediment that make up the Colorado Plateau. Through time the land lifted, causing the river to cut even lower, resulting in a gorge that is over a mile deep. Standing high up on the South Rim, gazing 10 miles across to the other side, we could just make out the grey-green river threading its way through the canyon far below us, a shining silver thread in the watery sunlight. The walls of the canyon have been eaten away by wind and weather to produce a magnificent and colourful landscape made up of rock layers of varying hues. Sunset tinged them rose, red and orange and, with no one else around, it became a mysterious, silent place. The grandeur was breathtaking, but it was bitingly cold and, as dusk fell, a young mule deer strolled across the road in front of us and posed for photographs as it grazed on the highway verge.

After supper in the Canyon Village, we drove to the Nevada border and at midnight on US 93 we crossed the Colorado River on the floodlit Hoover Dam, stopping to view this man-made marvel, built in the early 1930s in the teeth of the depression. A couple of hours later, we were in Las Vegas and discovered how the electricity being generated by the dam's great turbines was being used. Even at 4 a.m., all the lights were blazing and the casinos were still haunted by hard-bitten gamblers and all-night pleasure-seekers. We strolled through the downtown gaming halls, starting at the 'Golden Nugget' and ending at 'Circus Circus'; I had seen both earlier in the year in the James Bond film, *Diamonds Are Forever*. To satisfy Tim's curiosity, we drove along the strip, past 'The Sands', 'Caesar's Palace', 'The Tropicana' and the 'Desert Inn', just to see who was playing there.

As the sun rose, we followed the road to Death Valley, stopping at a 'ghost town' which boasted as many souvenir shops as it did abandoned mines and deserted buildings. As the road descended into the valley itself, we could see a range of hills enclosing the great depression, obscured by the early morning mist. The lowest point in North America, 282ft below sea level, is at Badwater Basin – at 200 square miles it contains some of the largest protected salt flats in the world, the thick salt crust taking on rough and varied forms and strange surface patterns. We didn't experience the legendary fierce temperatures – the highest ever recorded being 57°C – as it was no warmer than around 15°C. It took hours to drive through this huge, bare and seemingly endless moonscape, with the snow-capped mountains in the distance rising to over 11,000ft. By late afternoon, we were back on the main highway and heading for Bakersfield. After stopping for dinner in Fresno, and with John driving through the night, we arrived in downtown San Francisco in time for breakfast on New Year's Eve.

Dick had arrived several days earlier, having had a surprisingly uneventful time getting the bus out of the docks at Long Beach and secretly smuggling our over-height vehicle 400 miles to San Francisco along Interstate 5 without being spotted, all on his own and quite illegally, as he didn't have a permit. He arrived on Christmas Eve and booked into the Beresford Hotel in Sutter Street, which had an English-style bar called the White Horse that boasted a real log fire and which became one of our favourite haunts in the city. The bus was hidden in P&O's cavernous shed on Pier 44 until our official 'arrival' in a few days' time.

We saw in the New Year in San Francisco's colourful Chinatown, with its gay lanterns and amazing dragons and, next day, did a mixture of sightseeing and getting the bus ready for its North American debut. Gale and I moved into Dick's room – which gave everyone else somewhere to wash and shower as well – while, to save money, the others decided to sleep on the bus in the open behind the shed on the pier. Tony arrived the next evening and took a room in the Beresford. We were all back together again. A detailed schedule of our tour – which ran to over twenty pages and was continually being amended – became our bible for the next three months. BOAC had booked us into the prestigious Mark Hopkins Hotel on Nob Hill, arranging for the bus to be parked in a prominent position on the hotel's small forecourt. Named after one of the founders of the Central Pacific Railroad – whose Victorian mansion on the site was destroyed in the fire that followed the 1906 earthquake – it was completed in the 1920s and is one of San Francisco's most celebrated luxury hotels. Meanwhile, some of us were dossing on the bus. On Sunday morning, while they were washing it down, the police appeared. 'You're not sleeping on that bus here, are you?' they asked. 'Oh no,' lied Clive. Convening back in the Beresford, Tony flatly refused to share his double bed with any of them, so Tim and Dick went off to find a cheap hotel a few blocks away and booked a room in a dreadful, downmarket place called the Empress Hotel – described by Tim as being 'in the middle of the breast and bum quarter of the town' – which was so seedy that Dick eventually chose to squeeze into the camper with Bob, Clive and John, who parked on the side of the road that night after failing to find a caravan park outside the city. Years later, the Empress Hotel was home to people who were in transition from homelessness, addiction and mental illness.

The next day, we called at Hastings, the menswear store near Union Square, to collect our Austin Reed suits. We had assumed that they would be sober British business suits, but we were quite mistaken. They were, we were assured, the very latest in British fashion, and not only did we each acquire three suits, all beautifully tailored with fashionably wide lapels, but also three sports jackets, three pairs of casual trousers, plus shoes, socks, shirts and ties. All that was missing was new underwear. I ended up with a reasonably modest-looking, medium-weight, mid-grey business suit, another almost silver-coloured suit, and an amazing Prince of Wales check suit in a brown, cream and blue material, which could have been made for a bookie. They all retailed at well over $125 each. Two of my polyester and wool sports jackets were cream and mid-blue, while the third was a more conservative light brown-patterned wool mix. Suddenly, we were transformed and, although most items needed alterations – which were done within twenty-four hours – we rapidly got used to our new wardrobes, which must have been worth well over $1,000 to each of us. That evening, Tim celebrated his birthday by buying us all drinks in the 'White Horse' bar, and a quick-witted Bob quickly conjured up a cake from nowhere with twenty-nine candles blazing on it. We raised our glasses to the success of Pillock Ltd's American venture, but with little idea of how it would all work out. I was highly nervous about it all, for we would be giving our first-ever press conference the following morning, heralding the start of the biggest, most important and most highly paid venture of the whole world trip.

31

Into the American South-West

The next morning, we were back at Hastings, the menswear shop, to collect our new clothes, and were photographed in the store wearing the fine suits and jackets we'd been given, adopting the poses and deadpan expressions which we thought most suited our new role as professional male models. Alan would have hated it! Then we drove to 155 Post Street and P&O's offices for our first-ever press conference, which our sponsors considered to be a great success. The BTA had issued a press release, including a large, glossy photograph of The Philanderers and their bus, which was widely used by newspapers across America. As the US had no national newspapers, this was something that we repeated in most of the cities we visited. San Francisco's principal newspapers, the *Examiner* and the *Chronicle*, gave us good write-ups, and we posed for photographs with the bus in the street. *Travel Weekly* was there, too, as were two television stations, ABC's Channel 7, and KTVU Channel 2 – both of which carried stories about us in their news programmes – as well as several radio stations, including KSFO, San Francisco's top station, which recorded the conference and had announcements about us on-air shortly afterwards. Alan Wade, feature writer for the *Oakland Tribune*, rode around town with us on the bus: 'They're intelligent, talented, personable, these seven young men of solid British families and in whose breasts there existed a fierce desire to see the world ... (and who) regale people of many lands with song and music ...' Two of his weekly columns were devoted to fulsome appreciation of our travels and musical abilities. On Fisherman's Wharf, at British Rail's insistence, we posed with the bus next to the historic British steam locomotive, the *Flying Scotsman*, which, having hauled its British Pullman train across America, was stranded because the money had run out. Its owner, Alan Pegler, was reduced to charging people to look over the train, which had become a rather sad static exhibit. All Avis were able to rustle up for their photograph with the bus was a big Plymouth sedan, and British Leyland only managed a Triumph Spitfire. During the afternoon, publicity photos were taken for each of our sponsors, following which we drove to the opulent Mark Hopkins Hotel, checked into our highly expensive rooms and met up with BOAC's Peggy O'Keefe – who would be with us in California to distribute leaflets and add a bit of glamour in her uniform – and Barry Barratt, who would accompany us on the first leg of our tour, and who treated us all to supper at a extremely expensive steak house.

The next couple of days were just like our time in Australia with Integrity Paints. A rather sullen crowd of students watched us in the warm sunshine on 'The Commons' at San Francisco State College, but no one was really interested either in us, or in travelling to the UK with BOAC, despite my enthusiastic sales pitches between the songs. We visited two shopping malls, the Stonetown Shopping Centre and Ghirardelli Square, a former chocolate factory near Fisherman's Wharf which was now full of restaurants and boutiques, all to little effect. Our biggest achievement in San Francisco was a wildly successful open-air lunchtime concert at Union Square in the heart of the city, amidst greenery and palm trees, beneath a tall column, the Dewey Monument, crowned by the Eros-like Goddess of Victory, commemorating America's colonial adventures in the Philippines. Here we entertained a large crowd for more than an hour. 'They were enthusiastically received at Union Square,' wrote Alan Wade, complimenting us in his column, 'and Union Square audiences are known to be severely critical. Even the pigeons seemed pleased.' That evening, our last in San Francisco, we appeared at the Marines' Memorial Club, a splendid twelve-storey 1920s hotel built in the Californian Spanish Revival style on Sutter Street, at the first of the BTA's travel trade events, where a tape/slide presentation entitled 'Great Great Britain '72' was followed by half an hour's entertainment by The Philanderers. Our performance was somewhat undermined by the opening of the free bar as soon as the slide show was over, which immediately diverted a large slice of our audience. However, the slide show itself created a warm glow amongst the audience of hard-bitten travel agents, all of whom were falling in love with Britain until the slides, accompanied by an appropriately jangling soundtrack, illustrated a new and typically quirky British sport – a piano-smashing competition. Even the tough American travel agents blenched at the wanton destruction of what looked like perfectly serviceable musical instruments and found it very hard to take – the gasps from the disturbed audience were highly audible – and it took several minutes for them to settle down again and stop thinking that the British were a race of complete Philistines.

The next day, we set off for Fresno. It had been difficult getting approval to take what was described on our permit as an 'extralegal height' bus through California. The Director of Public Works of the State of California ('Ronald Reagan – Governor', the notepaper proclaimed) wrote explaining that it was only because he received confirmation of our official status from the British Tourist Authority that he was prepared to authorise our permit. As it was, we could only travel between the hours of sunrise and sunset, or 9 a.m. to 4 p.m. in San Francisco. Our permit cost us $2.50, had four pages of minutely printed regulations, and a further special restriction in bold type on the front that 'no advertising or messages will be permitted on the exterior of this bus while on any state highway'. Tony fell foul of this one on the day we were leaving, while driving the bus to a trailer park. He was in a hurry to beat the 4 p.m. deadline and, with the adverts exposed for all to see, was pulled over by a police car. The cops studied the permit and insisted that all the signs be covered immediately, which took Tony a good half an hour and involved a lot of brown paper and masking tape.

Our arrival in Fresno was covered by the local press and two television crews, who filmed us ceremonially tearing off the brown paper to reveal the bus adverts – giving our sponsors a good visual plug on the local TV stations. We entertained large crowds in two of the town's main shopping areas, the Fulton Mall and Fashion Fair Mall, where Tim and I shared the chore of doing the introductions. In the evening, we were at Pardini's restaurant at a BOAC travel trade event similar to the BTA's, except that the food was better. Fresno travel agents seemed to appreciate our music and humour, although some of the rousing Irish rebel songs in our repertoire, such as 'Dublin in the Green', had been deleted by our sponsors because of references to the IRA. We parked in front of Liz Esterly's house at 1485 East Englewood Avenue. Liz – whose cockroaches I had inherited when I was at West 17th Street – had only recently relocated from San Jose to Fresno, where she worked at the Valley Medical Centre. As she had only moved in a few days before, the place was sparsely furnished and, with the electrics not working, was lit by candles. The ever-resourceful Bob quickly got some power on and made safe the worst of the ancient wiring in her old weatherboard bungalow, while the rest of us went sightseeing. We drove in the camper deep into California's mountain forests to the Sequoia and Kings Canyon National Parks, high in the snow-covered Sierra Nevada 50 miles east. Here we saw stands of giant sequoias, including the majestic General Grant and General Sherman trees, almost 3,000 years old and the largest trees in the world, rising to heights of almost 300ft. We walked through the deep snow amongst these awesome giants, some of the oldest living things on earth. Scottish-born explorer and naturalist John Muir was one of the first Europeans to visit these remote redwood groves, and it was due largely to his efforts and those of Hale Tharp, the first European settler there, that, after fifteen years of campaigning, the area was designated as America's second National Park.

Early next morning we said goodbye to Liz, and also farewell to Gale, who was returning to Montreal. I had already incurred the formidable Ouida's wrath by allowing Gale to accompany us down to Fresno to see Liz, and our relationship with BOAC would have become severely strained had she continued with us to Los Angeles. Late that afternoon, the bus turned off lengthy, tree-lined Wilshire Boulevard onto the forecourt of one of Los Angeles' legendary hotels, the Ambassador, meeting place of film stars of the 1920s and '30s and home to the famous Cocoanut Grove nightclub. On a grimmer note, it was also where Robert Kennedy had been assassinated three-and-a-half years earlier. Tim described it as having 'the air of a mausoleum, a gigantic turreted building in pink stone which looks like a nineteenth-century folly converted to a mental institution or perhaps a prison'. He conceded that at least the beds were comfortable. We were booked in for three nights, in company with Barry Barratt and other

BOAC staff. The following day, we pulled into the parking lot of the Los Angeles Press Club on Hollywood Boulevard for our press conference. Here we met reporters from the *Los Angeles Times* and the *Herald-Examiner* – the latter quoting me as saying: 'What started out as a big joke has put us into business. Travel is the most broadening and interesting experience in the world ...', and referred to us as wearing 'mad, mod clothes and bowler hats ...' We featured on all the TV stations in Los Angeles. The NBC film crew recorded us singing 'Fly Away' over and over again, crammed into the lower deck while John drove the bus round and round the streets of Hollywood for what seemed like hours. 'They all left responsible jobs to make this trip and they'll go back to the jobs once it's over,' reporter Ray Duncan told viewers, 'but first they wanted to see the world before the world closes in on them.' Next day, Tim and I appeared on the city's top-rated breakfast TV show and were interviewed live outside the studio, in front of the bus, by the show's popular host, Ralph Story, who took a genuine interest in us and our trip and allowed us to mention all our sponsors. In contrast, the impish little man on KHJ-TV's *Tempo* programme – another breakfast news-talk show – simply went through the motions, interviewing us in front of the bus in the yard behind the studio, but we were still able to mention our sponsors.

We were in Los Angeles for just under a week, appearing at several up-market shopping centres, the best of which was Century City Plaza on Santa Monica Boulevard. We also performed at branches of Broadway Stores at the Panorama City and Northridge shopping centres. We sang in the street at Westwood Village in West Los Angeles, and to some mildly belligerent students at the San Fernando Valley State College, some of whom were not the last to somehow blame us for the troubles in Northern Ireland. We performed a couple of times at Northridge, a vast shopping complex in the San Fernando Valley that was still being built – one of many we were to visit that were billed as 'the largest in the world'. In our mail, forwarded to us from New York, was a letter from my mother: 'My cousin Nadine Dyer seems to have a new address in Pine Valley Pl, Northridge, Ca., but I don't suppose you will go anywhere near there. If you do just try to give her a ring ...' 'Talk about coincidence,' I replied, 'your letter with Nadine's address came the day before we visited, of all places, Northridge Shopping Centre ...' I phoned Nadine. She had seen us on television, lived about five minutes from where we were playing and came to see us on the bus bearing a big bottle of Scotch! The Los Angeles BTA Travel Trade presentation was held in the Mobil Building downtown, where we reprised our sing-song around the piano which had been so popular in Sydney – our stage performance having been undermined, like the one in San Francisco, by the lure of free drinks after the slide show. Our final appearance in LA was outdoors under banana fronds at a private function back at the Press Club, entertaining pre-dinner drinkers for John Sullivan, the local Avis representative. Before leaving LA we noted that the bus had 61,594 miles on the clock. We'd been so busy that this was the first mileage reading we'd actually taken in America.

Los Angeles was a wide, sprawling place, home to twelve million people, but without a real centre, and had become a victim of its own success. The wonderful climate and warm sunshine in this idyllic coastal valley, originally filled with palm trees and orange groves, made it the ideal location for the infant film industry. But now the whole place seemed to be covered in buildings, concrete and tarmac, and criss-crossed by freeways, with the surrounding hills trapping the ever-increasing pollution created by millions of cars which sat over the city as a thin, brown, hazy smog. As Los Angeles continued to grow, so did pollution levels – causing eye irritation and asthma – which were reported daily as part of TV and radio weather reports. Tim, in his bus diary, noted that unless something drastic was done, according to some ecologists, the place would become uninhabitable within ten years. Yet many residents appeared to go about their daily business seemingly blissfully unconcerned and in denial about what was happening to the environment around them.

We'd checked out of the Ambassador and, after a free supper at the Press Club following our performance there, drove the 65 miles to San Bernardino to the home of George and Evelyn Mazon, a contact of Adrian's with whom he had stayed during his visit. Tim described George as:

> A delightful wry American, a grandfather and by profession a computer engineer, and with his long lined face rounded off with an Abraham Lincoln beard, he looked the typical American backwoodsman, backed up with down-to-earth beliefs such as his firm contention that standard and premium petrol both come out of the same tank underneath the pumps.

George spoke with a slow drawl reminiscent of the cartoon character, Deputy Dawg, and he and his attractive wife, Evelyn, who cooked us a splendid breakfast the next morning, made us feel very much at home. Other than a TV interview in Palm Springs, our next commitment was at the end of the following week in Phoenix, giving us seven days for sightseeing along the way. George drove Clive and me to Palm Springs to do the live interview on KPLM-TV's early evening news magazine. We met Barry Barratt and, while Clive chatted up a local beauty queen – all teeth and lipstick – who was also appearing on the show, Barry, George and I went over the road to a diner to grab a hamburger before the interview. Wanting to add some ketchup, I shook the bottle vigorously, the cap came off, and the entire contents shot all over the counter, splattering the mirror behind the bar, as well as George and Barry, but it also ended up all over my nice new silver suit. It looked as if gangsters had machine-gunned the place. We rapidly sponged the suit to remove the ketchup, but it then looked so blotchy that we decided that the only way to disguise where the ketchup had been was to sponge the whole suit down. Ten minutes later, Clive and I were in the studio being interviewed, with my damp suit visibly steaming under the hot studio lamps. We didn't mention who had provided our clothes. The next day – with the exception of Bob, whose tolerance of sightseeing was very low – we borrowed one of George's cars and spent a day at Disneyland. Tim was so taken with the place that he devoted five pages of his bus trip diary to describing its many attractions, and John and I shot some film of the others as we wandered up Main Street. Our time with the Mazons was very relaxing and we were sorry to leave. There was so much more to see in Southern California which we would miss, and we were beginning to find that our tight three-month schedule was restricting the freedom we had previously taken for granted. On our last morning in San Bernardino, George Mendoza, a reporter from the *San Bernardino Sun*, joined us for breakfast. 'Richard King is the group's spokesman,' he wrote, '"only because he talks the most and has the biggest mouth," the other six shouted almost in chorus from the breakfast table ...' The article was headed 'Philanderers – Music a Driving Force'. '"We don't consider ourselves a professional group at all," said Clive. "We're just a load of Englishmen who are touring the world."' The article was well illustrated, with one photo captioned 'Bob Hall ... A Philanderer'! The same afternoon, a lady reporter for the *Indio Daily News*, in an eastern suburb of Palm Springs, caught up with us. '"We just don't stay in one spot long enough for the girls to get to know what nice guys we are," quipped dark-haired Bob Hall, in a clipped British accent,' said the front-page story about us the next day.

We were heading for Lake Havasu and London Bridge. Originally built in the late 1820s to cross the River Thames, it had been moved stone by stone and re-erected as a tourist attraction here in 1971. It was rumoured that the purchasers, McCulloch Oil, thought they were buying Tower Bridge and were rather disappointed when they saw what they had acquired. The bus and camper drove across the semi-desert of Southern California on Interstate 10, past groves of orange trees and date palms, crossing the Colorado River at Blythe, where we stopped for our first night alone together on the bus since leaving Australia. The next morning, we entered Arizona and paid $46.25 to register our 'foreign vehicle' and obtain the 'oversize permit' which allowed us to drive through the state on our pre-arranged route – something we would have to do on the borders of every one of the twenty states that lay ahead of us. I drove ahead of the bus on the road to Lake Havasu and set up the camera to film the bus driving past. I waited hours for them, only to find they had taken the wrong road and were already miles ahead of me in Lake Havasu City. With no way of us contacting each other – mobile phones had yet to be invented – I was fuming by the time I finally caught up with them. We arrived on Interstate 40 and the iconic Route 66, stopping the night in tiny Ash Forks before driving to the Grand Canyon, where we unexpectedly met Barry Barratt, who seemed delighted to see us. We drove the bus along the South Rim, visiting the various viewpoints and filming our progress along the way, before parking and cooking a meal overlooking the canyon's edge. The sun was shining, highlighting the contrasting layers of multi-coloured rock which form the canyon walls and causing the Colorado River to sparkle in the distance as it flowed through the deep gorge below. Tony, Dick and I stayed on for a few hours with the camper, and walked into the canyon along the Bright Angel Trail, where we met tourists on mules coming up from the canyon – a trek of 9½ miles one way and a rise in elevation of over 4,000ft. For the rest of the trip, whenever there was a natural wonder, Dick would say, 'When you've seen one Grand Canyon, you've seen them all!' The bus drove eastwards along the South Rim to Desert View, where there were breathtaking vistas into the canyon and beyond towards the Painted Desert. At just under 7,500ft above sea level, this was the highest point it had reached since crossing the mountains of eastern Turkey.

So far, the bus engine had performed perfectly, but on the way to Flagstaff it began giving trouble, which Bob traced to the drive to the injector pump, where steel shims in the flexible coupling had broken up. Undaunted, during a dark, chilly evening in a trailer park in Flagstaff, Tony and Bob made a temporary repair by unwinding a reel of masking tape around the joint, and the next morning Tony and Clive accompanied Barry Barratt, who was staying at a local motel, to Phoenix to get some replacements made. Meanwhile, I wanted to film the bus driving through beautiful Oak Creek Canyon, with its sheer walls and spectacular red sandstone formations, including the dramatic Cathedral Rock. It was a bright day with blue skies. I drove to the viewpoint at the head of the gorge to film the bus descending the canyon's hairpin bends. The bus disappeared from view and instead of stopping, as we'd arranged, they drove on, and I finally caught them up an hour later in open country way beyond the end of the canyon. I was furious and, despite everyone's protests, insisted they drive all the way back to the head of the canyon again. The result was a sequence of shots of the bus travelling through some of the most beautiful scenery in the American South West and was well worth the effort.

It was dull and cold as we crawled out of our bunks in pitch darkness at 5.30 a.m. on the morning of Friday 21 January in a dismal trailer park near Phoenix and got ready for a gruelling day's work. First stop was KTAR-TV, the NBC affiliate, where, after a quick coffee, we were on air at eight o'clock for thirty minutes, singing three numbers and giving lengthy interviews. Then, without stopping for breakfast, we were whisked off by BOAC's Tom Kraft to Hanny's, Phoenix's Hart Schaffner & Marx store, to collect another pair of slacks each, before meeting KOOL radio personality Len Ingebrigtsen in the street outside the studios to record an extended and very jokey interview. Next was a performance to a handful of people outside a local travel agents, which seemed to satisfy everyone except us. With no time for lunch, we drove to Scottsdale Fashion Square, in an upmarket Phoenix suburb, where a large and very responsive audience of shoppers clearly enjoyed our music, partly filmed for KOOL-TV's evening news programme. We were flattered when told afterwards that we were wonderful ambassadors for England. Still not having eaten, we took off for the Safari Hotel for a radio interview on KDOT, an 'easy listening' station which had its studios there. As we entered the hotel, we saw in disbelief that the grass surrounding the entrance – and anything that happened to lie on it, such as cigarette butts – had been sprayed with lurid jade-green paint! We were guests there at the Annual Dinner of the Scottsdale Chamber of Commerce, a gala affair where we ate our first and only meal of the day. After interminable self-congratulatory speeches from several self-satisfied local businessmen, we provided the cabaret before the dancing began. We each left with a small piece of English granite which had been put at every place setting and which we were told was a chip off the old London Bridge – originally stone from Haytor on Dartmoor.

Our next destination, Dallas, was over 1,000 miles east, our first commitment being on the evening of Thursday 27 January, which gave us time to sightsee along the way. We drove south to visit Old Tucson, passing through spectacular desert scenery filled with tall, gaunt saguaro cactus, some growing to a height of 50ft or more. Old Tucson had been created as a movie set in the late 1930s, was featured in many famous Westerns and TV series and, when not used for film-making, was an overpriced tourist attraction with stagecoach rides and incredible phoney gunfights in the main street to the accompaniment of piped 'Western' music, which we all found highly amusing and which caused Barry Barratt, who had come with us, to laugh uncontrollably, the tears streaming down his chubby cheeks. In contrast, we marvelled at spectacular examples of the native cactus and beautiful desert scenery in the Saguaro National Monument, staying the night in the park campground. After supper and a magnificent sunset, we sang songs round the campfire to the other campers. Crossing into New Mexico, the letter I had received from the director of operations at the State Motor Transportation Department, which stated that the requirement for an oversized permit in New Mexico would be waived, was duly stamped at Lordsburg, just over the border. The local police were very impressed that we had got such a hard to obtain dispensation. However, we had to pay for a fuel user's permit ($5) and tax on the fuel we were carrying ($1.40).

We were now travelling in three vehicles. As well as the bus and the camper, we also had Barry Barratt's rental car, and Tony and Clive regularly acted as Barry's driver. For the next couple of days, each unintentionally went its own way. After paying a quick visit to El Paso – which seemed to be an ugly industrial town – and having looked at the border crossing to Mexico, Tim and I drove north in the camper through a dry and parched landscape to visit Carlsbad Caverns, thinking the bus was ahead of us. But we were mistaken, and ended up spending the night in a cheap motel in Whites City, at the gates of the National Park, wondering what the hell had become of them. Meanwhile, back in El Paso, the rest of the crew had met the local press and TV reporters, alerted by Barry, outside a steak house called the Branding Iron, whose owner subsequently invited them all in for drinks and a huge Mexican meal. That night they got no further than the campsite near the border with Arizona. The next day, Tim and I visited the caverns and, as foreign visitors, were admitted free of charge. We were amazed by the vast underground caves with their fantastic limestone formations looking like petrified waterfalls, and the great stalactites and stalagmites, some combined into huge columns, all glistening with dripping water in the subdued artificial light. The biggest cavern is one of the largest underground caves in the world, and nearby are situated an underground cafeteria and restrooms, the waste from which is pumped back to the surface some 700ft above. Later that day, the others also reached the caverns, where hundreds of thousands of bats emerge at twilight from the gaping cavern mouth in a great fluttering cloud. We finally congregated for a drink with Barry in the bar of the Ramada Motor Inn at Big Spring – 'Capital of the World', I was informed by a large and rather loud Texan in a ten-gallon hat. 'How do you like America?' he asked. 'I like America fine but I like Texas better,' I replied. He then insisted on buying us all drinks. The next morning, we all set off for Dallas, where a much more intensive stage of our American trip would begin which would make everything we'd done so far seem like a holiday.

32

Freezing in America: From Tailors in Texas to a Pawnshop in Pittsburgh

The big, flat, open emptiness of West Texas slowly gave way to more wooded countryside as we approached Dallas. The blue skies which had accompanied us for most of the 2,000 miles since leaving San Francisco clouded over and the daytime temperatures plummeted to below freezing. The local BOAC representative, Chris Haas, a straightforward and unassuming young Englishman from Surrey with a pretty and heavily pregnant American wife, Lucy, insisted that we park the bus at his house during our three-day stay in Dallas. It was too cold to work on the bus, Bob decided, and it was several more weeks before he managed to fit new shims to the injector pump coupling – which, to our relief, soldiered on held together with a wodge of masking tape – and replace the washers on the wheel studs which kept the back tyres away from the springs with some spacers he'd had specially made. Tony, Dick and I visited the *Dallas*

Times Herald, where we were photographed posing with the BTA's large Triang model bus for an article headed 'The British Are Coming In Round-the-World Tour'. That night at the Sheraton Dallas Hotel, we finally persuaded the BTA to keep the free bar at their travel trade show closed until we'd finished our performance, with the result that we received a warm reception from a lively and appreciative Texan audience, who had nothing else to divert them. The following morning, it was so cold that we had to push the bus along the street outside Chris and Lucy's house to bump-start it, much to the surprise of their neighbours. Several of the local TV stations filmed us performing at the American Airlines terminal at Dallas and Fort Worth's international airport, and press photographers covered our afternoon performance at Town East Mall. Here, we could hardly keep a straight face. Tim noted:

> Barry, having heard of Tony's alleged predilection for large girls, amused himself by seeking the largest girl in the shopping centre and bringing her to watch the group playing, and then wickedly pointing Tony out to her. This inevitably had everyone in the group in a fit of ill-suppressed laughter, but it certainly cheered the performance up.

The cherubic Barry was soon to leave us, though, and return to New York. Press adverts heralded our appearances at Precision Motors, the local Triumph dealership, and at the *Dallas Morning News* free travel show, where we were the 'star' performers for a capacity audience in a large school auditorium. We saw little of Dallas, though, other than the venues at which we played, and were so tired that when we did have some free time we simply spent it resting. It was a pattern that was to continue throughout the rest of our tour of the US.

We left Dallas on a freezing Saturday afternoon and headed for Austin, the state capital, through flat, scrubby cattle country with big skies on a straight, open road. We stayed at a 'Kampgrounds of America' campsite. There are over 600 of these privately owned KOA campgrounds across America, and we were quite taken with their splendid facilities, which included good-quality showers, an extensive laundry with coin-operated washing machines and dryers, a small grocery store, often a comfortable TV lounge and sometimes even a restaurant. At $3.50 a night for two, plus 50 cents for each extra person, they were good value, and whenever we stayed in them we usually managed to do all our laundry and catch up on letters home while watching the clothes tumble dry! On Sunday evening, we played to a lot of empty seats in the Texas Union's huge ballroom at the University of Texas in Austin. Poor publicity had resulted in a small and unresponsive audience, and when we finished we were told that Sunday was probably the worst night for a concert there. The next morning, we were invited to the state capitol building, where we posed with the bus for the press at the foot of the capitol steps and were honoured by being given scrolls proclaiming that we were appointed Honorary Citizens of Texas. We were given a tour of the impressive 85-year-old building, which houses the State Legislature and the office of the Governor. The mosaic floor under the great dome shows the State's Great Seal, surrounded by the seals of the six countries whose flags have flown over Texas – Spain, France, Mexico, the Republic of Texas, the Confederacy and the US. It took three hours to drive the 100 miles to College Station, home of the Texas Agricultural and Mechanical University, where we appeared on the local TV station's women's chat show that afternoon. The host, sparkly-eyed Betty-Jo Smith, took such a shine to us – and to Bob in particular – that she invited us to park at her home that night, where we were set upon by her seven children, fed all the hamburgers we could eat and given a hearty breakfast the next morning. We were to perform at the university, where her husband was head of the psychology department. We really enjoyed our concert that night, playing to a large and responsive audience of Aggies (as the college students were known), believing this to be our most successful campus appearance so far in America.

In Houston, the BOAC representative, Jock Anderson, had booked us into the prestigious Houston Oaks Hotel, which was way beyond our budget. However, the canny Scot, anticipating that we would baulk at the price, had already lined up alternative accommodation for us at the much cheaper Surrey House Motor Hotel, near the Astrodome, Houston's multi-purpose domed indoor sports stadium. We spent six nights in Houston, our five days of hectic activity starting with a shambolic press conference in the car park of the Sakowitz Department which was called off, then resurrected, and at which no one from the press appeared until an NBC film crew turned up to cover our booked lunchtime appearance in Sakowitz's restaurant. The reporter, Elsa Ransom, petite and charming, interviewed us on the bus and asked some pretty naive questions: 'How do you get the bus from one country to another?' Answer: 'We drive it, actually ...' 'Do you have any interesting tales to tell about your travels?' Answer: 'I suppose we have one or two ...', and the question almost every reporter asked us: 'How did you come to get the name "The Philanderers" in the first place?' Answer: 'It was pure wishful thinking ...'

We collected even more suits and sports jackets at Leopold, Price & Rolle's menswear store, who featured us in a big half-page advert promoting Austin Reed and our appearance in The Galleria shopping centre, where their store was situated. These were to be modelled by us at a prestigious fashion show at the National Men's Sportswear Association's Convention at the Astroworld Hotel. We were interviewed and sang 'live' on three more TV shows and a couple of radio stations, and performed one evening in the popular pub-like bar upstairs at the Surrey House – where we met Pam Gernsbacher, an English woman who insisted that when we reached New Orleans we must park outside her home there – and gave concerts at two colleges. When we appeared at the stylish Galleria shopping mall – which incorporated a large indoor skating rink – we found that nobody knew how to turn off the awful piped music when it was time for us to play. There was another well-received BTA presentation and a reception and dinner held at Houston's World Trade Center hosted by the British Consul General, Roy Dean. Here, a stony-faced Ouida Huxley, who had just arrived from New York, obviously disapproved of my risqué comments and jokes when introducing our songs, although most of the guests laughed heartily.

By Friday we were exhausted but, on Saturday, which dawned dark and rainy, we still had to appear at the menswear convention for Austin Reed. Before lunch, our first brief performance in the large conference hall – designed to whet the appetite of the press to come to the show in the afternoon – drew a rapturous response. We shared the bill with Johnny Carson, host of NBC's legendary *Tonight Show*, who came on straight after us. A consummate professional, he quickly had the audience eating out of his hand promoting Hart, Schaffner & Marx. Then came lunch, when each of us was required to 'host' a table – Bob, to his delight, had the attractive Elsa Ransom on his. We had rehearsed our afternoon appearance the day before with Peter Reed, over from England to promote the family business, and the firm's young American manager, Terry Kalish. Peter sat on the stage with a borrowed bulldog at his side describing the clothes in a smooth English accent as we minced up and down the catwalk mixed in with professional male models. We didn't take it seriously, sending things up by striking exaggerated poses, which at first surprised and then delighted the jaded audience of press and buyers. We then topped this by unexpectedly coming on and singing. As we finally left the stage amid wild applause and cries of 'More!' echoing round the room, we were urged back for an encore – Austin Reed and The Philanderers had given the audience far more than just a fashion show. Tim wrote:

> The Hart Schaffner and Marks people – and Ouida, were ecstatic with the success of the whole thing – indeed The Philanderers had saved the afternoon from being a complete drag – and Richard's introductions laced with lines like 'The suit, subtly styled to point up Tim's deformities' ... were spot-on.

That evening, while Bob, Clive and John went off for a night on the town with girls from the pub at the Surrey House, the rest of us enjoyed the warm glow of a highly successful day as dinner guests of Peter Reed and Terry Kalish, where we discovered that Peter, who was not much older than us, had hitch-hiked overland to India some years before.

Our next assignment was in New Orleans. Crossing the state line into Louisiana, for the first time we were required to have a police escort. Interstate 10 was unfinished, so we were routed on US 190, which was broken down and potholed. In murky weather, we passed through the swampy Mississippi Delta country, a state trooper leading the way with the blue lights on his car flashing in the teeming rain, our escorts being changed every 20 miles or so. Pam Gernsbacher lived at 12 Central Drive, Metairie, about 5 miles from the old French Quarter and, taking up her offer, we parked outside her house for the one night we were in New Orleans. She dished up a splendid crabmeat gumbo before we set off to play to the students at Tulane University in Der Rathskeller, about 4 miles away, which resembled a German beer hall. After initial disinterest, we eventually gathered a big student audience, who warmed to our eccentric English folk music. The second half of our performance was recorded for WTUL, the student radio station. Afterwards, John, Clive, Dick and Tony investigated the nightlife in the French Quarter in company with some college girls and found some authentic jazz, while the rest of us, exhausted, returned to Pam's house. Next day, BOAC publicity man Bob Klan had fixed an appearance on the *Midday Show* at WDSU-TV at studios deep in the French Quarter, but had made no arrangements for parking the bus, and the police refused to let us take it there without somewhere to put it. I'd already driven there in the camper with Tony and Tim, so Pam Gernsbacher came to the rescue and ferried the others to the studio from her house, together with her son Kim and his friend, who had both skipped school to watch us. After placating the show's host, a precious, fussy little man called Al Shea, we played a couple of numbers, I was interviewed, and we closed the show to great acclaim with a burst of 'Wild Rover'. We left New Orleans less than twenty-four hours after arriving there, disappointed at having seen little or nothing of one of the most historic settlements in North America.

There were less than forty-eight hours before our press conference in Atlanta, 500 miles north and, on the way, after a night in a trailer park in Mobile, we made a pre-arranged stop at the Alabama State Tourist Office. The article in the *Mobile Register* read:

A tall bus swerved into the parking lot of a Mobile shopping centre on Wednesday, and seven hyperactive young

> Englishmen hopped out, smiled flashingly, exchanged
> greetings and gifts with the natives, offered a lightning
> tour of their vehicle, posed for pictures and dashed away.

... which pretty accurately described our visit to Mobile. After photographs were taken, we were off east again – our Alabama state trooper escort's car flashing red lights this time – along Interstate 85. Tony and I had driven ahead in the camper, but it broke down and we had to get a bracket made for the dynamo before we could continue. Bus permit problems in Georgia held us up still further and, with the press conference now aborted because of the delays, we arrived in Atlanta late on Thursday afternoon, just in time for the BTA travel trade presentation at the Sheraton Biltmore Hotel. We parked that night at a girls' university, Massey College, amid their small fleet of ex-London Transport RHL double-decker buses (a low-bridge model that, unlike ours, was within the state height limit and was about the same age as Hairy Pillock 2), and a group of female students took us for a late-night trip to Underground Atlanta, the city's popular nightspot. The next day started at 8 a.m. at a TV station, WSB-TV, to appear on *Today in Georgia*, followed by a performance in a hall packed with appreciative teenage girls at Massey College. By an amazing coincidence, our host, an Englishman, Reg Mitchell, the director of fashion studies, was in Vienna in October 1969. 'I remember seeing you lot playing in the street there and thinking: "Those lads won't get that bus very far,"' he told us. We then visited the Perimeter Shopping Mall, out in the country amid wooded rolling hills, where they seemed really delighted to have us play, and in the evening gave a concert in a huge empty hall at the Georgia Institute of Technology, which was made bearable by the busload of girls we'd brought with us from Massey College, who formed most of the audience and who partied with us afterwards in their dormitories until late. During the night, a thief crept onto the bus and ripped from its mounting on the back platform the body of the brass peacock we'd been presented with by the staff of New Delhi's Oberoi Intercontinental Hotel. It was a souvenir we dearly treasured and we were deeply upset that it had been stolen. The next morning, we left Atlanta for Athens, 70 miles north-east, and a performance at the University of Georgia, driving through a wintry land of fields and forests, a pretty landscape and one which altered little as we drove on through the Carolinas.

The next ten days followed the same pattern: up early to appear on a breakfast TV show, a shopping mall appearance, press and radio interviews, and one or two college performances each day, then on to the next town. The discipline of having to perform every day, some days playing for several hours, had tightened up and improved our act no end. Barry Ward, BOAC's local representative who accompanied us, seemed to have a special relationship with all the exclusive girls' colleges along our route, and had arranged for us to give concerts at a great many of them, some of whom provided us with accommodation. Our itinerary took us to Greenville, Charlotte, Winston Salem, Greensboro, Chapel Hill, Danville, and Richmond. Also tagging along was Tony Brazil, British Rail's terribly British representative. Night after night we found ourselves playing to audiences of attractive young females, who then invited us all to parties. We all succumbed to the charms of these nubile young students. Tony, finding himself alone with a couple of sexy teenagers late one evening, jokingly suggested an orgy and found himself with more than he bargained for! During the 650-mile journey between Atlanta and Washington, we were appearing on TV almost daily and were featured in dozens of local newspapers, all of which sang our praises. The correspondent in the *Guilfordian*, the newspaper of Guilford College, Greensboro, wrote:

Last night in the Union Lounge, we were treated to over
an hour of good time music and fun by 'The Philanderers,'
a group of touring-for-the-hell-of-it-just-to-see-the-world-
and-have-a-good-time musicians ... singing English and
Irish bawdy folk songs in a style that has seemed to have
disappeared for too long a time. Clowning around, cracking
dry British humor, and damn good picking, they thrilled
us ... The place was packed and walking in late made no
difference, since they made everyone feel so good. It's so
nice when people that full of life perform so well, and their
feeling goes out to all in the audience ...

Our scrapbook was filling up with press cuttings of fulsome
praise for our performances.

While we were in North Carolina, Bob replaced the dynamo
brushes – the batteries had not been charging properly –
and changed the injector pump shims. Bill Homewood took
over as our BOAC representative, and Roy Hopkins, head of
BOAC's Washington office, also appeared. The weather was
becoming increasingly cold, and by the time we reached
Richmond, the frequent, cold rain slowly turned to snow. We
were booked into the Holiday Inn there – the big sign outside
saying, 'Welcome The Philanderers.' In a coffee shop one wet
afternoon, Tim and I fed the jukebox with enough money for
it to play 'Take Me Home, Country Roads' over and over again
to enable us to write down the words, but we failed to realise
until it was too late that, no matter how much money you
put in, it would only play the record once. I finally learned the
song, and raised a laugh when we first performed it at the
Virginia Commonwealth University because of my English
accent, sounding quite unlike John Denver, whose record was
then high up in the charts. By the time I'd finished, though,
our audience were singing along with us and cheering.
Then it was on to Washington, the nation's capital, driving

through open parkland and stands of leafless trees on a dull, gloomy afternoon.

In Washington we did more damage to the bus than anywhere else on our world tour. It was beginning to snow. Tony, Dick and I drove in the camper to the Holiday Inn we'd been booked into just over the Maryland border in Chevy Chase, where we had coffee, with the endless free refills that seemed standard practice in America, looking through the coffee shop window at the worsening weather and waiting for the others to arrive. For some reason they had decided to drive through the centre of Washington. The snow turned into a blizzard as they neared the city, obscuring the view from the frozen upstairs windows, apart from a small section kept partly clear with the help of a large candle. It was getting dark and the road dipped into an underpass. The blizzard and the snow-covered front window made it almost impossible for Tim to see properly. Using the phone, he told Clive, who was driving, that this one was too close to call, but to give it a try, anyway. Clive edged the bus slowly underneath and, just as it seemed as if it would make it, there was a sickening crunch and a screaking sound. The bridge had torn a great hole in the roof, smashing the top of the wardrobe and shattering the centre support for the right-hand bunks. Clive stopped. Bob and John tried to hold up the traffic while Clive reversed backwards to reach the exit ramp. Snow was already falling into the upper deck and blankets had to be stuffed into the gaping hole as the bus drove bleakly through the blizzard to the Holiday Inn. Here the snow was several inches deep. I was livid at their stupidity in not having taken the ring road as we'd agreed, and a miserable evening full of recriminations and self-doubt followed.

The hole in the roof featured heavily in some of the TV coverage from the Washington press conference, but mostly they filmed us singing on the pavement outside BOAC's

Farragut Square office in front of the bus. A good number of radio stations and papers, including the *Washington Post*, covered our story and promoted our appearances in the capital. Our four days in Washington were bitterly cold, with no time for sightseeing other than an extended photoshoot on a dismal afternoon in front of the Capitol building – the top of the dome is the highest point of any building in the city – and an hour spent filming the bus driving past Washington's famous landmarks, most of which are situated in the park-like downtown area around the National Mall. The centre of Washington is very impressive, being full of iconic buildings and monuments, but is surrounded by an awful urban sprawl and slums in a sad state of disrepair. The roads were in bad condition, too, half of them being dug up for the construction of the city's new metro system. There was another BTA evening, performances in front of college and shopping centre audiences and, on our last day, a booking at Precision Motors, the British Leyland dealership in Rockville, Maryland. They had smartened the place up for us, even putting down a red carpet in the gents' toilet. Bob, as resourceful as ever, had quickly sussed out that they had the materials and tools to enable him to repair the bus roof so, while we were performing, Bob and John changed into their working clothes, took the bus to the yard behind the showrooms and set to work. The rest of us were about to start playing to a select audience of salesmen and friends when an unassuming little man stepped up to the microphone. We thought he was someone from one of our sponsors when he said, 'I'd like to welcome these young men from England ...' but quickly changed our minds as he continued, 'but I must protest about the presence of British troops in Ireland ...' Tim and I immediately dived on the amplifiers and turned them off. We'd already had problems at some of the more militant colleges we'd visited with students supporting the IRA, all of whom, when we talked to them, seemed to know little or nothing about the real issues in Ulster. The same applied to this little man when we spoke with him afterwards. Then a band of IRA supporters marched into the showroom with placards proclaiming 'End Internment Now', but several heavily built motor dealers swiftly hustled them out of the door. Meanwhile, in the yard at the back, John and Bob were marooned on the roof of the bus by other protesters chanting 'Freedom for Ireland' and even more abusive slogans at them. Clive and Dick tried to reason with some of them but the debate sank to the level of 'What are you singing Irish songs for? Sing your own bloody songs ...' However, when the police arrived, the protestors soon melted away.

The next day, we drove to Philadelphia. We were booked into a large room with seven small beds in it in the impressive 1920's Benjamin Franklin Hotel, in Philadelphia's historic downtown area, a small enclave in what Tony described as a 'ghastly place, a very ugly city full of people who are almost mad – it is foul'. Apart from the usual TV performances and another BTA reception – this time in the city's famous Barclay Hotel on Rittenhouse Square – The Philanderers' most memorable appearance was at Wanamaker's Department Store. There, to our amazement, we found ourselves playing in the organ loft of the biggest pipe organ in the world, suspended some 40ft above the store's Grand Court, the main shopping floor, where we followed the resident organist, who did his bit for Britain by playing things like 'A Foggy Day in London Town'. The Wanamaker Organ was a Philadelphia institution, originally built in 1904 for the St Louis World Fair, but the organ loft was the worst place for us to sing as we had absolutely no contact with our audience, being perched so high above them. Few of them had any idea where the singing was coming from and we soon stopped. The following day, we drove along the Pennsylvania Turnpike to appear at a shopping mall in a town with the strange name of King of Prussia (named after the historic local pub), not far from Valley Forge, the famous site of George Washington's headquarters during the War of Independence, which was now a Historic State Park. We saw nothing of this, however, as we spent most of our time trying to get the bus off the turnpike, built in the 1940s with dangerously low bridges. Jacob B. Kassab, Secretary of Transportation for the Commonwealth of Pennsylvania, confirming our route, wrote that we would not be able to travel on the turnpike due to our height, but Clive, in charge of our routes and permits, seemed to have missed this, and it took two police cars and a hair-raising 2-mile drive in the wrong direction up the turnpike's emergency lane to divert us away from an impassably low railway bridge.

The rest of our 300-mile journey to Pittsburgh was along the old road, past rolling farming country dusted with snow, through pretty little towns and villages into a vivid red sunset. We spent the night in the small town of Lebanon and later the next morning pulled onto the side of the wooded road to enjoy a cooked meal, which I filmed. It was the last meal we would ever eat together on the bus. The filming ended with Tony opening the bonnet and pushing the fan blade round to turn the crankshaft before the bus would start, something we had to do regularly, because some teeth had sheared off from the starter motor gear-ring.

We arrived at Pittsburgh's Sheraton Motor Inn, having driven through the beautiful Appalachian countryside, with the sun glistening off the snowy fields and hills and making the tumbling river that ran beside the road sparkle. Clive, John and Tim had driven ahead in the camper to find a replacement for Clive's banjo, which had been stolen after our performance at Washington's Trinity College, souring Clive's previously positive view of American students. Clive eventually discovered a pawnshop which had one which he bought for $40. Tim, a knowledgeable aficionado of popular music, delightedly wrote about this using the lyrics of the old Guy Mitchell hit, having Clive buying it at 'a pawnshop on the corner in Pittsburgh, Pennsylvania'. The next day, the weather turned, rain lashed down and by nightfall it was freezing and snowing hard. We'd appeared on KDKA-TV's *The Marie Torre Show*, when I was interviewed by Marie Torre herself, one of America's first women TV news presenters, who was famously jailed in the 1950s for contempt of court for not revealing the source of her story about Judy Garland turning down a TV show because she thought she was too fat. Accompanied by local BOAC man, Lee Vetlesen, a Norwegian, and John Lampill of BOAC's PR department, we then performed at a shopping centre and finished the day at yet another BTA reception before returning to the Sheraton in the camper in a blizzard, slithering about on icy, snow-covered roads, thankful that we weren't driving in the bus and had warm hotel rooms to go to. It was early March, and bad weather ahead of us could easily disrupt our heavy schedule. We'd run ourselves ragged and our reserves of stamina and tolerance of each other were at an all-time low. Our next appearance was in Columbus the following evening, over 180 miles away. I was beginning to wonder if we – and the bus – could continue to stand the pace, or whether we had bitten off more than we could chew.

33

The American Tour: The Mid-West in March and the Auto Show in April

When we awoke, the world outside was silent and bright, the frozen ground covered by over 3ins of snow. With two thirds of our tour of the US now behind us, we still had a lot of miles to cover and a tight timetable to keep. The door on the back platform of the bus was frozen solid. The roller shutter door opened sideways, and the bottom channel was full of snow and ice. Bob climbed into the cab, squeezed through the small sliding glass window into the lower saloon and worked on it from inside, while the rest of us got kettles of boiling water from the Motor Inn's kitchen to melt the ice. Twenty minutes later, it finally opened – but then the bus wouldn't start. Eventually, a friendly local trucker gave us a tow and the bus was on its way. Clive and John were to follow with the camper, but that wouldn't start either. We'd been having problems with the camper in cold weather and often had to push-start it. This time they had to call a garage out, and even then the mechanics failed to start it. Clive, who tended to leave things until the last minute, still had to collect the bus travel permits for West Virginia and Ohio, and arranged to meet us on the West Virginia border. This sort of thing had occurred before, resulting in delays and frustrations, but this time we were working to a really tight deadline. With the camper refusing to start, Clive used his initiative, rented a car from Avis, picked up the permits and – hours late – chased off to catch up with the bus, leaving John to sort out the camper. Meanwhile, Hairy Pillock 2 and its crew had been sitting in the snow on the West Virginia state line with tempers fraying. Clive, John, the camper and the permits were nowhere in sight. Against my better judgement, we decided to drive through grey and snowy West Virginia without the required papers, and on into Ohio. I was extremely uneasy about using the bus illegally and eventually insisted that we stop at a public phone and find out what had happened to Clive. Several calls later, I'd established that our permits had been issued, that Clive was on his way, but that we would be breaking the law if we continued further without the documentation on board. An hour later, Clive appeared. Now with the correct papers, the bus lumbered on to Columbus, hours late, but there was still no sign of John and the camper with all our sound equipment. Fearing he'd broken down, Clive and I retraced our steps in the car but couldn't find him. But John, having got the camper fixed by another garage, had driven hell for leather to Columbus, somehow missing the bus on the way, and was already at the Ohio State Campus when the bus rolled up, half an hour after the advertised start time of our concert there. With few people attending the poorly promoted event, it didn't matter much, and the evening was a bit of an anticlimax. Having not had a proper meal since breakfast, we then found that our campus accommodation had fallen through and instead we were booked into a Sheraton Motor Inn several miles away. The suggested route there was blocked by a low bridge and, as we groped our way around dimly lit suburban Columbus, tempers flared and an almighty row broke out. Even Bob – normally immune from such things – lost his rag. I began to despair as we retired to bed totally fed up with each other's company and shortcomings. Everything seemed to be falling apart.

What happened on that Friday in early March was typical of about a quarter of all the days we worked for our American sponsors. Problems regularly arose. Some appearances were so casually arranged and poorly promoted that the venues didn't even know we were coming. There were delays in getting our over-height vehicle permits – often, it seemed, due to Clive's laid-back attitude, with him apparently doing just enough for us to escape serious trouble. Accommodation was sometimes re-arranged at the last minute without our knowledge, and our sponsors regularly had unrealistic expectations and made unreasonable demands of us, often because their local representatives were badly briefed or lacked interest in the promotion and regularly underestimated the time it took to get the bus anywhere, failing to appreciate the problems caused by low bridges. Early on we took this in our stride but, as the pressure relentlessly mounted, our ability to cope was sorely tried, and nowhere in our schedule was there the opportunity for us to rest and recover. However, two-and-a-half years of working and living together, and our past experience of overcoming setbacks, enabled us to deal with it all and carry on. Even though we were often exhausted and exasperated with each other, the strong bond that had developed between us kept us going – we were, indeed, a 'Band of Brothers'.

The 400 miles from Pittsburgh to Chicago took us through Columbus, Cincinnati and Indianapolis, visiting more shopping malls, TV studios and college campuses, including the University of Indiana at Bloomington. In Cincinnati, we were guests on NBC's locally popular entertainment show, *Bob Braun's 50-50 Club* – which was networked throughout the mid-west and always attracted visiting 'A-list' entertainers. Bob Braun interviewed me at length in front of a large studio audience of blue-rinsed ladies, who thought The Philanderers were wonderful and applauded our singing wildly, including 'Galway City', another new song, introduced by John on the banjo, and we came away with an excellent audio tape of our performance. The next day, in Indianapolis, we appeared on WFBM-TV's long-running music and chat show hosted by Jim Gerard, another local celebrity, and unexpectedly received a cheque for $112.50 for our trouble. It was the only TV appearance for which we were paid on the whole tour. Early that evening in the Indianapolis Hilton, Tim and I were cheered up watching *The Wizard of Oz* on the big colour television in our room and, leaving for supper afterwards, found the others waltzing along the hotel corridor, arms linked. They had also been watching it, and together the seven of us, our spirits lifted, skipped through the dark, empty streets of Indianapolis singing 'We're off to see the Wizard ...', ending up bemusing the waitresses in a large, cheap restaurant with our clowning and high spirits. I went to bed that night in a happy glow, sensing for once that indefinable something which unites a collection of individuals and turns them into something more than the sum of their parts.

The next day, Dick, Clive and John drove the camper to Chicago, 200 miles north, with the bus following on. BTA's Jim Turbayne took great delight in warning me about all the difficulties he had had with Chicago's low rail bridges during their London bus tour twenty years before, and for hours that afternoon we had a similar battle with the city's

extensive rail network. Time and again, low bridges blocked
our progress, and we finally arrived for the BTA presentation
at the Ambassador West Hotel fifteen minutes late, Bob
having driven all around the houses for the whole afternoon.
We rated Chicago as the best of all the events we had played
at for the BTA, for the travel agents gave us and the BTA the
warmest reception we had yet experienced – although they
were, like all the others, stunned into silence by the piano-
smashing sequence in the slide presentation. The youthful
Dick Batchelor, head of the BTA in the mid-west, served them
Pimm's and fish and chips, and the evening was a startling
success. When it was over we walked across State Street to
the Ambassador East, where we crashed out in the vast suite
of rooms BOAC had booked for us there.

After the next morning's press conference, with the bus
parked outside BOAC's offices in Michigan Avenue, Dick, Bob
and I travelled with the BTA to Milwaukee, 90 miles north
along Lake Michigan, to prepare for the BTA reception there.
Tony and Tim, accompanied by BOAC's rather cynical Tom
Kraft, the tubby Texan whom we'd first met in Arizona and
who caused us problems by continually misrepresenting us to
Ouida Huxley in New York, saying that we were difficult and
uncooperative, took the bus to park it outside Tom's home
in the north-west suburb of Schaumburg, in readiness for
taking it to the nearby Woodfield Mall the next day. They were
followed by John in the camper, who would then drive them
to Milwaukee. Clive, meanwhile, had flown to Detroit for the
day, where he had to physically check the bus route before a
Michigan permit would be granted. Driving along the recently
resurfaced freeway towards Chicago's O'Hare Airport, Tony
and Tim got the bus wedged under the Montrose Avenue
overpass, where Interstates 90 and 94 divide. They were
stuck in the fourth of six lanes, with cars whizzing past on
both sides. John went off in the camper to alert the police,

but Tom Kraft, assured by the Highway Department that all bridges on the freeway were over 14ft 6in and who had been making caustic comments about Tim and Tony being too cautious, freaked out, leapt off the bus, ran across the road and disappeared up the exit ramp bank. A passing press photographer took a picture which appeared in the following day's *Chicago Daily News* with the caption, 'Sticky Wicket'! Very soon, half-a-dozen big yellow emergency trucks came to the rescue and blocked the four nearside lanes, enabling Tony to reverse back to the exit ramp. Tom Kraft reappeared and the bus was eventually parked outside his house. A few weeks later, BOAC's Chicago office received a hefty bill from the Ohio Department of Highways to cover the incident, but responded citing our permit and nothing more was said. We did our bit for the BTA in Milwaukee and the next day appeared at the Woodfield Mall. It was huge – the largest in the world by floor area, we were told – and in a vast indoor amphitheatre played to more than a thousand people, then retired to the nearby Holiday Inn for the night before heading for Detroit.

The camper had to be returned to Toronto, where it was to feature in a motor show, and I set out to drive the 550-mile journey there at 4 a.m. the next morning, dropping Tim off in Detroit to rendezvous with Jan Reynolds, a girl he'd met in BOAC's New York office. Gale flew down from Montreal and we had a short weekend in Toronto away from the others and managed to see something of Canada's largest city. 'Richard looks awfully tired, and is as thin as a rake,' Gale wrote to her mother. 'He also seems much older ... I'm sure this tour has taken a great toll on him.' I flew back to Detroit on Sunday afternoon and met up with the others at the Sheraton-Cadillac Hotel, where the man at the reception desk greeted us as old friends. He remembered booking us in at the Ambassador in Los Angeles and had just relocated to Detroit. That evening, The Philanderers gave a candlelit concert to an elegant, middle-aged audience at a large and impressive historic house, now a War Memorial community centre on the shore of Lake St Clair in upmarket Gross Pointe. Rocky Yates, BOAC's local man, was delighted by our performance and how we represented the airline. The next morning, in pouring rain, we arrived for our press conference. No one came except *The Detroit News*, which resulted in a rather splendid photo filling the next day's front page: 'Seven British troubadours, on a world tour in a double-decker bus, dashed for cover from the raindrops to the BOAC office on Washington Boulevard in Downtown Detroit yesterday.' It listed all our appearances in the city. The paper's fashion writer did a big piece about us, illustrated with our po-faced fashion photo taken in San Francisco. By the next evening we'd played at two more shopping malls, the Wayne State University and another BTA presentation. It was Clive's birthday, and we'd secretly arranged for the hotel to make and decorate a cake which, unfortunately, they then dropped on the floor. Discovering this after 11 p.m., Bob and I decided to take immediate action. Much to the concern of our friend on the desk – who worried about us wandering around late at night in dangerous downtown Detroit – we shot out of the front door, hailed a cab and asked the driver to take us to a cake shop. Instead, he took us to a bakery and a freshly baked sponge cake was swiftly iced and decorated for us. Hurrying back to the bar, arriving just before midnight, we entered triumphantly with Clive's cake, which we then immediately demolished. Tim was sharing a room with Tony, who, like the rest of us that night, had had a few drinks too many. The street lamp outside gave the room an eerie glow and Tim woke with a start as Tony climbed out of his bed (Tim told us the next day), lifted the seat cushion of an armchair, peed into it, lowered the cushion again and returned to bed. Tony had no recollection whatsoever of this and was convinced that the telltale traces in the chair were Tim's, who had invented the story to conceal his own nocturnal activities.

On another damp, dreary day, the countryside west of Lake Erie was flat and monotonous as we drove south to Toledo, where we joined the Ohio Turnpike. The 40mph minimum speed here was rigidly enforced by the Ohio State Highway Patrol and our trooper escorts gave us some difficulty by driving 2 miles an hour faster than our top speed. After some 200 miles, we arrived at Cleveland's Sheraton Motor Inn. The manager gave us a ridiculously low rate for the hotel's very spacious but down-at-heel penthouse suite, which was awaiting refurbishment. That evening, being urged on by everyone else, Tony finally shaved off his unkempt beard, leaving him with a rather dashing moustache. TV filming and a BTA reception at the Keg and Quarter filled the next day, following which it was St Patrick's Day. We were advised not to go out, as US elements of the IRA had been stirring up anti-British feeling, but we still appeared on a couple of TV shows and at another shopping mall that day, shepherded around by BOAC's Mike MacNamara, a rather nervous Irishman. An extra appearance he'd privately arranged was at a party given by an expatriate club, 'Britons in America', in a prosperous Cleveland suburb, where people were celebrating the Irish festival by being British. They were all from the Midlands and the North of England, and each song we sang was received with prolonged and boisterous applause. We caused a bit of a riot with 'Toe-a-Tapper' and 'Farmer's Boy', two rather earthy, unaccompanied songs involving a lot of innuendo and suggestive gestures. I explained that we had learned them from a group we called 'The Venereal Folk Three', who had sung them at the Deers Hut some years before. Their real name was 'The Fennario Folk Three', I said, but we thought our name suited them better. In the gaps between our half-hour spots we were fussed over by the women, bought drinks by the men and fed by the club. We hadn't had this kind of attention since performing in working men's clubs in England. Fortunately, we'd left the bus in the Sheraton's parking lot and were being driven back to the hotel by BOAC's staff. As we left, the organisers slipped us a cheque for $105. It was like returning to our roots, but we were dog-tired and happy to get back to Cleveland and our hotel, only to be kept up drinking by Mike until 2.30 a.m.!

The south side of Lake Erie, muddy grey in colour but seldom in view, was an endless snowscape dotted with woods and farmsteads. The bus crossed into New York State without the permit we needed, but we carried on anyway. After an overnight stop at a roadside diner and an early start, I was driving the bus with Bob navigating and everyone else in bed when we were pulled over by a couple of state troopers. Luckily, they turned out to be just curious. 'How high is this thing?' asked one of them. 'Oh, a stick and a stone,' said Bob, casually. They didn't ask for our permit. Over the road was a diner, so we all went in for breakfast and, shortly afterwards, another police lieutenant looked in for coffee, chatted to a few locals and then joined us, saying his colleagues had mentioned the bus over the radio. We talked about our trip and gave him some leaflets, and when we came to pay for our food found that he had already taken care of our bill, which caused us to regard the New York State Police with some affection. In Rochester and Albany, BOAC, Air Canada and P&O joined forces and invited travel agents to lunch to promote, amongst other things, their fly-cruise packages. After drinks, food and a film about cruising, we came on stage, and during my introductions I gently rubbished all three sponsors – much to the delight of the travel agents, who were usually subjected to straight-faced presentations. I explained the origins of POSH (Port

Out, Starboard Home) which referred to the most desirable cabins on the ship's shady side on journeys to and from India in the days before air-conditioning, and suggested that P&O's boats were so ancient that their clients might benefit from tips like this when booking their cruise – which got a great laugh. Fortunately, Bill Schneider, boss of P&O's New York operation, had a good sense of humour. We left Rochester after appearances at two shopping centres, a British Leyland dealership, filming a TV interview, and a visit by some of us to a local folk club, where we sang a few songs which raised $25. Our route to Albany took us along US Highway 20 to avoid low bridges on the New York State Thruway. Thursday 22 March was another poignant landmark in our world bus journey. It was the last time that we used the bus as sleeping accommodation. After an excellent supper at a roadside restaurant and bar in Cazenovia, New York State, the seven of us slept on the bus for the last time, snug and warm in our bunks with snow falling silently outside.

Clive and Bob had scouted the route across New York State three months before in the camper, and Clive's ingenious detours to avoid low bridges included driving the bus through a farmyard. It was cold on the bus, and the woods and rolling farmland of upstate New York were blanketed in snow, with the roofs of rural America's distinctive red barns all wearing a thatch of snow. Rain in Albany turned the snow to slush as we settled into our accommodation at the State University of New York. In nearby Schenectady, we appeared on WRBG-TV's strangely shambolic *Pick a Show*, in company with a huge but very docile Canadian brown bear which had appeared in many films, including *Paint Your Wagon*, in town as an attraction at a local carnival, wrestling with anyone game enough to take it on. After a couple of songs from us, the show's genial but inept host, David Allen, persuaded Clive to wrestle with the bear, now muzzled by its owner. Clive took off his jacket and came to grips with the bear, which had just drunk – rather daintily – a large bottle of 7 Up. The huge bear immediately put its head on Clive's shoulder and started licking the back of his neck, interspersed with burps of 7 Up. The contest was judged a draw, but Clive said that he knew he'd been well and truly licked! Our concert at the university that evening attracted a large crowd, amongst which was Basil and Lorene Candela's pretty teenage daughter, whom I'd met the year before when I stayed with her parents, and who surprised the others by greeting me like a long-lost friend and giving me a big kiss.

Boston was the furthest east we took the bus in America. Both Gale and Leonie, Bob's Australian girlfriend who flew in from Sydney, were joining us there. Bob got a car from Avis and he and I drove to Boston to meet them, leaving the others to make their own way there in the bus. We were booked into the Bradford Hotel in Tremont Street, a large 1920s hotel that seemed a little past its best, the bus being parked securely at the airport for the weekend. Sunday was free for sightseeing, and Tony, Tim, Gale and I followed the 'Freedom Trail', a tourist walking route through historic Boston, starting at Boston Common, the oldest public park in America. We also visited the USS *Constitution*, a frigate launched in 1797 and the oldest fully commissioned ship in the US Navy. The snow had disappeared, but it was still freezing as we rose early on Monday to appear live on WHDH with Jess Cain, Boston's most popular radio personality. Everyone tuned in to his morning drive-time show, on which we were interviewed at length and played a couple of songs. We parked the bus outside the BOAC office at the Statler Hilton on Columbus Avenue, where we held another press conference. 'The seven young Englishmen who are currently singing for their keep in the Boston area are fulfilling many a young heart's dream – expense-free travel around the world,' wrote the reporter from the Boston-based *Christian Science Monitor*, which carried a large photo of us with the bus and devoted half a page to our story. A concert for Boston State College, another shopping mall appearance, and a BTA reception completed our Boston schedule and we were off to Hartford, Connecticut.

The bus roof sustained further damage, hitting another bridge. Bob had scrounged a large but dented sedan from Avis on the pretext of delivering it to New York and he and I, with Leonie and Gale, were following the others, and when I saw the damage I was unreasonably furious and had to be calmed down by Tony. Our only commitment in Connecticut's state capital was the BTA reception at the Sonesta Hotel, where we were staying. Here the travel agents were a highly animated bunch, possibly due to the amount of drink they'd taken. They were about the only group who didn't blench at the piano-smashing part of the slide show – in fact, they seemed to relish it. Later, while I was doing my cocktail piano bit, a somewhat blowsy, rather tipsy woman lurched across the grand piano, knocking several glasses over, one of which smashed onto the keyboard and shattered. I carried on playing, until the wife of one travel agent, standing at the end of the keyboard and wearing a long silver dress, let out a shriek. Her dress was splattered with blood and, every time my left hand reached to the end of the keyboard, so more blood flicked onto her dress. Sticking out of the back of my hand was a sizeable shard of glass, and there was blood everywhere – I hadn't felt a thing.

Then it was on to New York through pretty New England countryside, with its lanes, fields, woods, streams and beautiful little white wooden churches. Old white-painted weatherboard houses with their gables and verandas slowly gave way to the elegant suburbs of White Plains while, upstairs in the bus, John was working away patching up the roof as they followed Clive's route onto Manhattan island. In the gathering late afternoon gloom, they reached the Middletowne Hotel. '"The Philanderers are back!" said one staff member to another in a tone of pleasure, which was a nice greeting,' recorded Tim. The bus was parked on the lot opposite at the daily rate for two cars, $20. Next morning was Good Friday. We were up early to tidy the inside of the bus, while John touched up the exterior white paintwork on the damaged roof before driving the bus to the Coliseum, the city's main convention and exhibition centre at Columbus Circle, where Broadway meets Eighth Avenue and 59th Street. Here we were met by our old acquaintance, Lyman Gaylord, British Leyland's PR consultant, who briefed us about promoting them at the New York International Auto Show. It was press preview and dealers' day and the bus was parked in the street outside the main entrance. A 1940s MG TC sports car was a star attraction on the British Leyland stand in the centre of the exhibition floor. We also appeared at the show's first public day. We were filmed performing on the pavement next to the bus and on the British Leyland stand by TV crews from across North America and even as far away as the UK and Japan, and were featured on that evening's news on most of New York's TV channels. The press had a field day, and we even got a mention back in England in *The Sunday Times*. 'This year MG are celebrating the silver jubilee of sales in America. Side by side are a 1947 TC and a 1972 MGB surrounded by a splendid British group called The Philanderers and girls in silver catsuits,' wrote leisure columnist Judith Jackson in an article about the show. People back home had even heard us interviewed on BBC Radio 4's *Today* programme! The next morning, we were photographed by the press in the street outside, draped around an E-Type Jaguar parked in front of the bus with 'Miss New York is a Summer Festival' sitting on it. We spent the rest of Easter Saturday in the sunshine filming the bus driving around New York.

After a break on Sunday to celebrate Easter and join the crowds in Central Park and the traditional Fifth Avenue Easter Parade, we performed for the staff at the Allied Chemical works in Morristown, New Jersey, gave a concert for the New Jersey Auto Club and played to the students in their canteen at the Montclair State Teachers College. The highlight of our time in New York, though, was playing for the BTA in the ballroom of the prestigious Plaza Hotel. We arrived outside late on Tuesday afternoon, to be faced by a battery of TV film crews and press cameramen. As we prepared to step into the limelight, amazed that they would all turn out to see us, a large limousine pulled up, out of which emerged a white-haired but sprightly Charlie Chaplin. He was visiting America for the Oscar ceremonies after a twenty-year exile and was holding a press conference in another room in the hotel, where he was also staying. Everyone immediately followed him in, leaving us standing quite alone on the pavement. We didn't even get his autograph. After playing to more than 200 people at the BTA's Plaza reception, Ouida had invited us all, including the girls, to dinner at an exclusive private club, Raffles, just across Fifth Avenue, on the understanding that we would sing after the meal. 'Another non-live music spot is Raffles, where a septet of nice-looking lads from London, "The Philanderers", couldn't stand the canned music, grabbed their instruments (guitars, bass, banjos, flute), donned their bowlers, and enchanted the staid rich crowd,' wrote Jack O'Brian in his gossipy 'Voice of Broadway' column, which was syndicated all over America, slightly misrepresenting our appearance there.

The final day of our tour dawned. We had one engagement left and then it would all be over. On 5 April, we drove in the bus to play in the dining hall of an exclusive girls' college at Briarcliff Manor, one of the most affluent communities in Westchester County, situated 30 miles north of New York on the banks of the Hudson River. There, overlooking a green hillside dotted with big trees, with everything showing the first signs of spring, in front of an audience of attractive young females, our commitment to our sponsors – for whom we had just driven almost 8,500 miles across the US in our double-decker bus – finally came to an end.

34

Travels Without the Bus

'I am SHOCKED – shocked and APPALLED – that you could live in such SQUALOR!' said a disgusted Joe Smith, ranting at Tony and me about the filthy state of the bus, and worrying about getting his smart suit dirty. We were in the parking lot opposite the Middletowne Hotel. 'You are a GREAT disappointment to me. You've both let me down – AND your parents,' he said. Tony and I felt humbled and ashamed and tried to invent excuses, but he was right. Joe had invited us all to dinner the previous evening to celebrate the successful conclusion of our American tour and had asked to see the bus. It was a mess, made worse by the damage upstairs. Over the past three years, the tidy ones amongst us had fought a losing battle with those who simply didn't care, and it showed. Joe was even more upset when he saw the mess we'd made of our apartments in the Middletowne Hotel, and we'd only been living there for a week.

That evening, Ouida had invited our sponsors to join her in the Speedbird Club to spend a final evening reminiscing with us about the highs and lows of our three-month transcontinental tour. Everyone seemed extremely pleased, and it was a fitting way to round off the hardest three months' work we'd ever experienced. Some of us felt like BOAC or BTA staff, and it was with mixed emotions that we accepted that our American tour had ended. The next day, Tony and Tim took the bus to British Leyland's Leonia headquarters, where it would be safe until one of their staff drove it to the docks to be shipped back to the UK.

I could hardly believe that I could now stop worrying. I thought about all that we had been through to get this far and looked back nostalgically to our hand-to-mouth existence, pining for the experiences we'd had driving the bus to India. It seemed unreal, like a distant happy dream. We now had more money than we'd thought possible then, but to earn it we'd sacrificed seeing America on our own terms. Instead, we'd rushed frantically from one city to the next with little time for sightseeing or getting to know the country better. Gale still thought I was stressed and tired as we celebrated her birthday by visiting the splendid 6,000-seat Radio City Music Hall, with its unique film-and-dancing-girls show – a feature of the place since before the Second World War. Strangely, some of the Rockettes, the high-kicking chorus girls, were incongruously dressed as nuns as a gesture towards it being Easter. The next day, Gale and Leonie caught the Greyhound bus to Montreal, while the rest of us flew to Toronto.

Lewis Roberts, head of the BTA in Canada, was employing us to appear in Canada for five nights in an English pub setting, for which we would receive $2,000 plus meals, travel and accommodation. As my bass wouldn't fit in the hold, it sat next to me in the cabin of Air Canada's DC-9, ticketed as 'Large Bass'. 'What would your friend like to drink?' asked the cheeky Canadian stewardess. 'A gin and tonic, please,' I replied. We arrived at Toronto's Lord Simcoe Hotel and the next day went to the BTA's venue, opened the door to the ballroom and found ourselves entering a very realistic replica of an English pub, complete with a bar dispensing English beer, fake beams and ceiling, horse brasses, a dartboard, log fire and all the other things you would expect to find in a make-believe 'olde worlde' inn. That evening, in our bowlers and Union Jack sweaters, we sang pub songs around the piano to a host of drunken Toronto travel agents until the party wound down around 9 p.m., in time for us to grab some supper. Toronto seemed a pleasant enough city – clean, compared with the cities we'd visited in America, with wide avenues and open spaces and older, low-rise buildings between the taller tower blocks. The Ontario Parliament building – one of the city's more historic buildings – was an imposing brick and pink sandstone structure built in the 1890s, while the impressive curved twin towers of Toronto's New City Hall had only recently been completed. But the city lacked the French roots and distinctiveness of Montreal. The following evening, we repeated our performance in the 'pub', our audience including former Liphook YC, Rosie Cross, and her sister, who had both emigrated to Canada in 1968. We then flew to Ottawa, checked into the hotel, went to the ballroom – and found ourselves in the same 'pub' again. It had been dismantled, transported in trucks overnight and re-assembled there, ready for that evening's function. The same thing happened when we arrived at the Sheraton Mount Royal in Montreal. Once again, the 'pub' was exactly the same, and once again we sang the same pub songs. By the end of the week, having sung ourselves hoarse five nights in a row to tipsy Canadian travel agents, we could hardly speak.

After a weekend exploring Montreal, we returned to New York. Bill Schneider from P&O offered us a free cruise to Alaska in exchange for entertaining on board. We quickly agreed and I signed a contract committing us to join the 28,000-ton liner *Oronsay* in San Francisco on 24 June. We had all agreed that when the tour was over we would split up and take a long holiday away from each other, so we arranged to meet up again in San Francisco on 21 June. Our sponsors had made their final payments to us, and our account at Barclays in New York showed a balance of $28,373.74, the most money Pillock Ltd had ever had to its name. Between us we'd already received $4,500 against our allowances of $85 a week each, but each of us were still owed around $1,000 from the company account.

We rapidly got things ready for our return to Britain, tied up the loose ends from our tour, wound up our business in New York and packed everything away on the bus, including our files, papers, films and equipment, which left us with only our instruments and the clothes we would need for the next couple of months. We sold the two speaker/amplifiers, but kept the microphones, stands and mixers, which we would need on the cruise. Before we left, Dick took some film of me, wearing an old suit, walking around New York and using the subway system – pretending that it was the previous year and I was looking for a sponsor – to be used in the documentary film I was planning. I'd already used the facilities at British Information Services to splice together the film we'd shot in Australia and America to have copied. Dick organised shipping the bus to Liverpool on the *Atlantic Causeway*, a container ship famous later for its involvement in the Falklands War. It cost $1,662.22, and sailed on 8 June. 'Unpacked Used Leyland PD 2, Double-Decker Bus,' the Bill of Lading stated. 'Roof heavily dented & scraped, all front and rear side panels dented or reworked ...' The roof was in worse condition than ever because the driver from British Leyland, a Scotsman called Willie, had hit a bridge on the way to the docks so violently that it caused more damage than we'd ever managed to do ourselves in two-and-a-half years. Tim, by then all on his own in New York, had to dash to the docks and valiantly seal up the holes and tidy up the mess before the bus was shipped.

We all had different ideas about where to take our holidays. Gale and I wanted to see the rest of Canada. Tim chose to stay on in New York and experience big city life there. Tony decided to get away from it all and had been introduced to a farming family in Nova Scotia who agreed to have him work his keep on their farm for a few weeks. Dick, Clive and John had ideas about going to the Caribbean, Central America and Mexico, Clive and Dick eventually finding a cheap way of getting to Florida by doing a car delivery. To Clive's delight, it turned out to be a Porsche. Bob wasn't sure what he wanted to do. He asked for a company loan to buy a camper to enable him to tour America with Leonie. This met with a surprising amount of opposition from several of the group, and he went away to think things over. Bob was probably the most kind-hearted and generous of us all and, while the rest of us were frugal with the money we'd allowed ourselves, Bob would readily buy everyone drinks and meals. We found it difficult to stop him spending his money. As a result, he had little left at the end of the tour compared to the rest of us, and some of us worried that if we were to allow him to do so, Bob would spend his share of our profits before we reached England. We had all agreed that any money we might make out of the trip should be saved to give us a good start once we got home. Bob thought seriously and decided to go straight to England to earn some money. Leonie was also keen to get to London and start her job in the *Sydney Telegraph* office there. Always a man of action, Bob arranged to fly out the following evening but, in his usual generous way, insisted on returning for the cruise to Alaska, even though we said that we would understand if he didn't. By the beginning of May we had all scattered to the four winds.

In Montreal, Gale and I bought a smart little green 1968 VW van for $1,000 which we named 'Daisy'. I drove it down to New York to finish work on the film, help Tim conclude our business there and collect my double bass, the microphones, mixers and stands, the camera and tripod and the rest of my clothes, all of which would accompany Gale and me on our journey across Canada. We left Montreal in mid-May, equipped with air beds, a Coleman stove and other camping equipment, and spent the next six weeks driving 4,000 miles through pine forests and past the unspoilt lakes of Ontario to the northern shores of Lake Superior, North America's great inland sea. We crossed vast prairies west of Winnipeg, climbed over the rugged and beautiful pine-clad, snow-topped Rocky Mountains, and drove through farmland and the great gorge along the Fraser River to Vancouver in British Columbia – on the way spotting moose, deer, bighorn sheep, marmots, bears and bison. We took the ferry to Vancouver Island and from Victoria sailed to Port Angeles in the US and crossed the Olympic National Park in Washington State, a temperate rainforest dripping with lichens and ferns. The Pacific coast was shrouded in fog and mist as we drove south through Oregon to California, ending in San Jose at Liz Esterly's; she had just moved back there from Fresno.

We all converged on San Francisco on the same day, and I was surprised at just how pleased we were to see each other again as, one by one, everyone walked into the White Horse bar at the Beresford, where several of the regulars remembered The Philanderers from January. 'Did you ever see those crazy Brits touring the world in their old steam lorry on your travels?' we were asked. 'They were here last month ...'! Bob returned from England, with news of the 'Welcome Home' celebrations being planned in our honour, which filled us with trepidation. Everyone stayed at the Beresford that night, and next day boarded the *Oronsay*. Practising in the ship's ballroom, we were surprised how easily everything fell into place. The rest and separation seemed to have done us good, and we were glad to be back together again. To save money, Gale joined the ship in Vancouver and, after we sailed, travelled there by Greyhound bus. Liz was happy to look after our van for a couple of weeks, using it to move all her belongings from Fresno to San Jose.

Built in 1951, the *Oronsay* had a white hull and an upright yellow funnel with a distinctive 'top hat', needed to clear the smoke from the after-decks. Next morning, the passengers boarded, and John, Clive and the others cast hopeful eyes over the pretty girls coming on board amongst predominantly elderly couples. As sailing time approached, it dawned on us that most of them were only there to see their grannies off. As the ship left the dock, we were given a traditional send-off, with the Red Garter Band playing Dixieland from the back of a vintage fire engine on the quayside, and thousands of coloured streamers raining down from the passenger decks. We were allocated two tiny four-berth cabins and found ourselves sleeping in bunks again, with little room for guitars, banjos and a double bass. We were working for the entertainments officer, Ronnie Owen, and, as we headed south to Los Angeles, he briefed the on-board entertainers. Ronnie hailed from Blackpool. 'It's a first-class ship,' he told us, adding that Captain Crichton and crew were 'shit hot'! We were in company with dance instructors, lecturers on Alaskan folk lore, investments and beauty techniques, park rangers from the Tongass National Forest – the vast temperate rainforest covering the Alaskan shores we would be passing – a husband and wife team who gave bridge lessons, and a golf instructor. On the musical side there were the Marty O'Conlon Trio, The Saphires; an organ and drums duo, resident pianist Tony Pompa, Rosemary East, the ship's delectable 'Disco Dolly', and us, described to the passengers as a 'Fun Group – The Philanderers, a group of young Englishmen who will entertain with folk songs and music'. The ship's main band, The Denham Sound, turned out to be a highly versatile five-piece outfit, headed by good-humoured, bearded and burly Adrian Hopgood, a young, very talented musician and master of various instruments, including the trumpet, clarinet, and almost anything else that came his way. They could play almost anything in any style, too, and we rated them the best band we'd ever worked with during our entire world trip. Adrian explained the name: 'I had to get a scratch band together at short notice,' he told me, 'and as most of us lived around Denham it was the first name I thought of.' There was a happy family atmosphere amongst the entertainers, and we were treated like fare-paying passengers by the crew. We really enjoyed our time as ship-borne entertainers.

We docked at Los Angeles' San Pedro Harbor and took on more passengers. Tim, Tony and I went ashore to visit the *Queen Mary*. Built in the UK in the 1930s and relocated to nearby Long Beach in 1967 after a rich history of trans-Atlantic service, it was now a floating hotel and tourist attraction. In two days, we covered the 1,000 miles to Vancouver at a steady 22 knots. Most of the passengers were retired or heading that way, and the competition with the male crew members to win the favours of the small number of unattached young women on board was fierce, but by the ship's first Gala Ball almost all of them could be found at our table. Each morning, every cabin received a copy of the day's programme, an exhausting schedule which had to be fitted in between incredible bouts of eating and drinking. Lunchtime buffet tables groaned with mouth-watering food. There were six-course dinners, each day having started with a full English breakfast. In addition to all this, there was morning coffee, afternoon tea with delicious cakes from the ship's bakery, and a late-night cold buffet.

Tuesday was 'Pub Night' and our first 'official' performance. Between songs I announced the following day's programme: 'At ten there will be a flogging at the mast, Tim will be keelhauled at noon, followed by a burial at sea at 2.30 and, to celebrate the ship's first voyage into Arctic waters to view the icebergs, the cinema will show *A Night to Remember* ...' After midnight, when, unexpectedly, we were asked to give 'The Denham Sound' another break, the late-night audience so enjoyed our act that an enthusiastic Ronnie Owen told us in his broad Lancashire accent: 'Fabulous, boys. You've saved the evening!' From then on we were favourites, both of passengers and crew.

Gale joined us at Vancouver, a vibrant young Canadian city, where we visited historic Gastown, the city's oldest neighbourhood, where old buildings and warehouses now housed up-market boutiques, antique shops and cafés. We also visited Stanley Park, alive with joggers and cyclists, with its wide grassy lawns, stands of tall firs, totem poles and zoo. We then sailed north between Vancouver Island and the mainland, through the Seymour Narrows towards Alaska, weaving in and out between the coastal islands. We first dropped anchor at Ketchikan, then at Juneau and Sitka, before sailing into Glacier Bay. P&O had only recently started cruising here and none of the places we visited had docking facilities, so passengers were ferried to and fro in the ship's open tenders. Originally settled by Russians, Alaska was acquired by the US in 1867, who bought the territory for $7.2 million, the treaty, ratified by the US Senate, being signed by a distant relative of mine, President Andrew Johnson. In 1959, Alaska became America's 49th state. The tiny community of Ketchikan, our first stop, was summer home for the Tlingit Indians before it was settled in the 1880s, and was never a Russian settlement. Its pretty, brightly painted wooden buildings cling to the mountainside, with some on stilts above the creek overlooking an anchorage for local fishing boats, all connected by picturesque wooden stairways and boardwalks.

Juneau, the Alaskan State Capital, had a population of around 15,000. Like Ketchikan, it is surrounded by fir-covered mountains. 'I think I'll climb up there this afternoon,' said Tony, looking out towards a large hill south of the town. 'It would take you a couple of days to get up there,' scoffed Dick. Off went Tony, with Tim, Gale and me tagging along, completely unprepared for the mud and snow that lay across our path. We eventually reached a point with a marvellous view looking down at our ship, like a toy in the fjord far below. Here, some people were re-erecting a large wooden cross. I later discovered that this was Father Brown's Cross, originally erected by him in the early 1900s but replaced several times since. Although we had climbed to around 2,000ft, we were nowhere near the top. Tony could not be dissuaded from pressing on, and Tim, Gale and I followed. Over an hour later, we finally reached a peak, having trudged across snowfields and boggy grass in our very ordinary shoes. Before us lay a magnificent landscape of forests and mountains that stretched eastwards towards the horizon, across the border into British Columbia. To the west, the sun sparkled on the Pacific Ocean beyond Alaska's fjords and islands. Suddenly aware that it was rather late, we hurriedly scrambled all the way back down to the ship, arriving just in time for dinner. We were told that we had climbed to Gastineau Peak on Mt Roberts, 3,666ft above sea level! The next morning, we explored Juneau, which was far less picturesque than Ketchikan, and visited the beautiful little wooden Russian Orthodox church, octagonal in shape and with a golden onion dome. Strangely, it was built by the local Tlingit tribes in the 1890s, thirty years after the Russians had left, due to their conversion to Russian Orthodoxy.

The highlight of the cruise was undoubtedly sailing into Glacier Bay, proclaimed a National Monument by the US President in 1925. This was the first P&O cruise to visit –

cruise ships had only started coming here in 1969. We sailed right up to the face of the glaciers, and, when the ship's deep siren sounded, great blocks of ice fell from the glacier resulting in impressive tidal waves in the icy waters below. This environmentally unfriendly practice was subsequently forbidden, and we learned that all the glaciers were retreating, some having already left the National Monument, retreating back into Canada. A boat was lowered for crew members to collect chunks of ice which, allegedly, were used to chill passengers' drinks that evening.

Sitka was the most historic of the settlements we visited, still containing some buildings dating from Russian times, when it was known as New Archangel. Surrounded by spruce-clad islands, Sitka is dominated by the snow-capped volcanic peak of Mt Edgecumbe. An excellent museum was devoted to the Tlingit culture which, after years of suppression, was beginning to see a new renaissance, the values of the native population finally being recognised.

We had turned south and, after more than a week of being under-used, The Philanderers were at last given work to do. I had been filming the cruise quite extensively and, on the afternoon that we left Glacier Bay, we appeared on deck in our Union Jack sweaters, where Gale filmed us playing 'Galway City'. From then on we performed somewhere on the ship every evening. In the Celtic Room we supported The Saphires, advertised as 'Special Cabaret – the very versatile and happy Philanderers produce a mixture and variety of their own as they present their own special cabaret act ...' The small crowd when we started swelled to a capacity house but five minutes after we'd finished everyone had left, leaving The Saphires playing to just five people. The ballroom was full the next night when we provided cabaret support to 'The Denham Sound'. We sang 'Farmer's Boy' for the first time, turning the night into a triumph and leaving the stage to shouts for more. During the evening, seeing a P&O director in the room, I jokingly announced that we'd been booked to play on the maiden voyage of their new liner, *Spirit of London*. This was greeted by enthusiastic applause. 'How long are they on the boat for?' he asked. 'Just this cruise,' he was told. 'Hmm. Pity,' he said. Old-hand stewards were heard to say we were the best cabaret group they'd seen on the ships. We also played to the crew in 'The Pig', the room in the bow of the ship where deckhands and crew meet to let their hair down, and went down so well that they wouldn't let us stop. 'Best night's entertainment we've ever had here!' we were told.

The ship arrived in Victoria – a city of parks, flowers and pleasant open streets. Having seen Gale off at the bus terminal on her way back to Montreal, I crossed the road to visit Thunderbird Park, next to the museum, only to bump into Tony and Tim admiring the totem poles there. Quite by chance, Tony and I were wearing identical Austin Reed jackets and trousers. 'Are you in a group?' asked a girl lying on the grass. 'Sort of,' said Tony in his public-school accent. 'Oh, you're from England,' said the girl. 'I was in England recently; my grandmother lives there.' 'Where?' asked Tony. 'Oh, you wouldn't have heard of it,' said the girl. 'A little place near Sussex, called Liphook.' Her grandmother, Mrs Higgins, lived in the Headley Road, and Tony had nearly lodged with her. It was yet another of those strange coincidences that continued to take us by surprise.

'A fabulous report's gone in about you boys,' said Ronnie encouragingly over a drink towards the end of our last evening on board, and we talked enthusiastically about working as entertainers on cruises in the future. The next morning, the *Oronsay* docked in San Francisco. Our cruise was over, and the last of our overseas adventures was drawing to a close. However, the Deers Hut and our free pint of beer were still over 5,000 miles away.

35

Back Home Again: 'A Busload of Banjos in Downing Street'

In San Francisco, we said goodbye to each other again. Bob flew back to England while the rest of us would meet in New York before flying home together. Tim returned to New York that afternoon, Clive and John drove to Los Angeles with a girl John had met on the ship to travel east from there, and I headed for Vancouver in our van, taking Dick and Tony with me. I planned to sell the van there, where I knew I would get a higher price than I paid for it in Montreal. We arrived late on Sunday afternoon and stayed the night with an old college friend of Gale's, David Crossley. On Monday morning, the van was tested and re-registered in British Columbia and by mid-afternoon I had sold it for $350 more than we paid for it, which more than covered the cost of our holiday. That evening, we boarded *The Canadian*, Canadian Pacific's flagship transcontinental train, and slowly glided out of Vancouver en route for Montreal, with my bass and an old suitcase full of microphones, mixers and other kit tucked away in the baggage car. The train took us through the Rockies to Calgary where, during a twenty-minute stop, we caught a glimpse through the train window of riders parading on the streets taking part in the famous 'Calgary Stampede'. We'd bought the cheapest tickets, and spent three uncomfortable nights snatching some sleep on recliner seats as we retraced the journey Gale and I had made across Canada, and when we arrived at Montreal's Central Station she was there to meet us.

In New York, Tim was already installed in the Middletowne Hotel, and by the next weekend we had all gathered there before returning to England. We checked out on Tuesday 18 July and headed for the Speedbird Club for a final drink with Ouida, Barry and Jim Turbayne. Eighteen months after arriving in New York on a cold January afternoon, I was leaving the city for the last time in the sweltering heat of summer. Taxis ferried us and all our clutter to JFK Airport, where we boarded BOAC's overnight flight to Manchester. I felt so at home in North America that I really didn't want to leave. We all had mixed feelings about returning to England and were all a little scared about what we might find there. We thought we'd changed, but anticipated that our families and friends in England would expect us to be the same immature, naive and idealistic idiots that we were when we left. Perhaps we were! At 10.45 p.m., the VC10 rumbled down the runway, and, as we climbed into the sultry night sky, we could just see the lights of Manhattan's skyscrapers, and the twin towers of the World Trade Centre, now the tallest buildings in the world, twinkling in the darkness behind us. Then they were gone, and with them our final view of the New World.

On Wednesday 19 July 1972, after a short stop at Prestwick, we arrived at Manchester Airport at 11.40 a.m. Several weeks earlier, Alan, who had never actually driven the bus before, with my cousin Paul, had driven it from Liverpool docks to Warrington Corporation's depot at Wilderspool

Causeway, where Mr Mantle had agreed to store it to await our arrival home. Having cleared our considerable baggage through customs, we were met by a driver from Warrington Corporation, who took us in the newest bus in the fleet through the lush green English countryside to the Birchdale Hotel, a delightful old establishment on the outskirts of town, where we'd been booked in for the night. After phoning home to say we'd arrived in one piece, we were taken to a pub down the road for a hearty Lancashire lunch and some good English beer. We then changed into our old clothes and went to find our bus. It was an emotional reunion. It was parked in almost the same spot as when I'd first seen it in 1969 and it looked rather sad. We spent the rest of the day at the depot servicing and cleaning up the bus. It was in a pretty bad state following the damage sustained on the way to the docks in New York. During the evening, Bob arrived from Liphook and the seven of us were reunited for the last time. The next morning, we loaded our gear on board the bus. Bob worked on the brakes to make them good enough to pass an MOT test while the rest of us finished tidying it up. By midmorning, we judged the bus to be clean enough to show people round. A reporter and film crew from BBC Manchester appeared, so we smartened ourselves up, sang 'Wild Rover' for them, gave an interview, and were filmed being greeted by the 'high-ups' in Warrington's transport department. Sadly, Mr Mantle was away on holiday and unable to bask in the dubious glory of being on local television with us. We then drove in the bus to Warrington's magnificent Georgian Town Hall, with its beautiful grounds and superb wrought iron gates, where we were greeted by the town clerk and borough treasurer. The mayor sent his apologies. He, too, was away. Photographs were taken by the local press, after which we were given an excellent civic lunch and were joined by other dignitaries, including the chairman of the transport committee, Councillor Hayes, whose idea this was. Finally bidding our hosts farewell, we drove to the M6 and cruised south towards London, knowing that we would pass under all the bridges with plenty of room to spare. We headed for Essex and Greensted House, Tony's parents' spacious home near Ongar, where we stayed the night. For reasons which the rest of us would never understand, Tony's father had taken his entire family on holiday to Spain, ignoring his eldest son's homecoming, and the poor chap returned to be greeted only by the family nanny, who had been preparing for our arrival by making up beds and cooking us an excellent stew, which ensured a good night's sleep in comfortable surroundings on our second night back.

The 'Welcome Home' arrangements in London were in the hands of Conservative Central Office staff, and the next morning we donned our most sober Austin Reed suits and drove the bus to Smith Square, Westminster, where I parked it across a couple of empty parking metres right outside Transport House, the Labour Party headquarters. Over coffee across the square in Central Office, we learned that the Prime Minister, Edward Heath, would receive us and the bus outside 10 Downing Street at 1.15 p.m., and that the press, TV and radio had all been invited. It was warm and sunny as we returned to the bus to find a zealous traffic warden about to attach a parking ticket to it. 'You're not allowed to park that there,' she told us as I unsuccessfully tried to persuade her to tear it up. A friendly young police constable appeared to find out what the trouble was and, while being quite sympathetic – unlike the traffic warden – agreed that she was probably right, so she handed me the ticket. 'Stick the bus on the pavement in front of Central Office over there and I'll see that you don't have any more trouble,' said the constable when we explained what we were doing. A reporter from BBC Radio London came along and recorded an interview, and then at 1 p.m. we drove out of Smith Square, past the Houses of Parliament, into Whitehall and turned left into a then ungated Downing Street. John's sister, Pauline, was in the crowd and I quickly pressed our cine camera into her hand and showed her how to use it to film our historic encounter on the steps of Number 10. The police, press and party officials all gave conflicting instructions about where the bus should park, until it finally came to rest with the back platform right opposite the doorstep.

The scene was described with wit, concision and allusive humour by Philip Howard in the following morning's *Times* under the heading 'Busload of banjos in Downing Street':

An ancient Warrington Corporation double-decker bus pulled up outside 10 Downing Street yesterday. It discharged seven ageing Young Conservatives from Liphook, Hampshire, wearing bowler hats and carrying musical instruments. The Prime Minister came out of his front door, beaming and escorted by the Lord President of the Council, Leader of the House and Home Secretary. A crowd of tourists seethed, goggled and mis-identified the characters to one another. A dreamlike dialogue to suit the fantasy of the occasion was spoken. Mr Richard King, Leader of the bus party, handing the Prime Minister a parking ticket they had just collected in Whitehall, said, 'We have got something we want to give you.' Mr Heath heaved his shoulders and handed it briskly back. A police superintendent; 'We will have the press on this side and the banjo-players on that side.' Confused muttering from the crowd. Mr King: 'We would like to play you a song.' Mr Heath, blenching; 'Just one verse.' The musicians broke into tongue and twang with a hearty rendering of an Appalachian Mountain folk song called 'Fly Away'. When it was over, Mr Heath climbed aboard the first bus that has ever penetrated Downing

Street, inspected it, descended, and said: 'I will see you away, because it may not start.' The bus did not start for some time ...

The article went on to tell the story of our world trip in great, humorous style, taking three columns and concluding with an aside from Clive: 'We are trying to play down the Young Conservative connection, because it does not help us to get singing jobs in left-wing circles.' The *Daily Express* carried an even bigger photograph of Edward Heath smiling on the steps of Number 10 watching us play, accompanied by a short piece by showbiz correspondent, Judith Simons. 'It looks like a script that no comedy scriptwriter could invent ...' she wrote, 'but it HAPPENED yesterday morning. The folk band called The Philanderers ... are unique ...' while the caption under the *Daily Telegraph* photograph quoted the Prime Minister as saying: 'You must have influence to get that great vehicle in here.'

We showed the Prime Minister over the bus, and he expressed great interest in how we'd converted it. 'It's a bit like my yacht,' he said, 'but you've got more storage space.' After the Prime Minister's party had left, we spent more time with the press before returning to Smith Square and Central Office. We'd been surprised by the lack of television crews, but were told that this was because they were all covering the police action late that morning against illegal picketing in East London and the arrest of five shop stewards for contempt of court. We'd been mostly ignorant of Britain's escalating labour troubles while we were away. After waiting around for the rest of the afternoon, with no one turning up, we drove back to Essex for dinner as guests of Tony's grandfather, Sir Patrick Hennessy, at his impressive house in Theydon Bois. Without Sir Patrick's help in 1970, we might never have got to Australia, and I was grateful for the opportunity to thank him for his trust in us and to tell him how Tony had been such a key member of the team. 'We lingered long around the dinner table while Sir Patrick threw frequent abuse at his grandson and entertained us with tales of his time as Lord Beaverbrook's right-hand man at the wartime Ministry of Aircraft Production, while we drank his brandy respectfully,' Tim recalled.

After another night at Greensted House, followed by a hearty breakfast, the local press appeared, and the following week the *West Essex Gazette & Independent* and the *Brentwood Gazette & Mid-Essex Recorder* carried stories about us with photographs of us with the bus in Tony's driveway. 'A fantastic trip, showing most marvellous initiative,' Tony's grandfather was quoted as saying. 'It was not easy; they obviously had to work hard at times, but they came through wonderfully ... I would like to have done it when I was young,' he added. Alan drove up to Essex in his old London taxi to follow us home. A 'Pillock Welcome Home' committee had been formed in Liphook, with my father as chairman, and many of our parents and old YC chums had been roped in. They had circulated press releases, organised media coverage, had been in touch with Warrington Corporation and asked our local MP, Joan Quennell, to arrange our welcome by the politicians in London. My mother, and my sister Mary, the committee's secretary, had written to me with the details. They had done a great job. After lunch, we gathered our things together, climbed aboard the bus one last time and set off towards Hampshire.

'Global Pillock and crew due home next week,' proclaimed the *Haslemere Herald*, our local paper, the previous week. The paper had regularly featured our adventures in their columns from the day we left. The morning before our arrival in Liphook they told their readers, 'Global Pillock home tomorrow. Excited crowds will line the road tomorrow evening when The

Philanderers come home to Liphook after their world tour.'
By the time we'd reached the Guildford by-pass, we realised
that we were far too early. 'The reception committee invite
you to join them in welcoming home The Philanderers after
their successful trip around the world' read the flyer, which
said we would arrive at the Deers Hut at 6.30 p.m., so we
stopped at Milford, had a cup of tea and swept the bus out.
Eventually, we crossed the county border into Hampshire,
south of Hindhead, where a police motorcyclist pulled into
the road ahead of us. For a moment I panicked, as the bus
had no MOT certificate and no UK tax or insurance. We were
chancing our arm by using our Australian registration and
my uncle's trade plates. As a police car pulled in behind us,
I realised that this was our escort. We approached Liphook
Square, which was lined with people cheering and waving,
just as the newspaper had predicted. We turned into the
Longmoor Road and were soon approaching the drive to the
Deers Hut. It seemed as if thousands of people had turned
out to welcome us home. We'd actually done it! We'd actually
got ourselves and the bus all the way around the world and
back to the pub in one piece. Looking back on the whole
trip, I could not think of a single moment when I had felt so
nervous, and I'm sure the others felt the same.

The police motorcyclist pulled over and the bus sailed past
the side of the pub into the paddock, where we could hear
the Petworth Silver Band playing 'Congratulations'. We came
to rest in front of a banner saying 'Pillock Go Home' held by
Adrian and Alan. The red carpet laid out for us was exactly
in line with the back platform. We all piled out, wearing our
smart Austin Reed clothes and bowler hats and carrying our
instruments. Cheers, whistles and applause greeted us as we
walked along the red carpet towards the steps that led to the
deck of one of my uncle's large flatbed brick lorries, which
was being used as a stage. Don Eades, our photographer

friend, took a colour photograph for his paper, the *Petersfield Post*. 'Welcome Home Boys,' said the banner on the truck. Peter Greenyer, one of the old Longmoor Road gang and another YC stalwart from the 1960s, was acting as compere and introduced us all – quite unnecessarily, as the papers pointed out, as everyone there knew us anyway. He then handed the microphone to Joan Quennell, our local MP, who headed a delegation that included the vicar, the chairman of the parish council and none other than Bert Oram, landlord of the Deers Hut, who now, almost three-and-a-half years since he made the bet with us, owed us a pint of beer. 'The people's welcome is the best thing we can say to you,' Miss Quennell shouted above the cheering crowd. 'You have shown the flag for Britain all the way round the world and we are proud of you.' I replied that we were glad to be home, but the cheering drowned me out. 'Sing us a song, you stupid buggers,' one of our erstwhile friends shouted jokingly above the noise, so we picked up our instruments and launched into 'Fly Away' – the song we'd sung to the Prime Minister and to hundreds of thousands of other people on our travels around the world – for one last time. Sitting on chairs at the front of the crowd were our proud parents, who would have to wait a while before they could greet us in private. A few more songs and the formalities were over and it was into the pub. There, in front of the press photographers, Bert pulled each of us a pint of bitter, and we stepped outside into the warm, early evening sunshine at the front of the pub with Bert and Queenie, raised our glasses and at last savoured the familiar taste of Bert's well-kept Courage Directors Bitter. As we did so, we felt a strong sense of achievement. We'd received a hero's welcome and were back in the bosom of our families and friends. After travelling for 1,025 days and covering just over 47,000 miles, we had finally won our bet. We were home.

Several hours later, things had quietened down, people had drifted away, and we found ourselves sitting in the corner on our own at the same table we had occupied when we first decided to embark on our world journey. Suddenly, we realised that the thing which had held us tightly together for three years was over. 'You must have had some amazing experiences,' people said, but soon changed the subject. All our old friends seemed to want to talk to us about were the parochial issues of village life and we were beginning to feel that we didn't quite fit in here anymore. Each of us had the same feeling of anticlimax. We all looked at each other, then someone said: 'What the hell are we going to do now?'

Epilogue — Or What Became of Us All

A 'Welcome Home' dinner at the Welcome Inn, Petersfield, the following Monday and a charity concert at the Liphook Church Centre the next weekend ended the celebration of our return. We realised that the world tour in Hairy Pillock 2, and our success as The Philanderers, had changed our lives. 'They all left responsible jobs to make this trip and they'll go back to the jobs once it's over,' the NBC reporter had told viewers in Los Angeles. However, none of us did, and the money we'd made bought us some time to think about our futures and the direction our lives might take.

We were now all comparatively well-off. Most of us were better off than we'd ever been. Our world tour in a bus had cost around £35,000, but we had earned quite a bit more. In America, the seven of us had already drawn over £800 each from the company since December to cover personal out-of-pocket expenses and, after all other expenses had been paid, the company was still left with a surplus in our New York account of around £9,000. We decided to hold back a reserve of around £2,000 to cover accountants' and solicitors' fees, any potential tax liability, the cost of preparing the proposed film and book of the trip, and any other unforeseen expenses, which left £7,000 to distribute amongst ourselves. The seven of us felt that Adrian and Alan, having contributed to the success of our adventure, should also share in our good fortune. 'All for one and one for all' was the 'spirit of the trip', and this prevailed right to the end. The trip had taken thirty-four months to complete, so we decided that a fair division of the profit would be achieved by calculating each person's share by the number of months he had completed on the world tour. Adrian had been with us for eight months, Alan for nineteen months and Bob (who had left the trip for three months in Australia) thirty-one months. Those of us who were with the trip for the full thirty-four months received around £900 (at a time when the average wage in the UK was around £30 a week, or about £1,500 a year), and the others proportionally less. It was all paid in dollars from Pillock Ltd's New York bank account.

We toyed with the idea of continuing professionally as The Philanderers, but both Bob and Tony had already decided to move on, so we invited Rob Slingo, a guitarist and singer from Liphook, to take their place. We auditioned professionally for the BBC, where our performance had received sufficiently favourable reports for us to be added to the list of those available for broadcasting. We subsequently made some recordings which were used on the *Tony Brandon Show* on Radio 2, where we were billed as 'guests of the week'. We also appeared on *Woman's Hour*, BBC Radio Solent, BBC TV South and Southern Television's *Day By Day*, but our big break never came. We got a number of bookings, including performing a few times at a holiday camp and acting as the support band for The Searchers at the Savoy Ballroom in Portsmouth, but we soon accepted that English folk singers and double-decker buses were commonplace in Britain, and that success in the musical world was very likely to elude us. So we finally split up and went our different ways, but all still remained friends and kept in touch.

While we were away, Adrian had graduated from Cambridge and married Agy, Brinsley Smith's sister, whom he'd been courting since his student days, and had started a successful architectural practice in Liphook, where they live with their daughter. He was the only one of us who remained in the village and regularly drank at the Deers Hut.

Alan qualified as a teacher and he and Nola moved to Yorkshire, where their three children were born. Alan taught engineering at Royds Hall School, Huddersfield, played his accordion in a ceilidh band and invented and manufactured the Microvox, an acoustic musical instrument microphone system now used by many folk and other musicians world-wide. Alan and Nola were later divorced and he subsequently married Toni. Alan died in 2012.

The world beckoned for Bob, who worked extensively overseas, using his mechanical and management skills in north eastern Nigeria and Java. He married Libby, a Liphook girl, and they lived for seventeen years in Australia's Northern Territory deep in the Outback 200 miles east of Darwin in what is now the Kakadu National Park, initially as caretakers of a uranium concession holding. Here Bob became known as 'the real Crocodile Dundee' when Paul Hogan chose their facility as the location base for his popular films. They then opened a café in Jabiru, the local settlement. Bob and Libby retired to Australia's Gold Coast and then spent seven years in Normandy before settling in New Zealand.

Dick married Gill and, after managing a pub and owning a newsagent's in Sussex, pursued his dream of owning and running a small hotel in France for a number of years. They had three children, but later divorced. Returning to the UK, Dick worked in the pub trade again. He died in 2008.

After we got back, Tony returned home to Essex and travelled all over the world as a salesman for Howard Rotavators before marrying Beverley and settling in Suffolk with their four children. Tony helped to run the family Ford agency in Woodbridge before branching out on his own in the company acquisition business, finally working for a pharmaceutical retail chain as their new business director. Tony died in 2012.

Clive's musical ability took him to Bermuda, where he sang in a nightclub before returning to America and, after joining the 'New Christie Minstrels' as a banjo player – 'sacked after a few months,' he confesses, 'but then, so was John Denver' – ended up driving his own tourist double-deckers around Lake Tahoe. He had two children with his first wife, Judy, and returned to England, eventually to work as a commercial pilot, flying all over Europe and writing the definitive book about how to gain a commercial pilot's licence. Now retired, but still giving flying lessons, he lives with his second wife, Deborah, in Kent.

Having written over 350,000 words in his reports about our world travels, Tim set to and wrote a book about it. Sadly, after dozens of rejection slips, he failed to find a publisher. With his background in electronics, he joined the staff of *Computer Weekly* and was soon travelling the world as their chief reporter. He then launched the computer industry's first daily newsletter, founding and editing Computergram International, and became the renowned guru of the IT industry, regarded by his peers as a consummate and professional journalist. Tim died in 1997 at the age of only 54, greatly mourned by his journalist colleagues who revered him, and by the rest of us who travelled the world with him.

John settled down and started out on a career in finance by becoming the branch manager of a building society in Essex. But life in a suit wasn't really John's style and, after a few years and some matrimonial ups and downs (he was married twice), he worked at a series of jobs including living and working on barges travelling around Europe's extensive network of canals and rivers, driving large articulated trucks and as a ticket inspector for British Rail. John died in 2007 while living and working in Portsmouth.

As for me, Gale and I were married in 1974 and I pursued a career in broadcasting, ending up by working for the Independent Broadcasting Authority, firstly in Hampshire, before becoming their representative in the South East of England, living and working in Kent. Taking early retirement, I then became a county councillor and, after sixteen years became the chairman of the council. I still play my double bass in a folk group with my cousin Paul (on the banjo), and two old friends who were both part of the crew on our first trip to Spain, Peter (guitar) and Wally (accordion and guitar). Until his death, Tim was also a part of the group, which still sings the same old songs from over fifty years ago.

Pillock Ltd never traded in the UK and was finally struck off the register in the 1970s, leaving the ownership of the bus in doubt, as it was legally owned by the company! Most of us still got together now and then, although getting all of us in one place at the same time was extremely difficult as we had scattered all over the world. Nevertheless, we held 'Pillock Reunions' in a big marquee at the Deers Hut with several hundred of our old friends to celebrate the 20th, 25th, 30th and 40th anniversaries of the start of our bus adventures, but only once did all nine of us appear on stage together since our last night in the Little Hut nightclub in Bombay in April 1970, and that was in July 1988, when we celebrated the 20th anniversary of the creation of the Pillock Organisation and our first trip to Spain together.

'And what happened to the bus?' you may ask. Pillock Ltd loaned it to my cousin Paul, who had already been using Hairy Pillock 1 to take parties of students and young people on European holidays for several seasons. It then fell into a state of decay, ended up derelict on a friend's farm in Wiltshire and came close to being scrapped. But in 1982 it was given a reprieve. It had taken me ten years to edit the film of the trip, initially for the BBC, who in the end decided they didn't want it after all. So, in order to raise some money for the Liphook Carnival Committee, we held the Gala World Charity Premiere of *Pillock Conquers the World* in Haslemere's Rex Cinema in October 1982. 'How about having the bus there?' I was asked. A gang of old friends from the YC days in Liphook, including half the original bus crew, brought the bus back from Wiltshire, got it through an MOT test, cleaned it up, repainted it and put it on display outside the cinema. Every one of the 1,200 seats were sold, and eight of the nine of us – Clive being unable to return from America – were reunited for the first screening of our film. The local venture scouts then asked if they could use the bus to take them to camp. Paul and I rebuilt the roof and the scouts revamped the interior, the old Liphook gang built a barn on Andrew Luff's new farm in nearby Headley, and for the next few years the bus had a new purpose. But the scouts grew older and stopped using it, and once again it sat sadly neglected, until some friends from my local pub in Kent suggested we might use it again, which was the beginning of the rebirth of Hairy Pillock 2. Today, the bus is in better mechanical shape than ever, and each summer sets out on yet another small adventure, most years visiting a different European country. It has now travelled over 800,000 miles and has visited twenty countries on four continents. A tribute to British engineering, it seems that our 1949 Leyland PD2 double-decker bus, formerly number 10 in the Warrington Corporation fleet – Hairy Pillock 2 – is set to outlast us all.

Acknowledgements

I would like to thank all those who contributed, at different times and in many different ways, to the ultimate success of our journey around the world in a double-decker bus. When Mark Beynon, Commissioning Editor at The History Press, suggested we produce a book telling our story, my surviving companions from our trip, Adrian Bird, Clive Hughes and Bob Hall, all agreed that I should write it.

The definitive chronicle of our trip was written by Tim Palmer. His regular reports to the *Haslemere Herald*, starting at 'Day 1' and ending at 'Day 1,025' and our return to the Deers Hut, provided a detailed daily account of all of our activities and ran to hundreds of thousands of words. This record provided much of the source material for the book. Another detailed account was a diary of our journey from England to India kept by Tony Hough, and I am grateful to Beverley, his wife, for allowing me to quote freely from it, and from the letters that Tony sent home. Adrian, Bob and Clive contributed their thoughts and commented on my original draft, and Adrian suggested we use his cutaway drawing of the bus prepared for the souvenir programme of the Charity Premiere of *Pillock Conquers the World*, the film of our journey, in 1982. The accounts, letters, papers, press cuttings, photographs and other memorabilia in the Pillock Organisation's considerable archive in my loft filled in the rest of the story. Any errors, factual inaccuracies or omissions are mine alone.

Finally, I would like to thank my wife Gale for her comments, advice and help. Without her support and encouragement, I doubt if this book would ever have been written.

Appendix

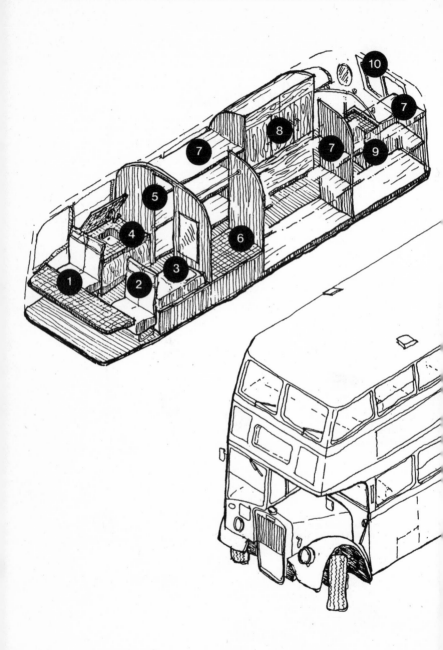